FAST TRACK
to the TOP

10 skills for **CAREER SUCCESS**

ROS TAYLOR   JOHN HUMPHREY

**KOGAN
PAGE**

First published 2002

Kogan Page Limited
120 Pentonville Road
London N1 9NJ
UK

Kogan Page US
22 Broad Street
Milford CT 06460
USA

British Library Cataloguing in Publication Data

A CIP record for this book is available from the British Library

ISBN 0 7494 3666 2

Typeset by Saxon Graphics Ltd, Derby
Printed and bound in Great Britain by Biddles Ltd, Guildford and King's Lynn
www.biddles.co.uk

contents

Contents

introduction

We all desire success at work. How to achieve it is the challenge. This book is about bridging the gap between the desire and the achievement.

You may want to get to the board of directors or indeed become chief executive. Some of you may not be as ambitious as that but would still like to know what it takes to reach those heights. Others may question the whole process. Who on earth would want the hassle of such seniority, and what might the compensations be for such hard work?

To answer these questions, and many others, we interviewed 80 business leaders to find out what made them tick. We analysed their skills, their attitudes, their backgrounds and their working habits. And yes, they do work hard, but the compensation is that they just love it. They adore the accompanying limelight and recognition, and they seem to have a lot of fun being in charge.

If these things are for you, read on.

The results of our interviews are a true guide to the characteristics needed to reach the top of a profession. We then used the findings to assemble practical programmes so that you, the reader, can also sit at the boardroom table.

You might, of course, have additional reasons to be interested in our findings. Perhaps you have responsibilities for employee training or development and want to ensure an adequate supply of director-calibre personnel in the organization. You may already be a director and would like to progress to the next stage. Or again, you may simply be curious to know what, if anything, separates those that direct from those that do not. Whatever your motivation for picking up this book, we are happy that you have. The skills that can be learned from these pages are great for self-development and will guarantee you success in whatever you undertake.

We decided to ask questions of the directors themselves, face to face. Of interest to us were their offices, the size, the décor, the art on their walls. Their secretaries were a fund of interesting information as they escorted us along corridors and into lifts. Their body language and often their replies spoke volumes as to whether the captain of industry we had just seen was a sweetheart to work for or a swine. We were able to make contact with a wide range of leading executives, far more than expected, and found them to be generally accessible and helpful. When they were not, we still attempted to talk to them to ensure that our results were not based on a self-selecting sample of 'nice' directors only. In general, we aimed at the top of the organizational tree and spoke to established chief executives, chairpersons, managing directors and the like. While you may not aspire to these dizzy heights, the people at the top have mostly passed through the lower ranks of directorship and, we reasoned, are most likely to epitomize the qualities of the ideal director at any level.

We quickly realized that we could not content ourselves with the simple, open question 'What qualities do you have?' Although we did always ask that, and were impressed with the responses, we wanted to dig deeper.

We also recognized a challenge with presenting the findings. The intention of this book is to give an accessible guide to directors' characteristics, not to ask the reader to wade through endless interview notes searching for nuggets. We therefore decided to test a range of hypotheses, and to ask directors to classify the importance of a range of qualities. The aims were to identify the real priorities, and to look for patterns of strengths or weaknesses, which seem to describe today's successful business leader.

Rather than reinvent the wheel, we looked at studies that had already investigated the roots of business success. The literature on executives and business leadership is voluminous to say the least, much of it generated by the top people themselves. However, for our purposes these publications are often limited by a focus on organizational, rather than personal, characteristics. Where they do become personal, they typically promote a particular philosophy rather than review the range of things that work in business.

In embarking on our work, we were particularly assisted by Jim Hindhaugh, formerly of Cranfield Business School. Ten years ago Jim interviewed chief executives in a number of countries. Cranfield have generously given us access to their data and this has been invaluable in setting the parameters for our own investigations. We modified the checklist they used – it was a little too slanted towards the public sector for our people – and this allowed us to quantify our interview data.

At this point we would like to acknowledge another interesting influence when we were developing our questions. This is the work of Dr Susan Dellinger on 'psycho-geometrics'. Dr Dellinger noted that, when people are asked to select a geometric shape (from a square, triangle, rectangle, circle or squiggle) which best describes them as an individual, their selection closely correlates with certain personality characteristics. While there is no suggestion that this is a comprehensive and analytical personality test, it met the important requirement of taking very little time to complete. It also happens to be intriguing and fun to do. We have included Dr Dellinger's test in our questions, and so far our interviewees have been fascinated with the results. Only one executive thought it too stupid for words. Everyone else has, if anything, been rather amazed by the accuracy of the results and demanded copies to try out on their team and the family at home.

You of course will have a chance to try the test and will have the opportunity to benchmark yourself against the great and the good. Later on we will reveal the results. To be truly experimental, select your choice first before you look at the others' choices.

The last part of the interview comprised the Personal Profile Analysis by Thomas International. We thought it would be interesting to discover whether there is a cluster of personality characteristics that correlate highly with success.

As you will see, *Fast Track to the Top* is presented as the '10 commandments' of business success. This is essentially a distillation of the findings that emerged most strongly and most consistently as the defining characteristics of the people we interviewed. However, our starting list was considerably longer than ten! We wanted to avoid imposing our own prejudices and preconceptions, and therefore included questions from a range of sources and influences. We included those which, before we started, we would have said were probably key to executive success – and were sometimes surprised by the results.

As well as using a variety of checklists, we asked a number of open-ended questions under the following headings, in alphabetical order rather than investigative importance.

Breadth of interests

How interested are you in things outside business? Do you follow arts, music, literature? Are you into sport, cooking, antiques or rollerblading? How important are these things and how do you find time to pursue them? Or do you just work all the time?

Emotional intelligence

Are you emotionally stable? Do you lose your temper or suffer fools gladly? Are you sentimental, romantic, good humoured? The life and soul of a party or cool and collected? Are you generally optimistic or pessimistic? Are you a stern moralist?

Family background

Do you have brothers and sisters? Which position were you in the family? Did your parents support your education and your career development? Do you regard your parents as an important factor in your success?

Financial awareness

Are you highly financially literate? Can you read a balance sheet intuitively and home in on key financial indices and issues? Is the financial performance of the business your own top priority? Are you aware at all times of the financial state of the organization? Was this skill the most important in your rise to success?

Health

Are you healthy? Is health important to you, and how far do you go to look after your body? Do you smoke? Drink? Exercise? Diet? Do you know your own weight? Blood pressure? Cholesterol level?

Humour

What place does humour have in the boardroom? Can humour be used as a business tool? Is humour ever inappropriate and should it be outlawed?

Knowing yourself

Are you self-critical, and do you feel that you know your own personal strengths and weaknesses? Do you take active steps to improve areas of weakness?

Love of change

Do you like a stable, steady environment or do you welcome change? Do you deliberately provoke change in some circumstances? Do you sometimes do everyday things differently just for the sake of change?

Networking

Would you agree that who you know is more important than what you know? Do you network whenever possible? Is your networking planned and structured? Do you often develop business contacts with people you don't like? Did your networking help your career development?

Prioritizing

How well can you home in on priorities for action? At any given time, are you dealing with the most important business issue? Can you separate the important from the urgent, as described in Stephen Covey's *The Seven Habits of Highly Effective People*?

Problem solving

Do you enjoy dealing with difficult problems? What approach do you use? Do you ever encounter insoluble problems? Are there some types of problems you are particularly good at? Do you involve your team in problem solving?

Risk taking

Are you a gambler by nature? Do you take business risks which have a real chance of failure, or are your business ventures sufficiently researched to be almost certain successes? Do you insist on comprehensive insurance against risks and losses?

Self-confidence

Do you have unshakeable confidence in your own abilities? Did you pop out of the womb confident or was confidence achieved gradually? Does your confidence go as far as arrogance, or do you ever doubt yourself? Have you ever had to pick yourself up from failure or depression?

Setting goals

Do you have clearly defined business and personal goals, or is your success largely based on being in the right place at the right time? If you have goals, how specific are they? How ambitious are they? Are they long or short term? Are they written down? Do you discuss them with others, or are they for you alone?

Success drive

How important is success to you? Is it important that you always win? Is success for its own sake important? Do you want to see your competitors fail?

Taking responsibility

Do you accept responsibility for the success of your business? Do you decide on your own actions or rely on others to steer you? When things go wrong, do you take the blame, or is this usually the fault of others?

Team work

Is your team of colleagues an important contribution to your success? Do they tend to be similarly skilled, like-minded people to yourself, or do they bring other skills and approaches? How do you find and retain your team? Do you mix socially or is the relationship strictly business?

Training and education

What are your academic qualifications? Have you been specifically trained for the job you are doing? If so, what was the training, who provided it and how useful was it? At what stage in your career was the training undertaken?

Values

Are personal values important to you? Do you follow a clear code of moral values? Where has this come from?

Work experience

How many different jobs and employers have you had? At what age did you take a management position? When did you control a significant budget? When and how did you become visible to senior management?

These headings formed the structure of our interviews. Initially we had worried that such senior people would be unwilling to give us enough time to complete all the checklists and questions. This rarely was an issue, but often they enjoyed the interview process so much that we ran out of time and they had to be left to fax back their checklists later. This they did with remarkable celerity. Two things contributed to their interest. First, how often does someone sit listening to them with rapt attention with no axe to grind or agenda to pursue? Second, these busy people hardly have a second to spare for navel contemplation, so the interview forced them to introspect in a way they had forgotten or, in some cases, had never done before.

The main structure of the book is a practical guide to the main findings, and how they can be utilized in practice. Let's conclude this introduction with some immediate observations about the size of the challenge. Is it possible to emulate the characteristics of successful people? Here are a few headlines which emerged time after time when we were reviewing our findings:

■ Board directors are not a race apart. As we carried out our interviews we found ourselves in the company of bright, hard-working people, but not creatures from another planet. They had a variety of IQs, expertise and backgrounds. In other words, directors are just like the rest of us – and their positions are up for grabs.

■ Interpersonal skills are all-important. Our directors were nearly always charming, persuasive and eloquent. Where they had faced challenges or found they had to acquire new skills, these were mostly behavioural rather than 'technical' subjects like computing and finance. These technical areas are like Herzberg's 'hygiene factors': you have to have them, but more of them does not lead to more success and does not guarantee success in the absence of interpersonal skills.

■ Energy is essential. We commonly found people working 80–100 hour weeks, with punishing schedules and little time for relaxation. They had a great drive for success, and a commitment to their businesses and their employees. To keep up the pace they needed to be aware of their health and to stay fit.

■ Directors are resilient. They cope with stress well, often saying that their work is not stressful. They often use distancing strategies by calling work a game, by retreating to other interests when necessary, or by using their domestic life as a cut-off from business pressures. They are also a very healthy group, with only 10 per cent having had any significant illness. John Spence, one of this 10 per cent, is a remarkable man who gradually became blind over the last few years. This disability did not deter him from becoming chief executive of Lloyds TSB Scotland.

■ Male executives need emotional stability to achieve business success, but women don't. The majority of men claimed that when things went wrong at home, they could not concentrate at work. In some cases their current stability had been hard won as they were into their third marriage. Women were different.

When women had trouble with relationships, they channelled their energies into work. In fact, one young female chief executive, Tanya Goodin, who had set up her own Web site company, was worried that her recent marriage would make her so happy that she would lose her competitive edge.

- Senior people do not set goals. This surprising finding is against the trend of conventional management wisdom. However, the fact is that relatively few of our interviewees had followed a planned road to success based on clearly identified personal goals. Most were essentially clever opportunists able to seize the moment when it came their way. When asked the reasons for their success, by far the most common answer was 'luck'. However, they did set goals for the business, just not for themselves.

- Directors aren't trained. Despite the 'learnability' of the ingredients of success, very few organisations taught these skills, and the group themselves had very little formal training for their senior positions. Once there, very few update their skills. If their organizations provide for continuous development, it is invariably for other people.

- Top people are fun and interesting. Despite their punishing work schedule, our group had a wide range of interests which they pursued actively. From sailing to opera, rollerblading to eggcup collecting, successful people live life to the full. It is clear that part of what they bring to their business is breadth of vision developed from a wide range of experiences.

- Successful people love work. A real secret of success is undoubtedly loving the job. Our group made no sharp distinction between their working lives and their social lives, and did not begrudge the intrusion of work into personal time. Charles Dunstone of Carphone Warehouse, when asked how he coped with the pressures of work, could not relate to the question. 'I just love what I do. There is simply no pressure involved in that.'

- Self-confidence goes with the job. Virtually all rated their self-confidence as 'high'.

- Patience and tolerance had to be learned. When asked what major skills had to be learned to execute their senior posts, overwhelmingly the two most common answers were 'patience' and 'tolerance'. It seems that these characteristics are not the natural behaviour of those who succeed, but simply have to be learned to make progress in the corporate environment. It is understandable that these thrusting, energetic individuals might expect everyone around them to be the same, and of course they are not. Claire McGrath, director at Pfizer, put it so succinctly when she said that she had to 'stop being a razor blade'.

In a nutshell, we did not discover a new species of human being. With the inside knowledge which this book provides, and a little practice, most people can emulate the skills and approaches needed to make it to the board.

After our interviews we were left with a huge volume of information to condense into key findings and then put together a programme that would give you, the reader, these key skills. The result is this book. The core of the book is the 'ten commandments of success' for the aspirant director. Of course, we could have made it nine commandments or 11 commandments, but the top 10 actually serve very well to demonstrate the attributes which most strongly and repeatedly emerge as the definers of board directorship. So here they are.

The 10 commandments

Problem solve

Our number one rated characteristic is the ability to solve problems in a crisis. Business success depends on being the person who stays constructive and creative when the going is tough. You need to see that there is always a way through, even when those around you have given up.

Deliver the goods

Successful people know what has to be done. And they *need* to achieve results. The key is the development of a results focus in which the end point is clearly understood and there is a sense of urgency in striving to get there. Once there, of course, new goals are set and the process begins again.

Want to win

Those at the top have a drive to become successful and see this as an objective in its own right. They enjoy winning for the sake of it and often think of business life as a game. Their secret is an understanding of the rules and a real desire to master them.

Relate

Our survey of leaders shows that they prize the ability to work with a wide variety of people. Leaders have learned to stay close to their customers and their employees. They take time to relate to other people and are empathetic, communicative and supportive. They also handle difficult people skilfully and value a happy domestic life.

Trust the team

Success is not achieved in isolation. Our directors knew that they had neither the time nor the ability to do everything themselves, and were highly dependent on finding and keeping the right team. Finding business partners and then trusting them is a key business skill.

De-stress

Directors consistently give a high rating to their ability to cope with stress and recognize that managing stress is now a business essential. There are many approaches to stress management, but the key is awareness and proactivity. In this, as in other aspects of business, successful people take control.

Love change

When we asked our sample of leaders whether they liked change – most people don't – they told us that not only did they love change, but they saw their ability to initiate change as crucial to their success. Embracing change, and recognizing that it is now a necessary part of business life, is an essential.

Know yourself

We were consistently impressed with the responses when we asked our directors what they saw as their strengths and weaknesses. Without hesitation they listed their talents, and then their failings. Confident self-knowledge is the building block for progressing in business.

Strike a deal

This commandment relates to the ability to negotiate. Leaders need to achieve 'win-win' outcomes with partners and providers. They have the creativity to construct a proposition from which everyone will gain, the toughness not to relinquish more than they can afford, and the charisma to steer the encounter to a successful conclusion.

Be confident

Some of the CEOs in our sample were born confident; for others it came with the job. Self-confidence seems to be an essential requirement since they need to speak up for themselves, to argue effectively with senior colleagues and to be the focus of attention in a range of business situations.

Our book develops each of these characteristics on the basis of our findings and from our own experience of working with, and developing, senior executives. Where there are tests available that enable individuals to rank their own capabilities, we have included them. Where there are proven approaches to improving performance in particular areas, we have described them. We hope you find the results interesting and useful, and wish you well with your journey to the top.

The 80 CEOs and senior directors interviewed

Dawn Airey	Channel 5 Broadcasting
Charles Allen	Granada Group
Sir David Barnes	Astra Zeneca
Crawford Beverage	formerly Scottish Enterprise
Ian Brindle	PricewaterhouseCoopers
Adam Broadbent	Arcadia Group
Andrew Brodie	formerly IRS
Chris Brown	Euromoney plc
David Campbell	Ginger Productions
Christopher Castleman	Standard Chartered
Georges-Christian Chasot	Eurotunnel Group
Richard Close	The Post Office
Dr. Steven Cole	Care Management
Nicholas Coleridge	Condé Nast
Sunny Crouch	World Trade Centre
James Cullen	Bell Atlantic Corporation
Susan Cummiskey	Bowne and Co
Brian Davis	Nationwide Building Society
Charles Dunstone	Carphone Warehouse
Ian Eldridge	Pizza Express
John Farber	ICC Industries Inc
Sandra Farber	ICC Industries Inc
Gwynneth Flower	Action 2000
Sir Rocco Forte	RF Hotels
Andrew Fraser	formerly Invest UK
Brian Gilbertson	Billiton
Tanya Goodin	Tamar Media
Lord Gordon of Strathclyde	Scottish Radio Holdings
Harry Gould	Gould Paper Corporation
Teresa Graham	Baker Tilly
Sir Richard Greenbury	formerly Marks and Spencer
Tom Hamilton	Hamilton Private Equity Partners
Sir Christopher Harding	Legal and General
Vivien Irish	NCR
Peter Jacobs	formerly BUPA
Bob Johnson	Bowne and Co
Pierre Jungels	Enterprise Oil plc
Iain Kennedy	New Medical Techologies Group

Angela Knight	APCIMS
Lesley Knox	British Linen Advisors
Philip Kogan	Kogan Page
Brian Larcombe	3i Group
Helen Ostrowski	Porter Novelli, New York
Malcolm Mackay	Russell Reynolds
Nancy Marino	formerly of Frederick Atkins
Sir Ian McAllister	Ford Motor Company
Claire McGrath	Pfizer
Tim Melville Ross	formerly Institute of Directors
Beatrice Mitchell	Sperry Mitchell and Associates
David Mitchell	Mitchell and Associates
Sarah Mitson	United Biscuits
Sir Bryan Nicholson	BUPA
Denise O'Donoghue	Hat Trick Productions
Ramon Pajares	The Savoy Group
Ed Palmer	IRI International
Diana Parker	Withers
Sylvie Pierce	formerly Tower Hamlets
Gail Rebuck	Random House Publishers
Sir Bob Reid	Bank of Scotland
Julian Richer	Richer Sounds
Dame Stella Rimington	formerly MI5
Christopher Rodrigues	Bradford and Bingley
Stuart Rose	Body Shop International
Colin Rutherford	Intelli
Vernon Sankey	formerly Reckitt & Coleman
Sir Patrick Sargeant	Euromoney
Alizon Scott	Scott Edgar Advertising
Mike Sheard	Garbane plc
Philip Simshauser	Centre for Executives
John Spence	Lloyds TSB Scotland
Seymour Sternberg	New York Life Assurance
John Stuart	Woolwich plc
Michael Teacher	Hillsdown Holdings
Sir Clive Thompson	Rentokil Initial plc
David Ure	Reuters
David Varney	BG plc
Joseph Wan	Harvey Nicholls
Sir Ian Wood	Scottish Enterprise Council
Rob White-Cooper	MMC Group
Ros Wilton	formerly Reuters

results

This chapter looks at how we acquired our sample of senior people, the breakdown in terms of age, sex, location and the outcome of a whole variety of measures used during the interviews. The measures comprised a structured interview, a business skills checklist, a personal profile analysis and psycho-geometrics.

The Times 1,000 compiled by FT Extel gave us our British sample and Crain's *New York Business Book of Lists '99* provided the American sample. We faxed an invitation to about 200 chief executives and managing directors asking if they would like to participate in research for a book which would supply advice to young aspiring managers about how they could reach the boardroom.

Of the sample there were 59 male respondents (75 per cent) and 21 females (25 per cent). The average age of the group was 52, with the women having an average age of 46. Sixty-six of our sample were based in the UK and 14 were American.

Educational background

Ninety-one per cent had degrees. The notables who did not go to university were Charles Dunstone, Julian Richer, Charles Allen and Sir Richard Greenbury. Thirty-seven per cent had second degrees or diplomas, MBAs being the most popular. We had expected accountancy, business and finance backgrounds to proliferate, but only 15 executives listed these as their primary field of study. Other subjects studied included veterinary science, American studies, psychology, social sciences, media, law, catering and tourism. Brian Davis trained as a rocket scientist. He strongly felt his early training developed a powerful analytical ability which has stood him in good stead as CEO of Nationwide.

Few respondents came from a human resources background, but Crawford Beverage was an exception. More than any other interviewee he was passionate about staff training and development as key to business success. All mentioned the variety of training available in their companies, but it was more for other staff than themselves.

Only six of our sample had been specifically trained for their role of CEO or MD, and of these four had completed a course at Harvard University. Colin Rutherford, one of these, waxed lyrical about the impact of his Young Presidents course. Not only did he meet the youthful great and good, but he received direct feedback about the shortcomings of his management style. Colin had always been that very rare commodity, an extroverted accountant. His Harvard experience taught him to listen to colleagues rather than talk at them. Gail Rebuck also enjoyed her Bertelsmann course, but Charles Allen thought the Henley CEOs course 'so awful' that he offered to sort it out and is now lecturing on it.

Dr Stephen Cole was allocated a consultant to help him develop his management skills when he became director of Care Management Group. The consultant encouraged a more logical and less emotional approach to performance and discipline than he had used as a physician.

However, the majority of our sample were like Peter Jacobs who 'went on management courses in mid career but not much in senior roles'. Many admitted to making huge mistakes 'on the job' when they first took over their senior position. The lack of training at top levels was, they felt, owing to pressure of time, as you had to hit the ground running. But according to Greg Dyke, Director General of the BBC, there may also be an expectation that executives should arrive complete to their CEO or MD role, despite the size, complexity or difference in market sector. The article in which he was quoted (in the *Sunday Times*, Jan 2000) described how angry BBC programme makers were when his Harvard leadership course cost £3,500 of taxpayers' money which they claimed could have been better spent on programmes: he 'has run companies for more than 10 years so why does he need to relearn the basics now?'

Our participants were also asked how they updated their skills in post. Hardly any mentioned any formal training or development input, apart from the occasional seminar or conference. Reading was the most popular updating tool, with a few mentioning learning on the job, learning from colleagues, the Internet, and one mentioning a mentor. John Spence, who is blind, gets his PA to read management books to him at the end of the day or when he is travelling.

When they acquired their first management job

Just over half of the sample achieved their first management job in their twenties. Pierre Jungels, for example, was made a young chief executive at a plant in Angola because no one else would take the job. Making a success of this first rung of the ladder, and grasping opportunities others refused, earmark much of the sample's experience. Many were aware that they did not offer the same chances to aspiring executives today.

Sixteen executives had remained with the same employer but had undertaken many different jobs. The rest had had up to eight employers. Sir Bob Reid had had the most individual jobs: 32, followed by Mike Sheard with 27 and James Cullen, Gwynneth Flower and Chris Brown with 20. Breadth of experience seemed more important than moving employer.

The impact of goal planning

The vast majority set no personal goals, and some were quite violently opposed to them. Only 10–12 per cent admitted to goal planning in any systematic way, although some had had short-term goals to take them on to the next stage. The group were overridingly ambitious, but claimed to have succeeded by opportunism and taking things one step at a time. Sir Richard Greenbury was emphatic that if colleagues even suspected you were pursuing your own goals or were self-interested, they would not support you. The success of the business was the thing, and any personal success was subservient to that. Sir Ian Wood said that goals led to inflexibility, and that people would often surpass goals if they had never been set. Adam Broadbent felt that long-term goals were 'no good as you might be dead'. One exception was Sir Clive Thompson, who claimed to 'plan everything', three to five years ahead, and wrote things down in 'a code no one else can understand'.

A network of professional contacts

The question of whether managers had a network which had helped them, split the group down the middle. Ian Brindle described himself as not a person who networks, and George Chazot said it was not the way he had conducted his career. Ian Eldridge felt networking was not the key to success, and Denise O'Donoghue described herself as the world's worst networker. Ros Wilton thought networking would have been easier had she been a man and played golf. Sir Bob Reid admitted to networking for advice but never for advancement. Dawn Airey disliked the implication of networking: 'I have got on by being exceptionally good'.

On the other hand, Sir Christopher Harding claimed to be one of the biggest networkers in London, sending over a thousand Christmas cards every year. It takes him a week to sign them all in green ink. Peter Jacobs agreed, saying that for him networking is key to success. Tom Hamilton had based his career on networking: his father's advice was to contact only the top people, what he called 'the purple route'. When he started he would wait for hours in waiting rooms just to see the right person. Some executives network like breathing. Ramon Pajares found himself networking at his daughter's party!

Driving forces

Achievement of results is a major driver for this group, and was mentioned most often in answer to this question. Richard Close felt he was almost programmed to achieve. They were a group who loved to come first, loved to win. They talked of loving the 'buzz' of success and the rewards that accompany it. Sir Richard Greenbury enjoyed the reflected glory of a successful business, whereas Sir Rocco Forte wanted 'money and lots of it'. Some were driven by quite different things: Andrew Fraser by being part of what is going on, David Campbell by creativity and being leading edge, Julian Richer by making his mark.

Many felt a commitment to others motivated them. Ian Brindle 'felt a responsibility to those who elected him as chairman', and Sir Bryan Nicholson talked of 'the sheer pleasure of being able to help people'.

Others, like Lesley Knox, did not set out for 'status, money or success'; and Charles Allen certainly surpassed his mother's aspirations: when she heard of his promotion to chief executive, she asked if that meant that he would have his own office.

Most just love work. Gail Rebuck has a 'passion' for it, Crawford Beverage attributes his drive to an inbuilt Scottish work ethic, David Mitchell at age 77 does not know how to stop. Most work in excess of 55 hours a week, 16 mentioned 80-plus and one more than 100 hours. Often they stated that they lived to work.

The job of CEO or senior executive

Staff management and people issues were mentioned as the most time-consuming part of the job by 50 per cent of the sample. Meetings and the preparation for meetings were cited by a further 25 per cent. Much time can also be spent on outside agencies and on PR and marketing. Some interviewees talked about having to deal with politics, politicians and government regulations. Delivering speeches internally and externally was seen as another major part of the job. Some respondents loved this directorial duty, while others were less confident of their ability.

Many directors travel a great deal. Sir Richard Greenbury loved this: getting round stores took him back to his roots in retail.

Six said they encountered no difficulties in their job. Sir Patrick Sargeant stated that he 'loved it all'. Others were more forthcoming about the challenges. People in all guises appeared to be the most challenging part of the job. Staff, clients, board members: all were cited. 'Dealing with illogical, backward thinking people' exercised the patience of James Cullen, and Sylvie Pierce admitted she was frustrated by people 'not thinking like her'. Choosing and keeping the right people constituted the most difficult parts of the job for some, whereas making people redundant still haunts the memories of many.

For Charles Dunstone, keeping the momentum of a business going is the most challenging part, and maintaining that personal 'buzz' is for Julian Richer. In addition Christopher Rodrigues said that 'thinking several steps ahead was the difference between a manager's job and a director's'.

At the beginning of the project, we almost took it for granted that directors would be pro-change and, to use consultancy jargon, happy to be 'change agents'. To a certain extent this proved correct, but agreement was not unequivocal. Teresa Graham of Barker Tilly did not like change ruthlessly instituted. She strongly felt that change must have a process and participation for it to work. Changing an organization when it is going well is very taxing, according to Colin Rutherford, CEO of Intelli, a much smaller streamlined operation than the nationwide accountancy firm RMD he helped to establish. Changing small is probably easier than changing big. Andrew Brode found change harder to cope with as time goes by, and interestingly he has just sold his Eclipse Group of publishing and conference businesses. Sir Patrick Sargeant drew on the wisdom of age to pronounce that 'like Palmerston I have seen many changes and most of them for the worse'. On the more positive side, Alizon Scott stated that she was 'comfortable with the discomfort of change. It was an inevitable, exciting, fun, roller coaster.' Several noted that they had a low boredom threshold and change kept things interesting.

Another surprise was that our directors did not rate financial expertise as one of their most crucial skills. Knowing Britain was one of the few countries where accountants become CEOs, we fully expected the financial side of the job to assume major importance. Only a quarter of the sample rated their financial skills as excellent. The rest varied from good to average; no one admitted they were poor. All mentioned how important it was to be able to read a balance sheet, but that they relied on their finance departments to supply the true expertise. The job of CEO or director is much more about people than numbers.

We asked our sample what it was like to be part of a board of directors and what they thought about their colleagues. Some of the replies contained inherent contradictions. Harry Gould described his fellow directors as 'irritating and useful', David Ure found 'something to admire and despise in all of them'. Professional partnerships were represented by Teresa Graham of Baker Tilly, accountants, and Diana Parker, senior partner with Withers, solicitors. Both were less than effusive about their senior colleagues. Quite a few directors mentioned what a lonely job it can be, especially for a chief executive. Andrew Brode was often driven to visit his lawyer or accountant just for a chat. Crawford Beverage admitted the job was so lonely that his fellow directors acted as a good sounding board.

Many interviewees of course valued their board thoroughly. Most organizations had at least one woman at board level, even if they were non-executives, with the exception of Ford, according to Sir Ian McAllister because 'we are very brutal at Ford – too brutal for women'. Some felt there were few differences between the sexes at a senior level, whereas others mentioned that a female executive was more likely to have better people skills, less ego, and a more practical orientation, and this helped to provide a board with interesting diversity. There were also comments that women were better at choosing a harmonious team.

The last word about boards must go to Sir Ian Wood, who emphasized the importance of the CEO and the chairman getting on. 'If they don't, sell your shares!'

Personal characteristics of senior executives

Our sample of successful people knew their strengths and weaknesses and were able to outline them instantly. The other notable thing was that there were always more strengths than weaknesses. Typical strengths were leadership, communication skills, delegation, getting on with a broad cross-section of people, having the capacity for hard work, being a team player, the ability to be enthusiastic, visionary, strategic, fair, analytical, loyal, tough when necessary, straightforward and honest. Typical weaknesses were impatience, having a low boredom threshold, not suffering fools despite trying hard, being too blunt or abrupt and sometimes too soft.

These people knew what they brought to the table and therefore what support they needed from their team. Sixteen said their level of confidence was moderate, whereas 38 declared that their confidence was high and had always been so. The rest admitted to previously low levels that had gradually increased on the job. Brian Larcombe was 'always' confident, Andrew Fraser 'appallingly so', Chris Brown 'far too self-confident' and Diana Parker 'totally confident in myself'. Some mentioned however that this confidence can be situation-specific. Lord Gordon of Strathclyde described himself as 'more self-confident than I should be in my ideas, less self-confident than I should be as a person'. Denise O'Donoghue said she was 'at work – fearless' but not elsewhere in her life. According to Christopher Harding 'the secret is to look confident'.

The vast majority declared that they were even tempered, and many admitted that this was a major area of learning when first reaching a senior position. As a group they were very aware that any job of management is about suffering fools and moving them on. To this end Claire McGrath had to learn 'not to be a razor blade with people', and Denise O'Donoghue had to 'contain her moods'. Dawn Airey reminded us that how you react when in a position of power influences people, Sir Ian McAllister that you cannot encourage people to be creative then humiliate them. If you do, it will be the last creative idea you ever receive. Richard Close 'loses the rag about once a year' while David Barnes last lost his temper 25 years ago.

Maintaining focus and identifying priorities were seen as important parts of the job, achieved by the group through a plethora of low-tech personal lists, despite their being surrounded by the latest technology. Julian Richer had a worksheet book, with his various projects outlined along the top so a day's notes are all on one page. Nicholas Coleridge preferred writing his five things to do on the back of his cheque book, and John Spence had an ideas register that was carried everywhere by his PA for additions at a moment's notice.

Brian Davis said he sat in the bath visualizing the future and developing catch phrases to help people concentrate on what needed to be done. Sir Bob Reid organized himself while shaving in the mornings, whereas Sir Bryan Nicholson advocated very careful diary management – at least an hour a week with his secretary.

This is a group of risk takers – not gamblers, as they were quick to point out. The majority claimed to take risks on a daily basis, but this was usually qualified by their desire to calculate the magnitude of that risk and the downside of failure. Dawn Airey emphasized that some jobs are risk-intrinsic. For her, going to Channel 5 was a risk, and commissioning every programme was a risk. In a similar vein, George Chazot had felt at times that his move to Eurotunnel was 'kamikaze'.

Joseph Wan talked of tolerable versus intolerable risk and the need for research. His recent decision to open a store in Edinburgh rather than Glasgow was questioned by a slightly partisan author, but he countered that he had been informed by his marketing people the only thing that would tempt the average fashion-conscious Glaswegian to travel to Edinburgh was the existence of a Harvey Nicholls store! He was right.

Many of the group took care to distinguish their risk taking at work from their home life.

Remaining healthy is important to such senior people, as great reserves of energy and resilience are necessary to cope with the job. Sixty-eight per cent exercised regularly at the gym, while others had a personal trainer. A few talked about watching their diet, some of reducing their alcohol intake. Ten admitted rather shamefacedly to doing nothing much to keep fit. Only eight had ever had a serious illness.

Many queried a question about how they escaped from the pressures of work. Sir Bob Reid and Dawn Airey did not regard work as pressure and so had no need to escape. Others escaped on holidays or to their families. John Spence relaxed by making the occasional soufflé and James Cullen by keeping work in perspective. He saw work as just a game, and said you must realize that you are going to look stupid to at least one person every day.

Despite working long hours, these people often indulged in wide-ranging hobbies. Nicholas Coleridge found time to write a series of novels based on his experiences in magazines and advertising. Sylvie Pierce enjoyed rollerblading, Harry Gould collected death masks, notably of James Joyce. Others' hobbies ranged from fishing in the Outer Hebrides to sewing tapestry and collecting contemporary art.

All with one exception felt that humour was important at work. Harry Gould suggested that without humour he would have to go into a monastery. Only Joseph Wan said he thought business much too serious an affair to be treated with levity. Perhaps that is an East/West cultural difference!

The effect of home life

This question received quite different responses from male and female executives. Men became disrupted and unfocused when there was conflict at home: Sir Richard Greenbury, for example, stated that he 'can't cope with pressure at home and at work'. Dr Steve Cole found that going through a divorce stopped him moving forward. It would seem that to many men, work is so important that everything needs to funnel towards it, and disruptive relationships are a distraction. Sir Bob Reid underlined this when he adjured young male executives to keep their lives simple and 'stay with the one woman and do everything you want to do with her'. It all sounds rather cosy, but many executives had had a number of tries before finding familial bliss. Both Tom Hamilton and Christopher Harding were on their third wife. These men do not always spend oodles of time at home, they just want to know it is ticking over. Brian Gilbertson admitted his son had said to him recently, 'I have added up the time I have seen you this week. It was 13 minutes.'

For the most part in our sample, executives' wives were homemakers. They had had careers in the past, but had relinquished them to foster families and their husbands' success. Notable exceptions were Andrew Fraser, whose wife runs her own PR company, and Brian Larcombe whose wife is a doctor.

Female executives told a very different story. Lesley Knox had used work as an escape when her first marriage was not going well. Sylvie Pierce very much felt that the failure of her home life in the past had driven her to succeed. Tanya Goodin said she was worried about being less driven after her recent marriage because she was so happy.

Ways to develop young managers

It was rare to find any formal progression planning. However Rentokil, the Marsh Group and Reckitt and Coleman did have structured programmes for the younger executive. Some admitted to having nothing, for example Eurotunnel and the Nationwide Building Society, and certainly saw it as a need.

Some answers revolved around broadening experience. Channel 5 had secondments with shareholder companies and Astra Zeneca sent young managers on overseas service. Marks and Spencer had a series of keynote addresses for their high fliers. Very few mentioned mentoring and coaching. 'Throwing in at the deep end' featured widely, with the caveat of lots of appraisals.

When executives were asked what were the key areas to develop in young managers, increasing self-confidence was mentioned most often. Some executives felt that there were differences between the sexes: young women required an increase in confidence, whereas young men needed to know that promotion did not come as a right. Responses also clustered around seeing the bigger business picture, becoming aware of business development and looking at strategic issues. For the most part, though, people skills and learning how to motivate and manage others were the main areas senior executives wanted to see developed. As David Mitchell said, 'Young people are often great technicians but they need humanizing.'

Analysis of personal profiles

The Thomas International Personal Profile Analysis is a structured questionnaire with 24 lines of four words, of which respondents have to select one as the 'most' preferred word and one as the 'least' preferred word to describe themselves at work. The 48 responses are scored and result in three 'profiles'. The first describes a preferred working style, the second how individuals may be modifying that style to be successful in a current working role, and the third how an individual may respond under extreme pressure. The system measures four main behavioural styles: dominance, influence, steadiness and compliance.

Dominance

Dominant people love a challenge, being considered reckless by some. Always ready for competition, they are at their best when something is at stake. They have respect for authority and responsibility. When challenge is not present they may stir up trouble. They will work long hours until they defeat a tough situation. In dealing with people, dominant individuals are usually direct, positive and straightforward; they can be blunt and even sarcastic, although they are not grudge holders. They can explode and take issue with associates, taking it for granted that others think highly of them. They like to be out in front and have the spotlight, and if they are not in the centre of the stage, they may sulk. They can hurt the feelings of others without realizing it. They tend to respond to flattery since they are basically egotistical. Usually they are rugged, self-sufficient individualists, who can be bullies and override others in order to attain their goals, often overstepping authority. They can be excessively critical and fault-finding when things or people do not meet their standards; however, after they have said what they have to say, they forget it. They will usually join organizations in order to further a goal rather than for social activity. They are interested in the unusual and the adventurous, curious, with a wide range of interests, and willing to try their hand at anything. They are self-starters and because of their multiple interests they prefer an ever-changing environment. They may lose interest in a project once the challenge has gone and prefer others to complete the job. They may spread themselves thinly. They will do the detailed work necessary to obtain a goal provided the detail is not repeated or constant. They are generally resourceful and are able to adapt readily in many situations. Dominance is active, positive behaviour, driving to accomplish in the face of opposition or antagonistic situations.

Influence

Influencers are outgoing, persuasive and gregarious. They are usually optimistic and can generally see some good in any situation. They are natural communicators. Principally they are interested in people, their problems and their activity. Being willing to help others promote projects as well as their own, they may lose sight of business goals. People tend to respond to them naturally. They join organizations for social activity. They meet people easily and are poised, becoming intimate and on first-name basis at the first meeting. Influencers will claim to know a tremendously wide range of people and may be name droppers. They can tend to appear superficial and shallow, switching sides of arguments to win, without any outward sign that they are aware of any inconsistency. They can jump to conclusions and may act on emotional impulse; decisions may be made on surface analysis of the facts. Because of their trust and willing acceptance of people, they may misjudge the abilities of others. They feel that they can persuade and motivate people to the kind of behaviour they desire to see. They usually perform well where poise and smoothness are essential factors, public relations and promotion being natural areas for them. Since they are reluctant to disturb a favourable social situation, they may have difficulty in disciplining subordinates. They exhibit active and positive behaviours in favourable and friendly situations, influencing others to positivity themselves.

Steadiness

Individuals with high steadiness are usually amiable, easy-going and relaxed, undemonstrative and controlled. Since they are not explosive or easily triggered they may conceal grievances and be grudge holders. They like to build close relationships with a relatively small group of intimate associates and will appear contented and relaxed, listening well and carefully. Patience and deliberation characterize their usual behaviour; they are good neighbours, always willing to help their friends. Steady individuals will strive to maintain the status quo, since they do not want sudden or unexpected change. Once in the groove of an established work pattern, they can follow it with seemingly undying patience.

They are usually very possessive and develop strong and loyal attachments for their work group, their club and particularly their family. They form deep ties and may be uncomfortable if separated from their familiar environment for long periods of time. They will operate well as members of a team, and can co-ordinate team efforts. Their style is one of passive behaviour in favourable situations, completing tasks and management responsibilities by obtaining consensus.

Compliance

Compliant individuals are usually peaceful, adapting themselves to any situation to avoid antagonism. Since they are sensitive and seek appreciation, others can easily hurt them. They are basically loyal and non-aggressive, doing to the best of their ability whatever is expected of them. Since they are basically cautious and conservative they may be slow to make decisions. This can frustrate quicker acting associates. They may wait to see which way the wind is blowing before acting, but they often display a good sense of timing, and shrewdness in selection of the correct course of action at the right time. Compliant individuals are able to mould themselves to an image that they see is expected of them. They go to extreme lengths to avoid conflict. They strive for order, stability, and clear working procedures, and being systematic thinkers, proceed in an orderly, predetermined manner. They are precise, paying attention to detail and using methods and expertise that have brought success in the past. They will avoid unfavourable situations, and when these occur they will protect themselves from antagonism by following rules and systems in a passive way to avoid trouble.

It should be noted that all respondents have all four characteristics in different combinations, some of which are 'working strengths'.

Of our sample, one profile analysis was 'invalid' in Thomas terms (since the responses were incompatible), and another was incorrectly completed and unusable. Of the remainder, approximately 42 per cent had dominance as their main working strength, 44 per cent had influence, 3 per cent steadiness, and 12 per cent compliance. Dominance and influence occurred as working strengths in all but two of the individuals who did not show these as a main strength. These are the two 'active' styles, and this indicates a style of 'results through people or working through people for results': a difference mostly of emphasis.

The detailed results suggested that 58 per cent of the respondents did not change their major working strength to be successful, and 82 per cent do not change their major style even under severe pressure. There were no significant gender differences in this sample, and the sample of American respondents was too small to draw any firm conclusions from it.

Overall, the clear and indisputable theme to emerge was that dominance and influence are very significant indicators of success as chief executive. This style, or styles, will involve drive, competition, forcefulness, inquisitiveness, direction, self-starting, assertion and/or influence, persuasion, friendliness, verbal ability, communication and a positive approach. There will be strong motivation for power, authority and/or recognition and praise, with a desire to avoid failure and/or rejection.

Executives' ratings of their own abilities

We asked our executives to rate their own abilities. The result is given here in priority order.

1. Ability to solve problems in a crisis.
2. Needing to achieve results.
3. Having a drive to become successful.
4. Being able to work with a wide variety of people.
5. Choosing and keeping a good team.
6. Coping with stress better than others.
7. Skill at initiating change.
8. Knowing your strengths and limitations.
9. Being able to deal and negotiate.
10. More confidence than others around.
11. Good family support – parents, spouse, children.
12. Willingness to take risks.
13. A desire to seek new opportunities.
14. Early responsibility for important tasks.
15. Breadth of experience before age 35.
16. Above average financial acumen.
17. Using business values to inspire others.
18. Ability to change management style to suit the occasion.
19. Dealing elegantly with conflict.
20. Having leadership experience early in career.

21. Being stretched in the past by a boss.
22. Fitter and healthier than average.
23. Having more ideas than other colleagues.
24. A network of contacts.
25. Setting yourself attainable goals on a regular basis.
26. Becoming visible to top management before age 30.
27. Being good at interviews.
28. A broad range of interests outside work.
29. Having a mentor or role model early in career.
30. Changing jobs at regular intervals.
31. Having special off the job management training.
32. Becoming a good 'committee politician'.
33. Being specially prepared/ trained for a top position.
34. Gaining importance through national committees.

Top 10 commandments from male executives

1. Ability to solve problems in a crisis.
2. Choosing and keeping a good team.
3. Having a drive to become successful.
4. Being able to work with a wide variety of people.
5. Needing to achieve results.
6. Good family support – parents, spouse, children.
7. Coping with stress better then others.
8. Being able to deal and negotiate.
9. Knowing your strengths and limitations.
10. Skill at initiating change.

Top 10 commandments from female executives

1. Needing to achieve results.
2. Ability to solve problems in a crisis.
3. Having a drive to become successful.
4. Skill at initiating change.

5. Being able to work with a wide variety of people.
6. Choosing and keeping a good team.
7. More confidence than others around.
8. Knowing your strengths and limitations.
9. Coping with stress better than others.
10. Willingness to take risks.

As you can see, the most striking differences between men and women are:

■ Women rated the need to achieve results as their number one priority, men as number five.
■ Men ranked the need for family support at number six. This was not rated by women at all in their top ten.
■ Women ranked having confidence as their number seven priority. This was not in the top ten for men.

To include the views of both males and females in our sample we combined the choice of having a happy home life and working with a wide variety of people as a single commandment – Relate. This allowed us to include Confidence, rated seven by the women, as our Commandment 10.

Our results are significantly different from those of the Cranfield study of American chief executives, where the top 10 were:

1. A need to achieve results.
2. An ability to work easily with a wide variety of people.
3. Challenge.
4. A willingness to take risks.
5. Early overall responsibility for important tasks.
6. A width of experience in many functions before the age of 35.
7. A desire to seek new opportunities.
8. Leadership experience early in my career.
9. An ability to develop more ideas than my other colleagues.
10. An ability to change my managerial style to suit the occasion.

This research was carried out some 10 years ago, and it is interesting to note that now the major skills for success are focused on problem solving, managing stress and skill in initiating change. A sign of the times!

Our combined top 10 provides the basis for *Fast Track to the Top's* '10 commandments', so it sets the structure for future chapters.

three

The first commandment: problem solve

The number one rated success characteristic from our business leaders is the ability to solve problems, especially in a crisis. Business success depends on being the person who remains constructive when the going gets tough. They see that there is always a way through, even when those around you have given up. The thinking associated with a 'can do' attitude and a number of creative problem solving techniques will be presented in this chapter.

Pierre Jungels, CEO of Enterprise Oil, said the quickest way to get to the top is to volunteer for a job that no one else wants, go in, be inventive and problem solve. He volunteered to work in Angola, remained there for four years and doubled production. However, he was very keen to emphasize that he worked for the greater good of the company, not for personal point scoring. This was a theme that continually emerged from our discussions: that the path to promotion was through the success of the organization, not personal glory.

Clearly being able to come up with novel solutions for the greater good of the company is a major skill for success, but what is creative problem solving? Ruth Noller in her book *Guide to Creative Action* says:

By creative we mean:
Having an element of newness, being relevant, at least to you the one who creates the solution.

31

By problem we mean:
Any situation which presents as a challenge, offers an opportunity or is a concern to you.
By solving we mean:
Devising ways to answer or to meet or satisfy the problem or
adapting yourself to the situation or adapting the situation to
you.
Creative problem solving is a process, is a method, a system
for approaching a problem in an imaginative way resulting in
effective action.

Everyone is creative in some way. If you have adapted an idea or
moved a concept from one discipline to another, you have been
creative. We often imagine that we have to be completely inventive.
This is not so, as the following demonstrates.

A railway company needed more guards on their trains. However,
they had overspent so there was no money in the budget for more
staff. The managers brainstormed the problem and came up with a
solution. Who was on the train every day except holidays? Who
knew more about the trains and their running than the staff? The
commuters, of course. So it was decided to give volunteers a cap, a
whistle and £5 for their trouble. The railway acquired cheap labour
and passengers got to live out their childhood fantasies. However the
unions have probably stopped it by now!

These skills can be taught: they are not just a genetic inheritance.
You may not emerge after reading this chapter a Leonardo DaVinci
or an Alexander Graham Bell, but you will be able to be creative to
order and be conversant with techniques of problem solving.

Problem-solving necessities

There are four areas for discussion and practice that will increase
your and your team's ability to problem solve:

- your attitude and thinking style;
- your ability to be creative;
- facilitating your team;
- establishing a creative environment.

First, let's identify any issues or problems which are around in your
personal or work life at the moment. We can use these throughout
this chapter to practise problem-solving techniques.

Tackle 'A sentence completion assessment of problems'. Try to work speedily. If some answers elude you, move on to the next, but try to complete as many as possible. They can be issues from work or home.

A sentence completion assessment of problems

My biggest problem is . . .
I'm quite concerned about . . .
Something I do that gives me trouble is . . .
Something I fail to do that gets me into trouble is . . .
A social setting I find most troublesome is . . .
The most frequent negative feelings in my life are . . .
These negative feelings take place when . . .
The person I have most trouble with is . . .
What I find most troublesome in this relationship is . . .
Life would be better if . . .
Working life would be better if . . .
I don't cope very well with . . .
What sets me most on edge is . . .
I get anxious when . . .
A value I fail to put into practice is . . .
I'm afraid to . . .
I wish I . . .
I wish I hadn't . . .
What others dislike most about me is . . .
What I don't seem to handle well is . . .
The department would run more smoothly if I . . .
A problem that keeps coming back is . . .
If I could come change just one thing in myself it would be . . .

Mark this page as you proceed through the chapter. We will return to it often for problem solving fodder.

Your attitude and thinking style

Some styles of thinking are conducive to problem solving, and some work against ever finding a solution to anything. The way we think is not something we consider often, but it is essential to the skill of tackling issues inventively.

Aaron Beck, the father of cognitive psychology, described thoughts as a kind of inner dialogue that continues in our heads even as we are talking about something completely different. This dialogue can propel us to great things, or talk us out of new situations and challenges. Although it is not easy to change, changed it can be. As soon as you embark on this transformation you will feel and act in a much more energetic and purposeful way, especially if you want to confront issues that have been around for a while in your life.

Let's take a look at faulty thinking, see if applies to you, then explore ideas to change it.

Types of faulty thinking

Exaggerating and catastrophizing

For example, if I say 'I am in a complete panic', 'I am totally useless' or 'The situation is a complete disaster', this dramatic language triggers an anxiety response and literally changes the biochemistry of the body. Rarely is anything a complete disaster, but because of this stress reaction our response time to problem solving is significantly longer, and we remain in headless chicken mode for longer than is necessary. We are also very irritating to be around.

A chief executive (not one of our sample) was nicknamed Mr Angry because he was always fulminating about something. Almost anything could trigger this response: the lateness of his mail, the temperature of his coffee, the stupidity of his clients. Every task he gave his staff was 'urgent' or in response to some 'crisis'. Those who were new to the company would work through the night to finish proposals, only to discover them in the CEO's in-tray several days later, unread. Eventually employees learnt not to respond to the words 'urgent' or 'crisis'. As a result, deadlines were sometimes missed, leaving the CEO enraged, calling his staff 'a shower of wasters'.

In times of stress and change, these thoughts proliferate. Coffee rooms in businesses and offices teem with exaggerated predictions of personal disaster as soon as the word 'reorganization' is mentioned. The fact that nothing, no matter how bad things get, comes near to these prognostications doesn't stop us indulging in such thoughts again and again. Part of the reason we do it could be that if you think the worst, it might not happen – a kind of superstitious thinking.

Ways to overcome exaggerating and catastrophizing

■ Analyze statements and situations rationally, assessing the potential catastrophe on a scale of 1 to 10. The situation is usually less than 5, unless you are being held up by an assassin with a balaclava and sawn-off shotgun.

■ It is important to describe feelings and reactions accurately, as this helps to maintain control. If you catch yourself using words like 'awful', 'dreadful' or 'disastrous', ask yourself, how awful is this really?

■ Learn to relax.

■ Do nothing, say nothing for 5 to 10 seconds till you have thought the issues through.

■ If something is lost, calmly review your movements and you will usually remember exactly where you left it. Anxiety interrupts your memory; relaxation restores it.

■ Try saying 'this is not a big deal, I can cope. I have before and I will again.'

TIPS FROM THE TOP

Christopher Rodrigues, Group CEO, Bradford and Bingley

■ What was the principal thing you had to learn to become successful?

To explain to people what I would like them to achieve in ways they understand. To think several steps ahead – the real job of the CEO.

■ What challenges did you have to meet along the way?

Learning how information technology can change a business. Recognizing that the business of the future will be less rooted in place and more in ideas.

■ What advice would you give to an aspiring manager?

Be straight – you will need ethics for staying power. Don't waste a life – help people to grow. Have a good strategic business plan and periodically review.

Table 3.1 gives examples of faulty thinking, when negative language is used in a situation such as a presentation or interview. The 'less effective thinking' is marginally better, as you are telling yourself to stop, but the negative language counteracts that advice. 'Useful thinking' on the other hand talks of 'coping', 'success next time' and 'beginning to make progress'. Add examples of your own faulty thoughts, past or present, using some of the problems you identified earlier, then change the language to more useful thinking. Note the difference in how these new thoughts can change the way you feel. Don't bother with less effective thinking. It is not good to learn the wrong or less effective way of doing things. Go straight for success and mastery.

Use positive words: for example, not 'I will not be disorganized' but 'I am usually organized and I will be again if I spend a day sorting myself out.'

All or nothing thinking

All or nothing is a thinking style that goes hand in hand with perfectionism. It involves seeing the world as black and white, right and wrong, and a 'nothing's worth doing unless you do it well' philosophy. This all sounds terribly laudable until you see how limiting and stressful it is.

A very bright manager in a microelectronics company was an all or nothing thinker. 'You win or you lose. Nothing else is relevant', he would say. Even in everyday conversation around the office he would have to win every argument. He would put people down

Table 3.1   From faulty thinking to useful thinking

Faulty thinking	Less effective thinking	Useful thinking
I'm so nervous. I've blown it!	Don't get anxious! You'll blow it.	I am usually calm and confident – I can cope with it.
I was a total failure – everyone will think I'm an idiot.	I wasn't a total failure, maybe next time.	Most of it was okay, I'll know what to do next time.
I didn't get anything I wanted. I'll never do any better.	I didn't get all I wanted, I should have done better.	I didn't get everything I wanted, but I did it and that's really positive. I'm making progress.

and actually say 'Are you stupid or something?' to ideas and suggestions not to his liking. That he might make a mistake was an alien concept, and he had no tolerance of mistakes in others. He was a very witty, intelligent guy when he relaxed, but the outcome of his thinking and behaviour was that he was roundly hated. Of course, when presented with feedback from his staff he was dumbfounded. He claimed that he wanted to challenge and stimulate a response in his team, but what he achieved was a surly silence, as no one wished to be humiliated when he 'won' yet another argument.

Life is full of grey areas and mistakes are unimportant.

Ways to overcome all or nothing thinking

■ Mistakes are unimportant – recovery is key.
■ Life is rarely black and white, but almost always shades of grey. Practise thinking grey.
■ You can have fun without winning at all costs. Start doing things for the hell of it, not to be the best around.
■ Relax and tolerate ambiguity.

Overgeneralizing

This is where, given one failure, you imagine you will only have others. At one end of the spectrum, overgeneralizing can lead to phobias like a fear of flying, when one bumpy flight leads to fears of the same happening again.

Robert was a travel agent who would not fly, despite an array of free flight incentives, because he recalled a difficult landing 15 years previously. He was convinced it would happen again. Changing his thinking to allow that his next flight might just be OK (or if not, he would cope with it) was the turning point for him. Robert proceeded to fly around the world, much to the envy of his friends.

At the more everyday end of the spectrum, this thinking style may not be as dramatic as producing phobias but can be just as limiting. Putting yourself forward for promotion and being refused an interview, auditioning for a principal role in the opera society to end up in the chorus, or writing a novel and being rejected by the publisher; we have all been there. It is humiliating, embarrassing, upsetting. But if you ever find yourself saying 'I'll never try that again', stop to ask if this is a reaction to failure or a genuine dislike of the activity.

Ways to overcome overgeneralizing

■ Tell yourself continuously that failure is OK. It may not be pleasant and may even feel profoundly uncomfortable, but it does not make you a bad person or even a lesser being – just human.

■ Be upset. Don't cover up your disappointment or control your emotions. You get ulcers that way. And don't pretend you didn't want the job/part/publisher in the first place. That is simply dishonest and stops you learning.

■ Ask yourself, next time how would I do things differently?

■ Ask for advice. The people on the interview/auditioning/publishing panel could be extremely helpful in directing you to where you might improve your skills.

■ If it helps, see yourself as a product requiring promotion or marketing: anything which stops you feeling destroyed as a person and increases your objectivity.

Become a reality thinker

What characterises all the faulty thinking described so far is emotionality and lack of objectivity. It is also very egocentric and entirely selfish. What helps is to objectify and realistically evaluate these thoughts.

Choose another faulty thought and reality test in the 'Reality thinking' box. Again focus on one of your problems or issues.

Reality thinking

Evidence

What evidence is there to support your thoughts?
What evidence is there to contradict them?

Alternative interpretations

How might someone else react in this situation?
How would you advise someone else in this situation?
What evidence is there now to support alternatives?

Effect

What is your goal in the problem situation?
Does the negative interpretation help or hinder achieving the goal?
What effect would believing an alternative have?

TIPS FROM THE TOP

Tim Melville Ross, former Director General, Institute of Directors

■ What was the principal thing you had to learn to become successful?

Over the years I learnt that there are two types of people – 'radiators' and 'drains'. Radiators give of themselves with enthusiasm to any project, whereas drains consume energy with negativity and moaning. Surround yourself with the former and you will succeed. Of course, you have to be a radiator yourself!

■ What challenges did you have to meet along the way?

When you start a new role as I did when I was CEO of the Nationwide Building Society, there is a temptation to rush at things. I now have a sense of pace and priority.

■ What advice would you give to an aspiring manager?

Take all the opportunities offered for training in self-awareness and development and get out and about amongst all staff. Everyone is important.

Ignoring the positive

The sales department of a consultancy firm was infamous for being critical. They had developed a new form for consultants to use when visiting clients on sales calls. Most were reluctant to use it as they had become used to the old one which appeared to be simpler. One consultant, however, tried out the new form for his week's call.

The sales team picked holes in the way he had completed the form, humiliating him in front of his peers. Neither he nor the others were the slightest bit motivated to try the form again. The team had ignored the positive and concentrated on criticism. This thinking style, often masquerading as academic rigour, flourishes to the detriment of human endeavour around our universities and professional institutions.

Sir Ian McAllister, Chairman and MD of Ford Motor Company, admitted during our interview that he did not suffer fools gladly. He demanded a certain standard and felt he should get it. However, when consultants worked with the top team, they fed back to him that his attitude was leading to a fear of speaking out at even the most senior levels. He has tried very hard to change his behaviour, as he is all too aware that when he is critical he inhibits any attempts at creativity in his colleagues. He now looks for the good in any idea they put forward.

At work, because you see the same people every day, it is particularly difficult to notice if anyone's behaviour has changed. Your initial negative perception of them tends to remain the same despite contrary evidence. When a manager does change for the better after years of complaints from employees, sometimes nobody notices, or even worse, they undermine the change with jokey putdowns.

Ways to stop ignoring the positive

- Ask yourself, is this situation all bad or are there some positive aspects which could be worked upon?
- If your sense of humour is based on putdowns and negatives, work hard to find an alternative. It might be clever, but ultimately it upsets and undermines.
- There are positives in almost any situation, even the most challenging. Often this is only in retrospect, but they are there nonetheless.
- Try some outcome thinking. Focus on the result.

Try this exercise and see whether you notice a shift in your thinking by the end of it. Think of a problem from your 'Sentence completion' exercise. Be specific in your problem choice: do not choose 'difficult people', for example, but choose a particular person or situation. Answer the following questions:

Problems

- What is your problem?
- How long have you had it?
- Whose fault is it?
- Who is really to blame?
- What is your worst experience with this problem?
- Why haven't you solved it yet?

Now complete the 'Outcomes' box. Notice how very different your experience is depending on which thinking style you use. What differences did you notice?

Outcomes

- What do you want?
- How will you know when you have got it?
- What else in your life will improve when you get it?
- What resources do you already have which can help you achieve this outcome?
- Think of something similar which you did succeed in doing.
- What is the next step?

If you noticed a change between focusing on your problems and exploring the outcomes, you need to indulge in outcome thinking more often. As one participant on a course said recently, 'It was liberating not to have to think of a complete solution, just the next step'. Others have commented that they felt less grounded by the problem. They knew what they ought to do but couldn't get away from focusing on the issue.

By using outcome thinking when you have a problem or a crisis, you are shifting to a much more positive frame of mind and a more creative way of operating. Also you are increasing the chances of finding solutions and becoming successful. Successful people overcome adversity, they don't avoid it.

Negatively predicting the future

A natural progression from faulty thinking is negatively predicting the future. This is especially a characteristic of people who call themselves worriers. They often have the notion, 'once a worrier always a worrier'. That is only true if you do nothing about it.

Two Scottish women started a curtain-making business in the spare bedroom of one of their homes. Their standards of workmanship were so admired that a national housing construction company asked them to supply the curtains for all their show houses. Despite financial and moral support from their local enterprise company, the two women could only envisage disaster. They had never borrowed money and started to fear the repercussions of not keeping up payments on the loan they needed. They talked constantly about their fears of losing their houses, of failure, of becoming too big and successful. So they are still making curtains in the spare bedroom. Of course, their business might have failed, but what a pity their ability only to predict the future negatively stopped them trying.

Ways to stop predicting the future negatively

■ Identify the words and phrases which start you on the path of visualizing depressing outcomes.
■ Stop these automatic thoughts as far up the chain as possible.
■ Replace them with alternative thoughts using reality thinking with coping language.
■ Follow this thinking chain till a more positive prediction of the future comes to mind.
■ Visualize success.

Visualization is so much more powerful a tool than most of us realize. If we visualize a successful outcome it is much more likely to happen: it is a kind of mental programming. Sadly, the opposite is also true.

The trick with visualization is to imagine good outcomes as vividly as possible. Think of your mind's eye as a television screen where you are increasing the colour and brightness controls to gain maximum impact. In a day-dreaming moment at the bus stop, coffee break or journey home, imagine successful solutions or positive possibilities to any issue or problem you might have. This raises your awareness and alerts you to opportunities, a little like when you buy a red car and that day you become aware of vast numbers of red cars inhabiting the roads of Britain. Our perceptions are heightened and honed towards our goals and desires.

Your ability to be creative

Everyone can learn to be more creative. There are a few simple things you can do to increase you personal creativity quotient.

Increase your energy

It takes a lot of energy to see things afresh and come up with new ideas on a consistent basis. Exercise has been shown, albeit in mice, to stimulate learning by increasing brain chemicals like endorphins. It does not have to be excessive: 30 to 40 minutes a day brisk walking does the trick.

Vitamins provide us with energy, and since we are not like plants and manufacture our own vitamins, we must get them from the food we eat. It would be great to think that we get sufficient from our food intake, but that is doubtful unless we eat our vegetables directly from the field or allotment, so supplements are good. For example, herbal extracts such as gingko biloba and ginseng were given to a group of students taking a maths test. They sat the test without the supplements, then were given either a placebo or the herbal pills. Those on the gingko biloba and ginseng showed dramatic improvements. Apparently the herbs increase the blood flow to the brain, which in turn improves concentration.

Take a new look at things

One of the major factors which stops us from seeing things differently is routine. It is a way of streamlining our lives so that we are not spending quantities of time thinking about tieing our shoelaces, for example. However, the downside is that we become inured to our environment. The freshness of perception of a child is captivatingly creative.

So take a new look at things. The following are some ideas. You can compile your own list.

- Take a new route home.
- Visit a gallery, park or zoo. This is especially good if you are unused to such diversions.
- Move your desk around at the office so that you are looking at a different view.
- Stir your coffee with your non-dominant hand, or practise using both hands at once.

Have ideas

Having ideas is terribly important if you wish to acquire a directorial role, but how do you generate ideas?

The more fanciful you can be, the better, as today's off-the-wall idea is tomorrow's reality. If you are quite 'ploddy', you need to learn to be spontaneous about the first thought that enters your head.

Visualize the ideal situation at work or in your personal life, and work back to ideas that would make those changes happen. The more relaxed you are, the more likely you are to have ideas. 'Eureka!' and baths come to mind.

Research what other departments have done about a similar issue, then add some modifications. This is just as creative as coming up with the idea from scratch. Tom Peters, the business management guru, talked about the adaptation of others' ideas as 'creative swiping'. So creatively swipe to your heart's content if it helps you to problem solve.

Learn to Mind Map

In 1974, Tony Buzan launched the concept of Mind Maps. Mind Mapping, he claimed, reflects the way our brains work using radiant thinking. Every brain cell is capable of embracing as many as 10,000 other brain cells at the same time. Radiant thinking reflects this internal structure. Every time you have a thought it is like trying to clear a pathway through a forest. The first time you have to hack your way through the undergrowth, but the second time is easier as you have travelled that way before. One thought may make countless connections irradiating from that initial input. Of course, making connections is the very stuff of creativity; the 'aha' we get when we see the significance of a fact or idea.

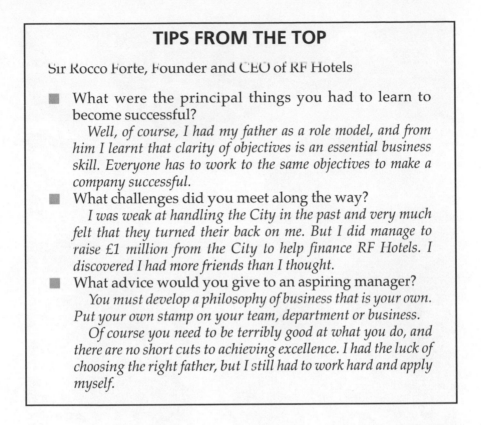

TIPS FROM THE TOP

Sir Rocco Forte, Founder and CEO of RF Hotels

- What were the principal things you had to learn to become successful?

   Well, of course, I had my father as a role model, and from him I learnt that clarity of objectives is an essential business skill. Everyone has to work to the same objectives to make a company successful.

- What challenges did you meet along the way?

   I was weak at handling the City in the past and very much felt that they turned their back on me. But I did manage to raise £1 million from the City to help finance RF Hotels. I discovered I had more friends than I thought.

- What advice would you give to an aspiring manager?

   You must develop a philosophy of business that is your own. Put your own stamp on your team, department or business.

   Of course you need to be terribly good at what you do, and there are no short cuts to achieving excellence. I had the luck of choosing the right father, but I still had to work hard and apply myself.

At school we were perhaps taught to take or make notes in a linear fashion, using sentences. The drawbacks of this method are:

- Full sentences obscure the key words with irrelevant ands, buts and sos.
- They are difficult to remember.
- They fail to stimulate creativity.
- They waste time by requiring you to reread them.
- You have probably had to reread this list.
- They may run to many pages.

Tony Buzan found that during his lectures on memory, when he used linear notes, he could not remember what he was trying to say. This led to his quest for a system that reflected the way we think and remember and at the same time stimulated creativity. The Mind Map was born.

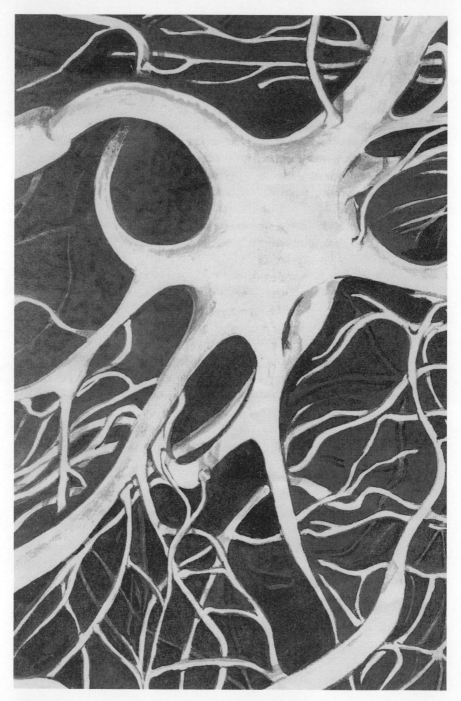

Figure 3.1 A single brain cell showing multiple linkages.

Advantages of Mind Maps

■ Mind Maps reflect the way we think, making connections from a central point.
■ They allow us to be more creative because they do not impose a premature structure on our thinking.
■ New information can be added without putting writing or arrows in margins.
■ Mind maps help us to memorize key points.
■ They are great for brainstorming for problem solving, report writing or preparing for a presentation. You put down anything that occurs to you, around a central theme and in no set order. It beats staring at a blank page pen poised waiting for inspiration to alight.

Mind Mapping guidelines

■ Start with a word or image in the centre of the page. It helps to turn your page sideways – there is more space that way.
■ Words should be printed in capitals, so you can read them easily.
■ You should only use key words, one word or two at the most per line.
■ Colours, images, action of any sort stimulate the memory.
■ Your mind should be left as free as possible during this process. Any thinking about where items should go will curtail the creative process of making unusual connections amongst the items. Analysing and ordering can come later.

In terms of creative problem solving, mind mapping is great at identifying where the real problem lies. Sarah, a human resources manager in a national bank, was unhappy in her job but felt unable to move as her husband had recently said how much they needed her wage. She volunteered herself as a case study to a group who were practising problem solving. They mind mapped all the issues, asking her questions to clarify the situation.

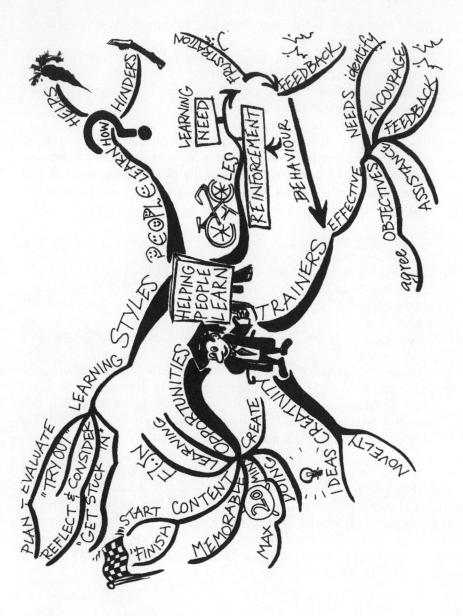

Figure 3.2 A sample Mind Map

Sarah's Mind Map

The group asked about her job. A colleague had left the department, and since there was an embargo on recruitment she had ended up doing two jobs with little training and no increased remuneration. The group discovered she had not discussed this situation with her boss. She felt he ought to know about the stress he had placed on her, and should have spoken to her or sorted it out. The reality was that he had not.

They then asked about her husband. Would he mind her being in another job, would he worry about the possibility of less pay, and if she chose to return to studying to become more skilled, would this be an issue for him? She had not discussed any of these issues.

Another thing which vexed her was a colleague who was not pulling her weight. Any conversations she had fell on deaf ears, so being Sarah, she just carried out the work herself.

Was the job or her husband the real problem? Reviewing the evidence, the group thought not. Analysing the Mind Map, it became clear that Sarah lacked assertiveness. She had not told her boss of her difficulties, had not asserted herself with her lazy colleague, and had not really discussed with her husband what she wanted to do with her life. She left the course with a plan of action to confront all these items. The latest we heard was that her husband really did not mind cutting back on their outgoings so that she could return to full time studying later that year. In the short term her boss cut back on the work she had to do, hired someone else, and the young woman who had not been pulling her weight left when it looked as if she was going to have an increased workload.

Having your problems analysed and brainstormed using a Mind Map is like being mentally massaged. It is revealing and inspiring and so motivational. We often get stuck in our thinking as we become submerged in routine lives.

Draw your own Mind Map

You could Mind Map one of your own problems or issues. Analyse it yourself, or if you're brave enough, reveal it to a colleague and suggest they brainstorm some solutions with you.

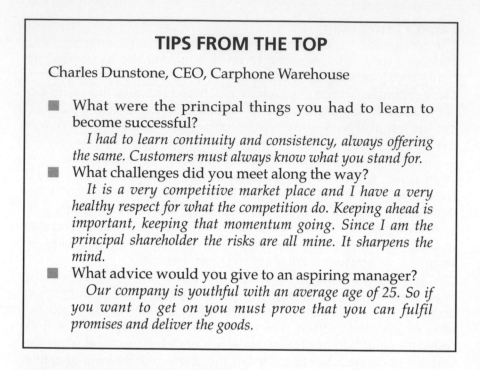

TIPS FROM THE TOP

Charles Dunstone, CEO, Carphone Warehouse

■ What were the principal things you had to learn to become successful?

I had to learn continuity and consistency, always offering the same. Customers must always know what you stand for.

■ What challenges did you meet along the way?

It is a very competitive market place and I have a very healthy respect for what the competition do. Keeping ahead is important, keeping that momentum going. Since I am the principal shareholder the risks are all mine. It sharpens the mind.

■ What advice would you give to an aspiring manager?

Our company is youthful with an average age of 25. So if you want to get on you must prove that you can fulfil promises and deliver the goods.

Facilitating your team

It is surprising how few business meetings contain creative problem solving. Sitting passively listening to a series of presentations, the chairman pontificating, the finance director number crunching, with actions no one agrees to and certainly no one intends to do anything about, still seems to be the norm. Of course spreadsheets are important and presentations useful, but they are not sufficient to involve and motivate those attending. The problem solving process called CREATE (see Figure 3.3) could signify the end to boring meetings.

The idea with problem solving is that you open up discussions in sequence using divergent techniques like brainstorming and mind mapping, then home in on priorities or actions. The whole thing looks like a series of fish tails. At each stage of CREATE, divergent tools are used first, followed by the convergent: closing in on the ideas that suit, fit the context or are doable.

Let's work through an example. Sales have slumped in a consultancy firm. The consultants and administration staff are meeting to

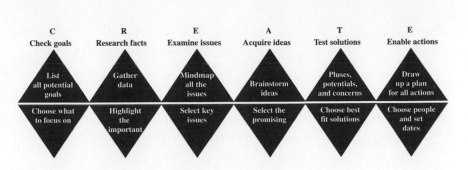

C	R	E	A	T	E
Check goals	Research facts	Examine issues	Acquire ideas	Test solutions	Enable actions
List all potential goals	Gather data	Mindmap all the issues	Brainstorm ideas	Pluses, potentials, and concerns	Draw up a plan for all actions
Choose what to focus on	Highlight the important	Select key issues	Select the promising	Choose best fit solutions	Choose people and set dates

Figure 3.3   CREATE – The problem solving process

come up with an action plan that will allow sales to exceed last year's turnover.

C R E A T E the problem solving process

*C*heck goals

There may be many reasons why sales have not been as good this year, so as leader or facilitator of this group you need to be clear about the main issues. Start by being divergent: ask the meeting what they are, and put the replies on a flip chart.

Even in the best of groups, some people contribute more than others. A technique which helps to ensure everyone participates is to ask people to write their suggestions on post-it notes which are then stuck on the flip chart or wall. Someone then clusters them into topics.

You can achieve convergence by giving everyone two ticks which they can place beside the list of topics. Choose to explore the most-ticked four or five areas. These might be:

- cold calling to achieve more clients;
- better follow-up after proposals have been sent to clients;
- more repeat business;
- becoming better known in the market place;
- finding out if clients like the company.

You are now clear what needs to be tackled, and can move to section two of the process.

*R*esearch facts

Before continuing, the group may have to check some facts. For example:

- How well has cold calling been carried out to date?
- How are proposals followed up? What is the time lag between sending a proposal out and winning the business?
- What is the repeat business rate? Are the statistics to hand?
- How well is the company known in the market place?
- What do clients think are the company's strengths, and are they exploited? Client survey results could be revisited.

Let's assume the major issue is that the organization is not well known in the world of consultancy. This is the issue which will be addressed by the group using the creative problem-solving method. Without going through this process, the group could have ended up dealing with the wrong problem: say, sales instead of position in the marketplace.

*E*xamine issues

The next stage of divergence is to Mind Map everything around the issue chosen, becoming better known. You are not focusing on solutions but still concentrating on the problem. Many branches might be attached to the map: poor PR, boring exhibition stand, too low a budget, difficult market sector, no research, other consultants doing similar things.

The group can then converge on what it would like to solve. Let's say it would like an exhibition stand that stood out from the crowd, but it has no budget.

*A*cquire ideas

The group brainstorms as many ideas as they can in two minutes. Wild ideas are the best, as they move you away from what has been done before.

Rules for generating ideas

- Go for quantity not quality.
- Do not worry about making mistakes or coming up with the right answer, just go for as many ideas as possible. The time for

analysis is later.

- Do not be judgmental.
  There are no right or wrong answers
- Freewheel with thoughts and ideas.
- Keep the momentum going with the first thing that comes into your head. The faster the pace the better.
- Make connections.
  Piggy back on others' ideas. Use them as prompts.

To put this process into practice, try to think of 100 uses for a table tennis ball in two minutes.

Now choose your best idea. Was it a very practical choice, or was it one of your more outrageous ideas? The latter is probably the better to pursue. As Osbourne and Parnes, founders of the Creative Problem-solving Institute, say, 'You can tame a lion but you can't make a cat roar'. In other words it is the unusual, weird, off-the-wall idea which you can modify to become something doable. The ordinary or commonplace has probably been done before and takes you nowhere new.

To get people into the frame of mind for brainstorming can take some time. The majority of our day, if not our lives, is taken up with logical thinking and giving reasons for our actions. To access the more creative right brain we need to leave all that behind, as creativity thrives on spontaneity and relaxation, so you should start with a mental limbering up exercise like the one above. You could brainstorm anything: uses for light bulbs, toilet rolls, bricks. To increase the fun, reward the team with the most ideas.

Convergence comes from getting the group to choose their best ideas, one of which has to be off the wall. The idea might be to rob a bank to get money for the exhibition stand. Taming this thought might be to get sponsorship from the company's bank or to ask for a loan or grant through banking contacts.

*T*est solutions
List all ideas and review which ideas have best fit for the group. Questions to be asked might be:

- How might these ideas be improved?
- What could we really see ourselves doing?

■ What reservations might we have about implementation?

How many meetings have we attended where everyone has agreed to solutions, only to disagree in the coffee room afterwards? If there are reservations, they should be discussed openly, and ways round them brainstormed, before finalizing actions. Then you are much more likely to achieve compliance from the group.

If our hypothetical group chose as their solution that they would seek outside investment for their exhibition stand from a venture capitalist or business angel, many in the company might be extremely worried about ownership and interference. Reservations would have to be treated seriously, with brainstorming around how the organization could maintain its culture and safeguards as to how much control and equity the outside investor would have.

*E*nable actions

What are all the action steps that can be taken to implement the solution? Who will undertake to do what and by when? It is a good idea to draw up an action plan as in Table 3.2.

Table 3.2 Sample action plan

Actions	Who	Timescales
Compile list of investors	Gary	End of the week
Talk to friends re investment opportunity	All consultants	Tomorrow
Write document describing opportunity	Directors	Tomorrow
Produce document	Liz	The day after tomorrow
Design and cost exhibition stand	Design company	Next month

There are a number of advantages of problem solving this way.

■ Everyone is involved. See below for the good outcomes of involvement.
■ What you end up with is often a surprise but is usually the best fit for the problem.
■ You achieve greater buy in when everyone considers possible reservations.

■ Everyone gets the chance to be creative.

Establishing a creative environment

Creativity is essential for business growth and change, and for establishing a competitive edge, but needs to be nurtured carefully.

The office
The traditional environment of separate offices and the lords and masters on the top floor is not conducive to spontaneity and invention. Open plan helps only if the senior team is part of that environment, and there are allocated spaces for relaxed meetings with couches, colours, pictures and plants. Creativity flourishes in a relaxed environment.

The culture
Ideas like a culture of respect, equality, reward and recognition. If the culture of your team or department involves put-downs and scapegoating, the chances of your getting an idea out of them will be remote. If ruled by fear, people simply hide their failures and toe the party line. Reward and appreciate, and you will be knee-deep in suggestions for improvements.

The team
Generating an atmosphere of fun and enjoyment means that you will have a group of volunteers not conscripts. Dull meetings should be eradicated and replaced by short sharp ones in the morning when everyone is at their decision-making best. The more participation you can achieve, the more enjoyment will be had and the more creativity you will get when you need it.

Keys

■ Ensure that your attitude and thinking are conducive to problem solving. Be aware of faulty thinking and change it accordingly.
■ Increase your ability to be creative by becoming more energetic, taking a new look at things and by learning to mind map.

■ Become familiar with the problem solving process CREATE and help your team become more creative.

■ Establish a creative environment by encouraging relaxation not stress, by rewarding not blaming, and fostering the involvement of everyone in the ideas-generation process.

four

The second commandment: deliver the goods

> Successful people know what has to be done, and they need to achieve results. The key is the development of a results focus in which the end point is clearly understood and there is a sense of urgency in striving to get there. Once there, of course, new goals are set and the process begins again.

In our survey of the characteristics of success, 'needing to achieve results' was the second most highly rated item overall. Among women, it was rated as the most important single characteristic.

The drive to deliver results is evidently built into successful people, and seems to exist almost for its own sake. When we asked people why they were driven to succeed, their answers became much more uncertain and diverse. Some simply turned the question round and said they had a 'fear of failure'. Others wanted to 'win', or loved 'success'. Patrick Sargeant declared that he was driven by 'greed and vanity', and Sir Rocco Forte unashamedly admitted a desire to 'make lots of money'.

Many felt an obligation to those who had put them into power, or to the people whose lives they now influenced. For Ian Brindle this was a 'responsibility to those who had elected him chairman', for Sir Bryan Nicholson the 'sheer pleasure of being able to help people'. Simple ego peeped out of many of the responses. Tom Hamilton acknowledged a 'touch of glory seeking', and Tim

Melville-Ross sought the 'glow of recognition'. Teresa Graham recognized that part of her job was 'being a role model'. Delivering results entitles the individual to demand recognition, approval and reward.

Often, the desire for results was taken to be a basic human drive. Adam Broadbent said, 'It's how you know you are alive – it's what human beings are meant to do'. More fundamentally still, Gwynneth Flower attributed the drive to 'pigheadedness', and Lord Gordon of Strathclyde anticipated having to account for himself on 'the day of judgement'. Some attributed the drive to the simple need to survive. Ed Palmer, brought up in the depression, believed this was a matter of 'feeding your children', and Colin Rutherford acknowledged the influence of humble roots and a 'competitive family upbringing'. Dame Stella Rimington felt she had simply 'inherited the work ethic from my father'.

Whatever its origins, the need to achieve results permeates the behaviour of those who succeed in business. So how is this developed? And how do you ensure that you choose the right results to go for, and behave so you are likely to achieve those results?

First, let's concentrate on the results to be achieved. In one of the most successful motivational books of all time, *The Seven Habits of Highly Effective People*, Steven Covey emphasizes the importance of differentiating things that are important from those that are urgent. Covey suggests we are too easily diverted by the immediate urgency of everyday things. An example is telephone calls. The price we pay for filling our days with this urgent clutter is a failure to tackle things which are truly important and might really develop our careers and ourselves.

How many of us would admit there are things we should be doing, but we allow the busyness of everyday life to postpone getting round to them? Perhaps we should be undertaking personal training, developing a business plan, writing to customers, mastering the computer, arranging a team meeting, making contact with a colleague, developing new products, publishing an article, writing a book. If you are feeling mildly guilty at this point (don't worry, even writing the list causes us pain), then continue. This chapter is about establishing a personal action plan that will deliver real results.

Exercise: finding the priorities

For a start, let's identify those things that would move us closer to the boardroom, rather than those that are wasting our time. This exercise has three stages.

Stage one is to list all the things that you _could_ do next week (assuming that is a reasonably typical week). Include the things you usually do, the paperwork, the meetings, the reports and so on, and the things in your diary and on your action list. Also include things that would be worthwhile if only you could get round to them. These might include making contact with influential people, signing up for a training course or writing a strategic plan. Make sure you add anything that you feel might be worthwhile, no matter how daunting or time-consuming it seems. Don't worry about making a judgement yet: if they occur to you, add them to the list.

Stage two is the judgement stage. Take a sheet of paper and divide it into four sections using two dividing lines labelled as shown in Figure 4.1. Now put everything on your list onto the matrix you have constructed. For each item you are making two assessments. First, does this really have to be done next week? If it's an absolute must, it goes over on the far right. If it could be

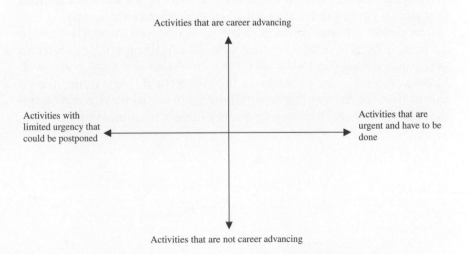

Figure 4.1 A career priority matrix

postponed without any problem, it's placed on the far left. In-between things are placed somewhere between the left–right extremes according to your judgement of their urgency.

The second assessment is the extent to which these items will enhance your career. How much closer to the boardroom will they bring you? Really useful career items go at the top of the page. The things that do nothing for your career go at the bottom. Again, make a judgement about the things that fall between the two extremes and position them on the page accordingly.

You will now have a page with all your options for next week placed in four quadrants, as in Figure 4.2.

- Quadrant 1 contains those things that are urgent and also career enhancing.
- Quadrant 2 contains the items that will promote your career but don't have to be done next week.
- Quadrant 3 represents the things that seem urgent in that they have to be done next week, but really don't deliver much in the way of career development.
- Quadrant 4 items don't have much going for them. They don't have to be done yet and they don't do much for your career.

Stage three, the final stage of this exercise, is to draw up a personal action plan. More paper is needed because this has to be committed to writing! Each quadrant needs to be considered separately.

The career-enhancing/urgent things (quadrant 1) clearly have to go on the list. If there is no time left for anything else, everything you do is developing you and your career in the way you want. However, if there is still space in the week (or if there are *no* urgent things that are career enhancing) then there is still work to do on the diary, and we need to consider some of the other quadrants.

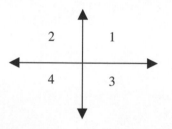

Figure 4.2   The four quadrants of the career priority matrix

The real challenge comes in dealing with those things that would add career value but which do not have urgency (quadrant 2). These are the items that prey on the conscience since we know they should be done but keep postponing them. Now is the time to grip them! *Somehow* they have to be scheduled, so make the decision on how and when. Perhaps they are too big and too daunting, in which case use the next exercise to break them down into manageable elements. If the problem is that they have been postponed too long, write them into the plan so it is clear exactly what you are going to do and when – and then commit to them.

This might leave an awkward list of the things that don't add to your career but still have to be done (quadrant 3). Often, these comprise the bulk of our jobs. A bit of creativity is called for here. Can these tasks be streamlined? Have we allowed them to fill the time available? Are we deluding ourselves that they have to be done? Can any of them be delegated so that some of our own time is freed up? Can they be done in a different way that is career enhancing? These items are like the scrappy files that fill up our computer memory. They need to be deleted or compressed to free up space.

Finally, ditch everything in quadrant 4.

TIPS FROM THE TOP

Sir Clive Thompson, CEO, Rentokil

- What was the principal thing you had to learn to become successful?

    Nothing in particular, 'though I am learning all the time. I don't go on formal training courses.
- What challenges did you have to meet along the way?

    Business is a continual challenge – you must take evaluated risks. But you don't have to change everything all the time – evolution is often better than revolution.
- What advice would you give to an aspiring manager?

    Plan ahead. Avoid vagueness. Integrity is your number one requirement.

Exercise: eating an elephant

The 'Finding the priorities' exercise may well have revealed a common problem: we know some things are genuinely important, but can't quite get round to them because they are too big or too radical. These are likely to be found in quadrant 2 of the prioritizing exercise. Confucius is reported to have said that 'The journey of 1,000 miles begins with the first step'. So the purpose of this exercise is to break down a daunting task into doable elements. It has four simple stages.

Stage one is to identify the task. What do you, or your business, most need? A degree? Increased profitability? Training in public speaking? A detailed five-year plan? The launch of a new product? Maybe nothing springs to mind, or maybe you have several ideas but are not absolutely sure whether they are right for you. In that case, you may like to return to this exercise after reading other parts of the book. However, if you have been able to home in on a task, move to stage two.

Stage two is to break the task down into deliverable elements. Sometimes this is obvious and straightforward. Increased profitability, for example, might comprise:

1. Detailed analysis of current profitability by area and product line.
2. Market research to identify most promising areas for future development.
3. Analysis of expenses to find opportunities for cost reduction.
4. Planned phase-out of unprofitable lines.
5. Setting up teams to introduce new, profitable, products.
6. Revision of bonus system to give better incentive for profitable performance.
7. Re-training of managers in budget control.
8. Revision of budget to reflect new programme.

This is a simplified version of a plan that might contain many stages and sub-stages, but it illustrates the way in which a daunting business challenge must be gripped: by conversion to deliverable, actionable items. Some tasks may be complicated to break down because the stages do not consist of a simple continuous sequence: a number of things may have to happen simultaneously, and the details of one stage may be dependent on the outcome of previous stages. The launch of a new product could well fall into this category. Planning for a really complicated task may require the use of special techniques such as the Gantt chart, which shows the progress of the various elements and the way in which they interrelate. Specialist books and dedicated software are available, so maybe the first stage of the exercise is to research the most appropriate tool.

Stage three is to set the timetable and make a personal commitment to ensure the job gets done. Did stage two break the task down into steps you are reasonably comfortable with? If not, break it down some more. Once you are happy with the stages, put them in your diary. It doesn't matter if the job is going to take a long time, provided it has become realistic. Time passes, and doing the job a step at a time is vastly better than constantly projecting it into the never-to-come future.

Stage four is to make that first step. Call the team together, explain the plan, set the ball rolling. It is the door to success, and will give you the heady thrill of taking positive action.

Now let's explore another key element of success, an imperative if real results are to be delivered. This is the vital factor of personal enthusiasm. We were talking with a young man, Stephen, who had not really settled into a career and felt that he might be suited for work as a consultant. As we talked, it became clear that he was really excited by the potential for a change in direction, but that only the analytical and financial elements of consulting work appealed to him. We suggested that he build his plan with these as the focus, and suddenly the discussion sparked into life. These were the things that Stephen enjoyed and was good at, and the idea of a career that directly delivered them kindled an enthusiasm that he had never really associated with work before. Stephen spent some time at an independent career assessment centre, and is now embarking on a career in accountancy with a passion and pleasure he had not thought possible.

We are unlikely to deliver results at work if we do not positively enjoy what we are doing, but sadly the business world is full of misfitting round pegs that have been driven into square holes. One common problem is feeling constrained by our qualifications. During our schooldays we may have been gently (or not so gently) steered towards 'suitable' subjects, but perhaps they were suitable for our teachers and our parents rather than for us. Suddenly we find that our GCSEs and A-levels have started to close doors rather than open them. We may even press on with a degree in a subject which, somehow, we never really seemed to choose. Then we find that all we are qualified to do is to design a chemical reactor, when all we ever *wanted* to do was run a bookshop.

Let's try a short exercise to see whether the things we do at work deliver sufficient excitement to drive results. This involves another matrix.

TIPS FROM THE TOP

Sir Richard Greenbury, former CEO and Chairman of Marks and Spencer

■ **What were the principal things you had to learn to become successful?**

I had to learn to develop and communicate a consistent vision and so I had to have a very clear idea of where the business was going.

I also learnt to acquire patience. Not everyone thinks in the same way or at the same pace.

During bad patches I can begin to question my decisions but I have learnt not to let that dominate my thinking.

■ **What challenges did you meet along the way?**

The climate for retail recently has been very tough, and as a result dealing with the press has been particularly challenging. They forget all that has gone before, that during my time as CEO, profits trebled at Marks and Spencer.

■ **What advice would you give to an aspiring manager?**

You need to grab opportunities if you want to get ahead. And if you achieve then you will be promoted. Do not be frightened of the 'big jobs' or the international assignments. That broadening is very important for success.

Get yourself around successful people. My Chairman's Executive development course at Marks and Spencer did just that by introducing high fliers to the great and the good.

Work on having the desire to go to the next rung of the promotional ladder, not an overriding desire to get to the top. Then you will make decisions that will help the business first.

Exercise: enthusiasm test

Stage one is to make a list of all of the things you *could* do professionally. Some creativity is called for here, since this is not meant to be a list of the things you actually do (although they should be down there) but anything you might have the capability of doing. Here is a possible list (yours may be longer):

■ Make presentations.
■ Prepare budgets.
■ Sell products to clients.
■ Participate in meetings.
■ Undertake employee reviews.
■ Interview job applicants.
■ Write reports.
■ Produce promotional literature.
■ Work on computer spreadsheets.
■ Train other employees.
■ Visit clients to advise on products.
■ Devise new products.
■ Check monthly returns.

Stage two is to construct the matrix. See Figure 4.3: this time the axes represent the extent to which you actually do the things on the list, and the level of excitement they generate.

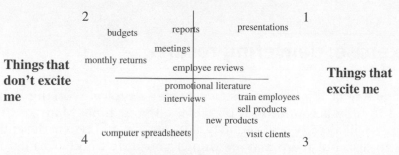

Figure 4.3 Enthusiasm test matrix

Stage three is to assess your business life as revealed by the matrix. In essence our objective is to lead a life in quadrant one. This involves developing a plan in which quadrant three items are cultivated, and quadrant two items are abandoned. The things we have written into quadrant four are not a problem unless someone is trying to manoeuvre them our way – to be resisted at all costs!

Our example shows someone who wants to interact with other people through selling and training, but is stuck with administrative tasks that give no pleasure. The only job feature that raises adrenalin is making presentations. It's probably time for a chat with the boss.

Now we should move on with the business of delivering results. The next aspect is that of efficiency. In science, efficiency is defined as the ratio of the useful energy output of a machine to the energy input. In a perfect machine, all the energy is converted to useful output, but there's no such thing as a perfect machine, or a perfect human. Some energy is always wasted; the question is how much?

In talking with our interviewees it was noticeable that they consistently disliked wasting time. This is not to suggest that they filled every moment with intense direct business activity. If that was the case they would have been unlikely to give us at least two hours of their time. But they often went to great lengths to ensure that their days were highly organized, and that the things they did contributed to their objectives. Much of the objective here is to avoid the lure of those urgent pressing things that can consume the week without delivering anything, and to ensure that the really important items are dealt with, even if their return will be some way in the future.

This next exercise is a measure of efficiency. How much of your time is really productive?

Exercise: delivering results

Stage one of this exercise is to consider a typical working month and to fully account for, if possible, all your time. Many of these things will already be listed in quadrants one and two of the enthusiasm test, but there may be things you didn't bother to itemize there like talking to colleagues, sorting the post and reading e-mails. Don't worry if this list is embarrassing: a study of this sort undertaken by Reams Office Personnel in Detroit contained items like 'chatting at coffee machine', 'making personal phone calls', and 'daydreaming'. Your list needs to be honest, and it is for your eyes only.

Stage two is to itemize your activities on separate lines in the 'activity' columns of an activity table. (Table 4.1 is a worked example.)

For **stage three**, first estimate the time spent on each item each month. The total should come close to the total time available (about 160 hours if you work eight-hour days and five-day weeks). (If it doesn't, think through your working month again.) Enter these times in the second column.

Now make a ruthless judgement about the extent to which each of these items contributes to your business results. We're not concerned here whether the things are necessary, just whether they deliver results. There has to be an element of subjective judgement in this estimation, and in the example in Table 4.1 someone has decided that checking e-mails makes only a 5 per cent contribution to results, attending committees makes no contribution at all, and presenting to clients is 100 per cent productive. The percentage efficiency estimates go into column 3.

Now multiply column 2 by column 3 to find the 'equivalent' productive time from each element. Enter these times in column 4. Then add the figures in column 2 and column 4 to give your total actual time, and equivalent total productive time. Finally, calculate the percentage of your time which is effectively productive by working out the column 4 total as a percentage of the column 2 total. The calculation for this is shown as a worked example at the

Table 4.1 Worked example of an activity table

Activity	Time spent each month	How much does this contribute to results?	Equivalent result-producing time
Checking e-mails	20 hours	5%	1 hour
Presenting to clients	15 hours	100%	15 hours
Attending internal committees	20 hours	0%	0 hours
TOTAL	55 hours		16 hours
Percentage of time productive = $16 \times 100 \div 55 = 29\%$			

bottom of Table 4.1, indicating that this individual is only 29 per cent productive. More illuminatingly, it shows where the problems are. The majority of time is spent on things that don't get anywhere: reading e-mails and attending committees. The majority of 'result' is delivered by something that occupies a minority of the time, presenting to clients.

The phenomenon of the majority of effect resulting from a minority of the input is known as the Pareto effect, after the Italian economist Vilfredo Pareto, who noted that most of the wealth in society was owned by a minority of the population. It leads to extremely useful observations about the way we spend our time, and the things that are worthy of our attention.

Stage four is to draw conclusions from the table and act on them. In the example, there is clearly a need to streamline reading e-mails and opt out of some internal committees, then increase the time spent presenting to clients and perhaps introduce some of the important priorities which were identified in the first exercise in this chapter.

If this chapter has succeeded in homing in on some action priorities that will really help to deliver results, there is one remaining question. How will you know when you have got there? Our final exercise in this section is to ensure that your 'results' have been defined with enough precision to be meaningful – and measurable.

TIPS FROM THE TOP

Nicholas Coleridge, MD, Condé Nast UK

- What were the principal things you had to learn to become successful?
  Learning about money and balance sheets.
- What challenges did you meet along the way?
  The challenge is to produce a beautiful object that is a magazine but at the same time running a profitable business.
- What advice would you give to an aspiring manager?
  You must always work for good people.

Exercise: how will you know when you've got there?

All being well, this chapter will have produced a list of actions which, if implemented, would further your career, enthuse and excite you, and deliver results for the business. But are these actions really achievable? Or are they rather vaguely defined, a good wish list but somehow removed from reality? This final stage is to convert the action list into genuine deliverables – items you can write in your diary and tick off when completed.

This exercise is important both as a reality test, and as an opportunity to set some deadlines. In our interviews, the need to make a budget, publish a magazine on time or prepare for a shareholders' meeting was commonly the driving force which spurred our leaders into action. In writing this book we used the 'eating an elephant' exercise (a chapter at a time), and imposed a deadline on ourselves for each part. All, of course, against the background of the publisher breathing down our necks!

Stage 1 is to write down the actions you have resolved to implement. For the plan to improve profitability we discussed earlier, in summary this would be:

- Analyse current profitability.
- Undertake market research.
- Analyse expenses.
- Phase out unprofitable lines.
- Set up new product teams.
- Revise bonus system.
- Retrain managers.
- Revise budget.

Stage 2 is to identify measurement or completion criteria for each of the actions. For example, 'analyse current profitability' might require a report detailing the contribution to margin from each product, each region and each client over the past three years. Many actions will have more than one measurable component. For example, the aim to 'retrain managers' could be measured by the number of people trained, as well as the achievement of satisfactory scores on the training assessments.

Stage 3 is to set a target for each of the areas of measurement.

Finally, **stage 4** is to set the timescale.

See the example in Table 4.2.

A word of caution: the timescales should be less than 12 months unless you are embarking on something like a company relocation

Table 4.2   Sample action list

Objective	Measurement	Target	Timescale
Analyse current profitability	Produce report analysing profit by product, region and client	Identify all items capable of delivering more than 15% margin	1 month
Undertake market research	Produce report showing services with greatest potential for development	Identify three new areas for profitable development	3 months
Analyse expenses	Produce report itemizing all controllable expenses for past 12 months	Identify opportunity for 5% cost reduction	1 month
Phase out unprofitable lines	Discontinue products not contributing to profitability	Closure of all lines contributing less than 5% margin	10 months
Set up new product teams	Set up teams charged with delivery of three new products	Product development plans capable of implementation within 18 months	3 months from completion of market research
Revise bonus system	New bonus system directly related to individual's contribution to performance	Linkage of bonus to profitability with no net increase in total bonus allocations	6 months
Retrain managers	Managers to be retrained in financial skills with emphasis on profit delivery	All profit centre managers to undertake two-day course. 90% of managers to meet course attainment standards.	12 months
Revise budget	Budget to reflect short-term investment in new lines, and medium term delivery of improved margin	Budget supported and approved by board	2 months

or a personal degree course. Ideally, all the items should be capable of almost immediate initiation. This was a key finding in our interviews: everyone was clearly driven by the tasks in hand, but generally unenthusiastic about long-term goals.

One good reason for keeping the timescales short is that it keeps the door open to new opportunities. The ideal is to have long-term ambition coupled with short-term goals which keep you moving forward. According to Adam Broadbent, 'Long-term goals are no good – you might be dead', and Sir Ian Wood was concerned that 'long-term goals lead to inflexibility'. However, all were driven by the need to produce results and all were actively working on projects and plans designed to take them and their businesses forward.

Some aspects of your plan will be for the business, and need to be shared with colleagues. Others will be for your personal development, perhaps to be shared with a mentor, partner or boss, but otherwise kept to yourself. Sir Clive Thompson, who plans everything over a three- to five-year time scale, writes his personal plans in a secret code which no one else can understand.

The actions and timetables that you have constructed during this chapter form your personal business plan. The important thing is that you now have some actions which excite you, which feel realistic and, above all, you can get on with.

Good luck!

Keys

■ Identify priorities that will deliver personal and business results.
■ Develop an action programme broken down into deliverable elements.
■ Find business areas that are matched to your skills and enthusiasm.
■ Ensure your daily activities are producing real results.
■ Set clear targets and timescales.

five

The **third commandment: want to win**

> Those at the top have a drive to become successful and see this as an objective in its own right. They enjoy winning for the sake of it and often think of business life as a game. Their secret is an understanding of the rules and a desire to master them. They are motivated and know how to motivate others. This chapter will look at what drives people, how to find life rewarding as a manager and also how to make work fun.

Our executive group were characterized by an overwhelming desire to be successful and by wanting to win. As business people this involved making profits, but also included bringing new ideas to fruition and of course trouncing the competition. Sir Ian McAllister of Ford explained that there was nothing to compare with the feeling when a new car went on sale. Seeing all the advertising or even better, the cars on the streets, were wonderful rewards for him and a tangible result of his labours.

Sir Richard Greenbury enjoyed walking around the outposts of the Marks and Spencer kingdom. Dawn Airey and Denise O'Donoghue enjoyed the benefits of seeing their television programmes created from nothing. For others the balance sheet or the increase in share price had to suffice. The majority certainly loved the status of their roles. The men in our sample especially had large offices: some were the size of small tennis courts with desks situated at the serving end. Of particular note was the office of James Cullen at Bell Atlantic. More football pitch than tennis court, the green carpet seemed to stretch for miles till one met the distant gaze of the secretary. The most luxurious were Sy Steinberg's New York Assurance offices in a building of such antiquity and carpets of such pile. The interview was conducted to the muted tick of a grandfather clock.

Views from offices were also desirable, the higher up the better. Julian Richer's penthouse looks over St. James's Palace, 3i the panoply of Waterloo station. James Cullen has a vista of most of Manhattan. Of course, not everyone's office was of *Homes and Gardens* standard. The women in our sample had smaller, more functional offices but they did contain more flowers, and Denise O'Donoghue, on the dark winter evening when she was interviewed, had a perfumed candle burning.

So is a drive for success just a matter of focusing on rewards, or is there something else operating?

Two things come to mind. These people focus on their successes past and present. They were not all necessarily outstandingly successful at sport or academia, although most had degrees, but they do know what they are good at. Charles Dunstone of Carphone Warehouse, when asked to what he attributed his success, replied that he was good at selling phones. So there is a mind-set that tells you that you are a winner. This was supported recently by a representative from *Readers Digest*. He stated that despite the often small competition prizes people won, the fact of winning changed their perspective. They ceased to be failures. Second, our sample love what they do, be that selling phones, managing people, producing cars or operating a global retail outfit. So this sets the agenda for the next part of this chapter. We will discuss how you can achieve the mind-set of a winner and love what you do.

The winner mind-set

To know what you are good at and have this knowledge at the front of your mind, complete the winner's checklist below:

The winner's checklist

- One thing I like about myself is . . .
- One thing others like about me is . . .

- One thing I do very well is . . .
- A recent problem I've handled very well is . . .
- When I'm at my best I . . .
- I'm glad that I . . .
- Those who know me are glad that I . . .
- A compliment that has been paid to me recently is . . .
- A value that I try hard to put into practice is . . .
- An example of my caring about others is . . .
- People can count on me to . . .
- They said I did a good job when I . . .
- Something I'm handling better this year than last is . . .
- One thing that I've overcome is . . .
- A good example of my ability to manage my life is . . .
- I'm best with people when . . .
- One goal I'm presently working towards is . . .
- A recent temptation that I managed to overcome was . . .
- I pleasantly surprised myself when I . . .
- I think that I have the courage to . . .
- If I had to say one good thing about myself I'd say that I . . .
- One way I successfully control my emotions is . . .
- One way in which I am very dependable is . . .
- One important thing that I intend to do within two months is . . .

It is worth keeping this list nearby so when you are going through a bad day you can reread it and lift your spirits. If you found it difficult to complete, a number of factors might contribute:

- You may not know what you are good at. If this is the case, ask a colleague or boss for some feedback as to your talents.
- You may be someone who focuses on the negatives or is driven by a fear of failure. All available research and our own interviews show that successful people concentrate on strengths not weaknesses, success not failure. Of course we make mistakes, and everyone has weaknesses, but the successful learn from the former and supplement the latter by hiring good teams with the skills they lack.

Related to this particular key to career success is of course problem solving in a crisis and being confident. All involve utilizing a thinking style that focuses on solutions and the personal and group ability to achieve them. About half of our sample claimed to be born with this ability, but equally as many said it was hard won. If our parents have a positive approach to life and were rewarding to us, it is more likely we will be the same. However, literature is full of examples of people from deprived and depressing backgrounds which have fuelled their motivation to become successful. If they can turn their thinking around, so can you.

Love what you do

To love what you do, you must gain an understanding of what drives you; what gets you up in the morning. We know from researchers and theorists like Herzberg that there are general circumstances which motivate: achievement, recognition, interesting work, responsibility and advancement. But we are also individuals with differing needs and drives. A questionnaire called 'Career drivers survey' from *Managing Your Own Career* by D Francis provides great insight into nine major drivers. Follow the instructions carefully and see how you fare.

Career drivers

A word of warning before you complete the questionnaire: sometimes you will find yourself struggling to compare two items which appear equally relevant or irrelevant, but please persist. The technique forces you to weigh difficult choices, and the discipline has proved worthwhile. There are no right or wrong answers; it all depends upon personal preferences, so please be as honest and objective as you can. Work through the questionnaire quite quickly: 10 minutes is usually long enough.

Instructions
In Table 5.1 are listed 36 pairs of motives often cited by people asked what they want and need from their career. You must evaluate the relative importance to you of the statements within each pair and allocate three points between the pair: so you might allocate all three points to one item, or two to one and one to the other. The letters given before each item are for the purposes of scoring and need not concern you at this stage.

Table 5.1   Career drivers

1. A... I will only be satisfied with an unusually high standard of living.
   B ... I wish to have considerable influence over other people.
2. C... I only feel satisfied if the output from my job has real value in itself.
   D... I want to be an expert in the things I do.
3. E ... I want to use my creative abilities in my work.
   F ... It is specially important to me that I work with people I like.
4. G... I would obtain particular satisfaction by being able to choose freely what I want.
   H... I want to make quite sure that I will be financially secure.
5. I ... I enjoy feeling that people look up to me.
   A... Not to put too fine a point on it, I want to be wealthy.
6. B ... I want a substantial leadership role.
   C... I do that which is meaningful to me, even though it may not gain tangible rewards.
7. D... I want to feel that I have gained hard-won expertise.
   E ... I want to create things which people associate with me alone.
8. F ... I seek deep social relationships with other people in my work.
   G... I would get satisfaction from deciding how I spend my time.
9. A... I will not be content unless I have ample material possessions.
   D... I want to demonstrate to my own satisfaction that I really know my discipline.
10. C... My work is part of my search for meaning in life.
    E ... I want the things that I produce to bear my name.
11. A... I seek to be able to afford anything I want.
    H... A job with long-term security really appeals to me.
12. B ... I seek a role which gives me substantial influence over others.
    D... I would enjoy being a specialist in my field.
13. C... It is important to me that my work makes a positive contribution to the wider community.
    F ... Close relationships with other people at work are important to me.
14. E ... I want my personal creativity to be extensively used.
    G... I would prefer to be my own master.
15. F ... Close relationships with other people at work would give me special satisfaction.
    H... I want to look ahead in my life and feel confident that I will always be OK.
16. A... I want to be able to spend money easily.
    E ... I want to be genuinely innovative in my work.
17. B ... Frankly, I want to tell other people what to do.
    F ... For me, being close to others is really the important thing.
18. C... I look upon my career as part of a search for greater meaning in life.
    G... I have found that I want to take full responsibility for my own decisions.
19. D... I would enjoy a reputation as a real specialist.
    H... I would only feel relaxed if I were in a secure career.

Table 5.1 (continued) Career drivers

20. A... I desire the trappings of wealth.
     F ... I want to get to know new people through my work.
21. B ... I like to play roles which give me control over how others perform.
     G... It is important that I can choose for myself the tasks that I undertake.
22. C... I would devote myself to work if I believed that the output would
         be worthwhile in itself.
     H... I would take great comfort from knowing how I will stand on my
         retirement day.
23. F ... Close relationships with people at work would make it difficult
         from me to make a career move.
     I ... Being recognized as part of the establishment is important to me.
24. B ... I would enjoy being in charge of people and resources.
     E ... I want to create things that no one else has done before.
25. C... At the end of the day, I do what I believe is important, not that
         which simply promotes my career.
     I ... I seek public recognition.
26. E ... I want to do something distinctively different from others.
     H... I usually take the safe option.
27. B ... I want other people to look to me for leadership.
     I ... Social status is an important motivator for me.
28. A... A high standard of living attracts me.
     G... I wish to avoid being tightly controlled by a boss at work.
29. E ... I want my products to have my own name on them.
     I ... I seek formal recognition by others of my achievements.
30. B ... I prefer to be in charge.
     H... I feel concerned when I cannot see a long way ahead in my career.
31. D... I would enjoy being a person who had valuable specialist
         knowledge.
     G... I would get satisfaction from not having to answer to other people.
32. G... I dislike being a cog in a large wheel.
     I ... It would give me satisfaction to have a high-status job.
33. A... I am prepared to do most things for material reward.
     C... I see work as a means of enriching my personal development.
34. I ... I want to have a prestigious position in any organization for which
         I work.
     H... A secure future attracts me every time.
35. F ... When I have congenial social relationships nothing else really
         matters.
     D... Being able to make an expert contribution would give me
         particular satisfaction.
36. I ... I would enjoy the status symbols which come with senior
         positions.
     D... I aspire to achieve a high level of specialist competence.

Scoring

To score the questionnaire, add up all the points that you have given to each of the A, B, C, D, E, F, G, H, I items. Write the totals down and check that the grand total is 108. Then copy these scores on to the Career Drivers Profile chart (Table 5.2) by circling the numbers you scored for each letter. Join up the circles to give a diagrammatic profile of your personal career drivers, and read the next section to interpret your profile.

Table 5.2 Career drivers profile

24	24	24	24	24	24	24	24	24
23	23	23	23	23	23	23	23	23
22	22	22	22	22	22	22	22	22
21	21	21	21	21	21	21	21	21
20	20	20	20	20	20	20	20	20
19	19	19	19	19	19	19	19	19
18	18	18	18	18	18	18	18	18
17	17	17	17	17	17	17	17	17
16	16	16	16	16	16	16	16	16
15	15	15	15	15	15	15	15	15
14	14	14	14	14	14	14	14	14
13	13	13	13	13	13	13	13	13
12	12	12	12	12	12	12	12	12
11	11	11	11	11	11	11	11	11
10	10	10	10	10	10	10	10	10
9	9	9	9	9	9	9	9	9
8	8	8	8	8	8	8	8	8
7	7	7	7	7	7	7	7	7
6	6	6	6	6	6	6	6	6
5	5	5	5	5	5	5	5	5
4	4	4	4	4	4	4	4	4
3	3	3	3	3	3	3	3	3
2	2	2	2	2	2	2	2	2
1	1	1	1	1	1	1	1	1
0	0	0	0	0	0	0	0	0
A	B	C	D	E	F	G	H	I

Find out what drives you

The nine career drivers are:

A	Material rewards	seeking possessions, wealth and a high standard of living.
B	Power/influence	seeking to be in control of people and resources.
C	Search for meaning	seeking to do things which are believed to be valuable for their own sake.
D	Expertise	seeking a high level of accomplishment in a specialized field.
E	Creativity	seeking to innovate and be identified with original output.
F	Affiliation	seeking nourishing relationships with others at work.
G	Autonomy	seeking to be independent and able to make key decisions for oneself.
H	Security	seeking a solid and predictable future.
I	Status	seeking to be recognized and admired.

Your top two or three highest scores are your main drivers, the sources of energy and direction that shape your life. If we are unaware of these career drivers the danger is that we seek jobs or promotion to positions because it is the next step or everyone expects it of us, but if a job does not satisfy our major drivers we become dispirited, apathetic, even depressed – the opposite of motivated. This is the time to keep your CV perked up and distribute it to a few agencies or head hunters. It is always good to know your value in the marketplace, and this is a strategy used by fast-track managers to negotiate their way to the top. You do not have to leave, but it will give you increased confidence to negotiate. On the other hand this questionnaire may have confirmed your desire for new challenges. If so, then you can use knowledge of your drivers to interview the interviewer. For example, those with high power and influencer drivers must ask who they will be reporting to and where their job fits into the overall picture. Those of you with a drive to be experts should enquire about the availability of training and coaching before ever considering a position, and so on.

Here is a list of things to look out for and ways to interrogate your score.

- The most important question to ask yourself is, does your current position satisfy all your main drivers? If not, you must change your role immediately, or as soon as is humanly possible. We know this is not as easy as it sounds: mortgages and rents must be paid. But there are often areas within jobs that you could volunteer for, or you could delegate the draggy bits of your job to someone who would be motivated by them. (Ask everyone in your department or team to complete the questionnaire.) You can then concentrate on the satisfying parts.

- Your top drivers will change over time. For example, if you want to leave a large company to set up your own business, your career drivers profile might reveal a high power/influencing score coupled with a high autonomy score. This pattern is predictive of entrepreneurial zeal. It may be coupled with a high money score but that is less predictive than the other two. Plan to do your own thing if this pattern is yours.

- Look out for conflict between your scores. If you have a high autonomy and security score, for example, it could be that you are sticking with the wrong job because it is steady. Or you might be working for a charity and have a high money score. Wrong place to be!

TIPS FROM THE TOP

David Campbell, CEO, Ginger Productions

- What were the principle things you had to learn to become successful?
  I hate to fail but I have had to learn patience.
- What challenges did you meet along the way?
  When you start something different or new, you set yourself up to be shot down. The biggest thrill though is to confound all the critics when you are a runaway success.
- What advice would you give to an aspiring manager?
  Key areas are the people skills involved in motivation and management.

Helping others to win

Of course if you want to reach the board you need to take others' motivation into account as well as your own. You will certainly not be able to win by yourself. In the book *The Fish Rots From The Head*, Bob Garratt states that the fatal error managers make is that when the pressure is on they start to do tasks themselves. They gravitate to what makes them feel comfortable rather than what the job demands. This dabbling rather than managing can be avoided if you have an understanding of what drives other people to give of their best.

This is not always easy. The mistake we make is to imagine that other people are motivated in the same way as we are. We need to understand what other people's drivers are, how we can motivate them individually, and how we can so easily demotivate if we do not take this information into consideration.

High **meaning** scorers need you to spend time with them so they understand what is going on. They are easily demotivated if you are too busy to meet them, or cancel appointments even for the best of reasons.

You might notice a head of department or team leader was over-worked and suggest splitting the role to help ease the pressure. This would be a bad move with a high **power/ influencer** who would be insulted that you had eroded their power base, even for the best possible reasons. You would need to find a way of making this person in overall charge while bringing someone else on board to help.

High **material rewards** scorers can be highly demotivated by a delayed pay cheque or a late or lesser bonus. On the other hand, they are very easy to reward.

Bringing another **expert** in to provide a boost for a department may seem a great idea, but what will the resident experts feel? They must be handled with care accompanied by a lot of recognition for their existing expertise.

To suggest to people with a high **affiliation** drive that they should work on their own will have them looking at the appointments pages before you put a full stop at the end of your sentence. However, place them in the centre of a team and give them the social events to organize and you will have happy employees.

The worst thing you can say to high **creativity** scorers is 'do it the way we have always done it'. Boredom will ensue. Purposefully using them to brainstorm ideas, finding new ways of doing things to save time and money, will keep them motivated for ever – well, almost ever.

Asking people who are high in **autonomy** to report directly to you so that you can oversee their project and steer it in the right direction may seem sensible but will profoundly irritate them.

Put everyone on short-term contracts and the high **security** scorers will have sleepless nights, so let them know where they stand. Promoting someone without giving them the title or any outward trappings will have the high **status** scorer digging for freedom. Be prepared to discuss titles, desks, office size and even car choice at length, because these are their motivators.

It might be worthwhile at this juncture to reflect on motivators and demotivators in your own life. Fill in the 'my way' exercise below, describing not only the people and circumstances but specifically what they did or what happened. To help you a little, try reflecting initially on your early years. Did your parents motivate you to greater things? What about an elder brother or sister, relative or friend? Then think about school. Which teachers inspired you and which ones humiliated? Add to that sport, hobbies, college or university, your first job. Who or what at that time motivated or demotivated you? And what had the greatest impact on your life; moved you forward incrementally in skills or beliefs or emotional development?

Also, can you think who you might have motivated or who you might have demotivated?

TIPS FROM THE TOP

Peter Jacobs, former CEO, BUPA

■ What was the principal thing you had to learn to become successful?
Handling isolation and finding quality advisors.
■ What challenges did you have to meet along the way?
Managing the political environment. It's difficult to get change out of the government. Almost equally difficult was managing the medical profession – doctors and their professional bodies.
■ What advice would you give to an aspiring manager?
Work hard, be honest and use common sense. Find good employers and good mentors as early in your career as possible.

Exercise: my way

Who or what has motivated you?
Who or what has demotivated you?
Who have you motivated?
Who have you demotivated?

This exercise helps to focus on what has happened in the past, and should generate a 'do as you would be done by' philosophy. We tend to be more aware of who has motivated and demotivated us than who we have motivated or demotivated. We keenly feel the put-downs and exult in the praise, but when it comes to others there can be a memory lapse .

Reflect on the demotivators you listed. Add to the list if you were not precise enough. We must emulate the motivators and expunge any behaviour we have learnt from the demotivator group.

Learn how to reward

Herzberg and Maslow, famous motivation theorists, talk of the generalities of what motivates. Herzberg's 'satisfiers', as he calls them, involve responsibility, recognition, opportunity for advancement and work that is interesting. Maslow puts forward a hierarchical process of motivation, in that it is useless to offer advancement or self-development to someone who does not have enough money to pay the rent.

Further information about motivation comes from learning theory. Dogs, rats, pigeons and many other animals have been utilized in the experimental process. All have learnt, changed their behaviour and successfully acquired their pellet or cheese through the process of **reward**. As students, we all probably read about experiments with pigeons which were taught to turn cartwheels by researchers rewarding successive approximations to a cartwheel with pigeon food. Psychologists could have electrocuted them, spoken sternly to them or beaten them to a pulp to make them learn. However, reward worked.

Humans are not dissimilar to pigeons. In recent research into reward, quoted by Roger Firestein at the Creative Problem Solving Institute in Buffalo, it was discovered that if tutors worked with students to maintain a consistent academic performance, they had to reward them **four** times as much as they criticized. To improve the students' performance so that their exam results increased incrementally, tutors had to reward them **eight** times as much as they criticized.

This emphasizes the profound effect of reward. As a management skill it is probably the most important. The guidelines listed below will help you make your rewards even more rewarding.

Rules for rewards

Learning theory research provides the following principles for rewards. They must be:

- *Intermittent.* Rewards are most rewarding when they are not predictable or institutionalized like pay rises or bonuses. A thank you, a card, a box of chocolates on completion of an assignment is much more compelling. A parallel is gambling. If you were rewarded with a win every time you bet on something, there would be no excitement and of course no addiction.
- *Specific.* Rewards should be 'for' something well done, or something you would like to happen again. To be truly reinforcing you should outline the behaviour you admired, like working late three nights in a row or cooking, cleaning and washing up, rather than just being nice. 'Nice' is difficult to achieve again if you don't know specifically what you did.
- *Contingent.* Thank yous of any sort are more powerful if they happen immediately after an event rather than a week later, at the end of the month or at the end of the year. We associate the good feelings that accompany the reward with the action that led to it, and are more likely to act that way again, or even better next time.
- *Consistent.* If you reward one person for going that extra mile, your must notice and celebrate other extra miles. Unfairness ruins the entire process and leads to accusations of favouritism.
- *Relevant.* Tap into your knowledge of the career drivers of your team or department to choose a reward that suits and will motivate. There is the cautionary tale of the MD of a shipping company. The organization had gone through tough times during the recession, but had recovered through the good

services of the staff who had put in extra hours and taken pay cuts. The MD had dreamt of rewarding the entire workforce and their families with a Christmas cruise to celebrate the turnaround, but as he jauntily put up the poster advertising the event, the workforce went on strike. He was devastated. He hadn't asked them what *they* would like to do. They would have preferred a less expensive party, and some money for presents for their kids who had been deprived of luxuries during the recession.

- *Genuine*. Flattery for the purpose of ingratiation or achievement can easily be spotted (especially in tone of voice and body language). Rewards and compliments must be genuinely felt and sincerely praised.

Julian Richer, the very successful owner of Richer Sounds, put reward at the top of his leadership skills list. He owns 11 houses. Two he lives in, but the other nine he makes available for his staff. Good performance by any employee is recognized with a holiday in one of his homes. He has written books about the pivotal nature of reward in any organization.

A great little book (and it is small) called *Motivating People* by Dayle M Smith is very readable because it brings these theories to life with great case studies you can relate to. We have put together such a case study below to test your powers of motivation.

Motivation case study

Read the case study below and imagine the set of circumstances outlined. Write your ideas and plans for your first month in the new role in the space provided.

Your new department is demoralized. Their previous leader became ill suddenly four months ago and has not been able to return to work. He was very popular with all groups, but less so with the director, as the department was never particularly effective and looks a bit of a mess. Since then the department has been managed on an acting basis by one of the section leaders, Helen. She applied for the job you have been given, but her performance did not impress the directors enough to make her position permanent.

At the moment the groups do not consistently meet any of their output and quality-related work targets, though they make some of them some of the time.

The department is under considerable pressure from other departments. This comes not only in writing, but also in the form of urgent phone calls and visits to individual members.

Your grasp of the department's work and technology is superior to, or in a small proportion of cases equal to, that of your subordinates.

You do not know any of the group and they do not know you.

What would you do to motivate this group?

Motivation in action

Here are some ideas you may have included, already or might now want to add to your list.

- *Communicate work targets.* It is hard to be motivated when you do not know what you are supposed to be doing.
- *Seek ideas.* Find out how your department thinks targets can be met.
- *Agree a plan of campaign.* When a group is demoralized, targets which seem impossible to achieve can destroy what little motivation they retain. It is the leader's job to help develop a plan for achieving the results in which members of the group can believe.
- *Provide feedback.* You must reinforce the importance of the plan by providing regular feedback on how the group are doing. Reward any improvement vigorously.
- *Seize opportunities.* Seize any opportunity, however trivial, to make concrete changes for the better. This will not only begin to establish your own position, it will also start to motivate the group by demonstrating to them what change is possible.
- *Protect the group.* When the group is demoralized and not performing well, it is the manager's job to absorb most of the heat to which it is being subjected from outside. Apart from improving working conditions by giving people a breathing space, this also establishes the leader's position.

■ *Tackle housekeeping issues.* No group of people can feel motivated if they believe themselves to be drifting. Everyone needs a certain sense of pride and direction, even if the scale of the feeling varies from person to person. The manager has to achieve a difficult balance in seeking people's opinions while at the same time giving the clear impression that he/she knows where they are going. Symbolic acts, like getting the place cleaned up, have an important role to play in establishing that impression.

■ *Talk to individuals.* It is very important for the first line manager to get to know the individual members of the group as soon as possible. Doing this in a way which motivates people, as well as making them feel more satisfied, needs some care. The main emphasis of these discussions must be on the work.

TIPS FROM THE TOP

Julian Richer, CEO, Richer Sounds

■ What were the principal things you had to learn to become successful?

I have always been entrepreneurial. Even at school I was selling things. But I had to realize that I could not do it all on my own. To grow a business I had to learn to motivate and delegate.

■ What challenges did you meet along the way?

Once the business has grown, keeping that buzz is the challenge. I now like working for charity and public services like the Prison Service.

■ What advice would you give to an aspiring manager?

Learn how to motivate the people around you. Understand what drives them and reward them when they reach their targets. It sounds simple but it works. Sadly most managers don't do it.

Exercise: celebrate winning

Life is so hectic that we have barely finished one project before embarking on another. Closure and the reinforcement of success is so important and raises morale. There is one last exercise for this section. Write down at least six ideas to celebrate winning. Half of them should be personal rewards, rewarding yourself for an achievement or completion of a project. If you work in a team, write down things you can do together to mark success.

These must be ideas you have never used before.

Keys

■ Adopt a winning mindset that concentrates on successes.
■ Become an expert in what motivates you in your career.
■ Understand others' drivers because they will more than likely differ from your own. Learn to reinforce these drivers at every opportunity.
■ Reward the people around you eight times more than you criticize them if you want them to improve.
■ Celebrate winning at every opportunity, and have fun in everything you undertake, especially at work.

six

The **fourth commandment: relate**

> *Our survey of leaders on both sides of the Atlantic shows that they prize the ability to work with a wide variety of people. These leaders have learnt to stay close to their customers and employees. They take time to relate to other people; are empathic, communicative and supportive. They also handle conflict elegantly because in many ways that is the job. This ability extends to the domestic front as the majority of our executives rated a happy home life as essential to their functioning.*

The vast majority of our chief executives and directors had fabulous interpersonal skills. They were very welcoming, gave their time freely and were focused on the interview when they must have had much more urgent and pressing matters to deal with.

Forming relationships, maintaining relationships, dealing with difficult relationships are all part of the job, be they internal or external to the organization. D A Benton in his book *How to Think Like a CEO* has as one of his vital traits the ability of the CEO to be 'nice'. It is based, he says, on a basic respect for people and a benevolence that helps you enjoy your work.

Dawn Airey of Channel 5 said she discovered when she became a senior executive that how you react to situations influences huge numbers of people. Denise O'Donoghue of Hat Trick Productions had to learn to contain her moods, Sir Ian McAllister of Ford to suffer fools and Claire McGrath to stop being a 'razor blade'. So it would appear that at least a third of these leaders were not born with people skills, but had to work to achieve them. Many mentioned that the key thing they had to learn was patience with people: David Campbell of Ginger Productions, Andrew Fraser formerly of Invest UK, Brian Gilbertson of Billiton, Stuart Rose of the Body Shop, Sir Bob Reid of the Bank of Scotland and Helen Ostrowski of Porter Novelli.

When we are talking about fostering friendships we are not talking of the schmoozing and networking which passes as friendship, but the genuine article. Mark Townsend in the *Daily Express* (Jan 2000) recently quoted a survey of 1,500 bosses conducted by Office Angels. They commented that 76 per cent of all attempts by staff to impress their way to success were completely misguided. Bosses liked to see good team working rather than solo stars. This very much reflected the views of the majority of our sample. Sir Bob Reid said, 'I have networked for advice but never advancement', and Sir Richard Greenbury was emphatic that networking for personal aggrandizement was the surest way to be sidelined as your colleagues would despise you.

Daniel Goleman, the New York psychologist who wrote *Emotional Intelligence*, would say all the relationship skills we have been talking about contribute to emotional intelligence (EQ). What psychologists have recently discovered is that EQ correlates with success. Let's look at this in more detail, realizing that we have covered some of the principles in other chapters.

The five domains of emotional intelligence

Understanding your own emotions

This is the self-awareness of recognizing an emotion as it happens. It seems on the face of it to be so simple, yet some of us may have been brought up to see emotions as unruly things in need of control. Signs of emotion in a man might be viewed as unmanly, in a woman as hysterical, but without emotion we cannot relate to our fellow human beings, and we are uncomprehending about a whole raft of information we need for decision making. And to recognize an emotion in someone else, you do first have to be aware of one in yourself.

Managing your emotions

This is emotional self-control. For example, it is the ability to pick yourself up after setbacks and failures, to go on to greater things rather than spend hours being depressed. Some people sincerely feel lacerated by the world's woes, but emotional intelligence requires you to limit that to situations you can do something about. This skill is intimately tied up with how we think, and in turn relates to solving problems. (See Chapter 3.)

Motivating yourself

To get up each morning, to move towards the distant goal of a degree or a promotion (or a book!) takes the emotional control of delayed gratification. With anything in life there are highlights and draggy bits. Motivation helps us raise our eyes to the horizon and work through the less exciting times for the goal at the end.

Chapter 5 tackles the concept of motivation.

Recognizing emotions in others

This is commonly known as empathy. You need to be self-aware before you can acquire the ability to be sensitive to others. It involves picking up on the subtleties of body language and emotional expression. The tenth commandment, be confident (Chapter 12) will investigate your own and other's body language, and what you can do with that information.

Handling relationships

This requires handling emotion in others (and yourself) over a long period of time. Popular leaders in business, politics and the services have the ability to inspire devotion and loyalty through superb social skills. They are what Goleman calls 'social stars'. This chapter will begin to ensure your own social stardom.

Essentially the fourth commandment will look at handling our own emotions and those of others, as well as dealing with the whole gamut of relationship building.

Emotions can be fabulous and thoroughly disruptive, often confusingly at one and the same time. At a conference a number of years ago, the MD of a large hairdressing organization said there was no place for emotion in business. Her statement was more wishful thinking than reality, as the workplace is a seething hotbed of emotional intrigue. People might pretend they don't care, but being given promotion or denied it, being humiliated or praised, engender feelings to kill for. How we handle these powerful stimuli may make a difference between success and failure.

How often, when asked by a superior about our views on a project, have we replied that we thought it was 'fine' while harbouring huge doubts as to its viability? Understanding that people often find it difficult to speak up, and that we must listen and encourage assertiveness, is crucial to good management.

Recognizing emotions in yourself and others

Exercise: emotional descriptions

A number of emotions are listed in the box. Describe as concretely as possible what you feel when you experience them. For example, how does your body react, what happens inside you, what do you feel like doing? (A couple of examples are given at the end of the list.) You do not have to complete the entire list: concentrate on the emotions you feel uncomfortable with, or which have exerted a powerful influence over you. Once you have described how you feel when you experience these emotions, you should have a wider repertoire of words, phrases and statements to describe your own emotional states and to identify emotions in others.

A list of emotions for you to describe

Accepted	Afraid	Angry
Anxious	Attracted	Competitive
Intimate	Inferior	Hopeful
Dutiful	Joyful	Lonely
Rejected	Trusting	Guilty
Jealous	Loving	Satisfied
Defensive	Free	Frustrated

Example: anger

When I feel angry:

- I want to do something about it now, though I know that would be disastrous.
- I can feel hurt.
- I can feel rejected.
- I feel alive.
- I can feel confused.
- I feel hot and bothered.
- I feel instantly vindictive.

Example: love

When I love someone:

- I feel exhilarated.
- I feel glowing.
- I can feel confident.
- I can feel vulnerable.
- I can feel less in control of my life.
- I feel giving.

Handling relationships

The last element of Goleman's recipe for emotional intelligence is the forming of close relationships, and this section focuses on how to make the relationships in your life more rewarding. So often we take those around us completely for granted. Countless favours from parents go unnoticed, domestic tasks from partners and children are merely expected, and at work colleagues' support can go unrecognized. If you manage a team, if you have anything to do with customers, both internal or external to the company; if you have to interface with superiors, colleagues or team members, then you need to recognize the input of others and find a way to reward it.

All of us can talk a good game, think and feel we have changed. but the proof is whether anyone else notices, especially those close to us.

We concentrate here on forming relationships quickly and effectively, while at the same time providing you with a framework for handling difficult people.

The mnemonic FORE was coined many years ago for a telecommunications company after it was privatized. The managers had not had to sell their wares before, as the company had had a monopoly. While they knew they had to indulge in PR events, they were reluctant to converse with their customers. As part of their training programme, they were taught to use FORE as a means of learning about other people:

F = family
O = occupation
R = recreation
E = education

On a 'Transformation' course, we give participants three minutes each to find out information about each other that they didn't know before. It's always amazing what can be discovered in that short space of time. One telecommunications manager who had had a little snigger about the FORE exercise found that a colleague with whom he shared a secretary and occasionally an office had won a marathon the previous weekend. He hadn't even known he was a runner.

In this fast-paced world we are so task- and target-driven that we can forget it is the people around us who help carry out tasks and reach targets. We need to know who they are and what makes them tick. That's the job of managing. If colleagues like you, they are much more likely to go to the ends of the earth for you, and let's face it, that's required most weeks!

FORE is just as good for use on the telephone as face to face. We put together a programme called 'Customer Bonding' for a drinks exporter. The staff only had telephone relationships with their customers, as they were scattered around the world. The 'getting to know you' aspect of FORE was a new concept for them. They had previously thought that anything not related to business or orders was wasting time. Now the whole department are relationship converts, and business is brisk.

A few additional tips for use with FORE:

■ *Focus on types of question.* Try to use open-ended and probing questions when FOREing people. You will get to know much more than with closed questions inviting yes/no answers. If you really want to bond, ask more probing questions like 'That's interesting, tell me more'. Once you grasp the open and probing routine you can just relax and listen, without wondering what to say next. It is a wonderful if forgotten social skill. Table 6.1 gives examples of different types of questions.

■ *Use emotional banking.* Sometimes people are – well – boring! If you were at a party, you would simply avoid them. If it is a colleague, you can sit elsewhere at lunch. But if it's the boss or a lucrative customer, avoidance is not an option. Laurence Clarke, consultant and writer, confronts this issue: he suggests trying some 'emotional banking'.

The emotional bank

Discover interest
Ask open-ended, probing questions till you find something in common, or a topic less boring than the rest. Avoid closed questions.

Table 6.1 Types of question

Closed	Open	Probing
Are?	What?	How?
Do?	Which?	In what way?
Have?	When?	Tell me more
	Where?	Describe in more detail
	Why?	For what reasons?

Build a credit balance

Reward all interesting facts and topics. Boring people are seldom rewarded, so this can have the amazing effect of helping them become enthusiastic and animated.

Deposit

You can invest information and self-disclosure into the conversation, or move the topic to more interesting territory. For example, if the chosen interest is football, which has you glazing over in five seconds flat, then you subtly move to the drunken/ sexual exploits of its stars (which might be of more interest). Try this out next time you are at dinner with the boss, or are travelling for hours with that all-important customer. Ask yourself, were you as bored as usual or did investing some effort into the relationship pass the time more interestingly?

Recently on a young managers' course, the group was split into pairs and one member of the duo was asked to bore the other as they had never bored before. The other was instructed to use the techniques of emotional banking. We thought our debrief of the session had been clear, but when we read the feedback sheets, one young manager wrote that this particular exercise had been a failure because nobody in the group of 25 was one whit bored despite all their best efforts! Her criticism was a great validation of the technique.

A colleague who was very practised at this skill was stuck beside a titled business executive throughout a long and boring dinner. Narrowly rejecting the option of drinking to oblivion, he decided to invest a little energy into the conversation. The only topic offering the barest flicker of enthusiasm for our friend was this man's hobby of butterfly collecting. So good was his emotional banking (he had never seen a mounted butterfly in his life) that the executive wrote to him the next day, offering him all sorts of books on every species of winged insect on the planet.

Having FOREed and banked and bonded, you may need to move on (or get away) sometimes. You may have been the only person to listen to that poor soul in years, and they now have you pinned to the wall at the office party, talking in intimate detail about their pet snake. The elegant way to extract yourself is to interrupt with a compliment, always genuine of course, look at a watch or a clock, touch the person's arm, move them slightly by the elbow if you have to, then keep walking. Anything less than this complete set of skills may result in your being held hostage by stories of snakes all night. This, of course, is a worst possible scenario. Usually FORE helps you to meet wonderful, exciting people to whom you might just have nodded before.

Two executives on holiday met at the pool while their wives were shopping. In turn they asked each other about family, occupation, recreation and education. At this point, one asked the other whether he was using FORE. They had both attended one of our courses, but with different companies. They became firm friends and still correspond.

Stroking

Stroking is a concept created by Eric Berne in his theory of 'transactional analysis'. Around the time he formulated it, psychologists were carrying out early behavioural experiments with monkeys, which revealed that if they were reared separately from their mothers, monkeys appeared comforted by a cloth substitute over a wire shape. They would rub up against it and hug it. If this were replaced by a wire 'monkey' without a cloth cover, the young monkey did not touch it and became withdrawn.

The implications for human behaviour are plentiful. We need from birth to be hugged and stroked, not only to provide us with a sense of security and well-being, but also to give us an awareness of the boundaries of our bodies. As we grow older, hugs and strokes are confined to intimate relationships, but we still desire metaphorical stroking socially and at work. Just like the motherless monkey with the wire replacement, if these 'strokes' are absent, then behavioural withdrawal or attention seeking results.

Giving feedback in the workplace to colleagues and staff is essential to help them feel comfortable with what they are doing and/or to help them change. Lack of stroking at a fundamental level can lead to an uncaring attitude and a 'psychopathic' organization.

Negative strokes

Negative strokes are ways of diminishing people. Ignoring or putting down others' ideas or contributions are common examples. Negative strokes are not to be confused with criticism, which can be very positive and helpful if delivered in a friendly and self-developing way. Negative strokes discount people. They help to make people feel inadequate. They erode self-confidence and lead to resentment and over-cautious behaviour.

Some examples are:

- keeping people waiting;
- not consulting or involving people in decisions which affect them;
- asking for suggestions when you are already clear on your decision;
- hurrying people up rather than listening to them;
- closing an issue before everyone feels heard;
- over-explaining obvious things;
- being condescending;
- refusing to acknowledge someone's expressed feelings;
- using jargon;
- name dropping.

When people discount themselves ('I don't know much about this but...') they have probably been exposed to negative strokes. They no longer feel secure and have stopped being clear, direct and open.

James was a staggeringly successful entrepreneur who built up an outsourcing company in London. We met him and his board to talk about staff development. James arrived late, interrupted the proceedings, walked about, talked over the presentation and was frankly rude. That was interesting enough, since he had asked us there, but more fascinating still was the equanimity with which this behaviour was received. No one was surprised or ashamed. This must have been his normal behaviour. We remember thinking how it must, at some time, limit his success. Some months later we visited a company in New York which had wanted a joint venture with James's organization. They called off discussions because of his 'untrusting and discounting behaviour'.

In transactional analysis it is observed that the strokes that work best are often unconditional, rather than dependent upon someone behaving in the desired way. Unconditional strokes are given simply because the person is OK with you, warts and all. The vital thing about strokes is not so much in the giving as in the receiving. However, it is important to observe whether stroked people accept or reject the strokes. If they are feeling depressed or low in self-esteem, they may reject the strokes by discounting themselves ('It was nothing, really'; 'It didn't take me long'; 'I'm sorry it was incomplete'). If this happens, you may have to work at building up their self-confidence sufficiently to receive the praise.

Characteristics of strokes

Strokes are:

- 'units of recognition' or rewards;
- the ways we demonstrate our awareness of the existence of another human being;
- a biological necessity – although the level of stroking needed varies between individuals.

Strokes may be:

- Positive:
  - life and growth encouraging;
  - inviting the recipient to feel okay about themselves and others.
- Negative:
  - life and growth discouraging;
  - inviting the recipient to feel not-okay about themselves and/ or others.

Strokes may also be:

- unconditional: given for just being or something over which we have no control;
- conditional: given for doing something over which we have control, or an aspect of our behaviour such as work performance.

Strokes are given and received via the senses:

- Hearing:
  - the things we say to each other;
  - the sounds of music, singing;
  - tone of voice (angry or friendly).

- Sight:
  - facial expression, gesture, posture;
  - via painting, ornaments, scenery;
  - through written comments (eg memos, performance appraisals).
- Touch:
  - shaking hands;
  - holding, hitting;
  - through textures and temperatures.
- Taste and smell:
  - through food and drink;
  - perfumes, air fresheners;
  - tobacco.

Individuals and organizations develop characteristic patterns of stroking, and this more often than not emanates from the top. One chief executive of a distribution company was mercurial. He indulged in a kind of unconscious game playing where he would reward you with the beam of his attention one minute, then cast you into outer darkness with a comment designed to humiliate the next. Clever staff quickly realized that only good news received approbation, so they would massage sales figures and cover up crises. He would then fly into a rage and castigate them for not being direct and honest. Organizations become extensions of their owners and leaders: an awful thought in this case.

Exercise: stroking patterns

Choose six people who are significant in your life: three from home, three from work. You may want to select a partner or spouse and at work, a boss as well as colleagues.

Giving strokes

- When did you last give each of your chosen colleagues and family/friends a significant stroke (more than a polite greeting)?
- Was it positive or negative? Did it invite them to feel OK about themselves and others, or was it a put-down of themselves or others?
- What prompted it? Work, personal, hobbies, appearance? Your preferences or theirs?

Receiving strokes

- When did you last receive a significant stroke from each of these chosen people?
- Was it positive or negative?
- What prompted it?

Review

Review your answers and become more aware of the ways in which you give and receive recognition. Consider first your choice of six people. Are they a random selection, or have you included only those people you like most? What interactions do you have, or not have, with the colleagues you like least? And have you included your boss as someone you work with? Do you stroke and reward your staff but forget to stroke people in authority? They are human too, despite perhaps having more status or being paid more than you.

Next, review your responses in the section on giving strokes. How might you appear to others? How much time is spent in put-downs rather than positives? Note that constructive criticism is a positive stroke: it implies that the person can do better, and you care enough about them to let them know how. How varied are your reasons for strokes? Do you range over work and personal matters, or do you only comment on whatever interests you? People who get on well with others target their strokes, making sure that they pay attention to whatever the other person values.

Consider how you receive strokes. Are you getting a reasonable quantity and variety? Do you feel comfortable with your working group? Is there a lot of joking and put-downs so that genuine praise is outlawed? Check also for any tendency to swap strokes, as this can devalue them. Swapping occurs when we automatically return a compliment, such as when we say, 'Yours is nice too'. The overall effect is to cancel out the original stroke, leaving both parties feeling vaguely dissatisfied or disappointed. And lastly, do you reward being given a stroke by saying 'thank you' and showing sincere appreciation?

Do you stroke more at work or at home, and where do you receive the majority of your strokes? Why is this? Where you stroke less, you are probably taking these people for granted. And if you can't remember when you last gave a stroke to anybody, then you really need to change.

Edification

Of course stroking does not have to be confined to individuals: you can reward an entire group or team, or an individual in front of a team. If you need to get someone accepted as an expert so that a client or colleague can cease to rely on you, reward their skills openly. This is the true nature of delegation. It often falls apart when we are insecure enough to enjoy the accolades for ourselves and so deny them to others.

It's a bit like being at a conference. You can hardly stand up and tell an audience how wonderful you are and how lucky they are to be benefiting from your expertise, but someone else can, which is why conferences are chaired and speakers introduced. This process of third-party credibility is called edification. It is so powerful a tool that it can make all the difference between success and failure.

Culture

If individuals, groups, and entire organizations could change negative emotion to positive, they would have an entirely different culture. In Table 6.2 the difference between a caring and blaming environment is outlined, to help you identify which is yours. If yours is more blaming than caring, you may have to create your own environment in your team or department, with a bit more

Table 6.2   The caring–blaming environment

Caring	Blaming
I like people	I find people wanting
I compliment people	I discover faults
I do not judge	I judge constantly
I can only change myself	Other people should do what is expected of them
I allow others to be equals no matter who they are	Few people deserve my respect
I listen to others' ideas	There is a right and wrong way of looking at things
I allow others to be right	I am invariably right
I assume responsibility for what goes wrong	I blame others for anything that is wrong

recognition and a little less cynicism. Staff often blame 'senior management' for the critical atmosphere in their company, and they may well be right, as a culture usually is established from the top. However, you can make a difference. Make your team the most motivated and stroked in the company, so everyone is asking what your secret is.

At a conference for chief executives in Northern Ireland about reward and culture change, the seminars focused on how rewarding they were as people, how often they stroked their staff and what they did to celebrate winning. At the end, the feedback was that they wanted to know about employee of the month and financial incentive schemes. If only they realized that caring for your staff, saying 'thank you', rewarding them more than criticizing, costs nothing and produces infinitely more effective culture change than any incentive scheme on the market.

TIPS FROM THE TOP

David Varney, BG plc

- What were the principal things you had to learn to become successful?

    I had to learn to trust my instincts about business. I also had to create a persona that others would want to follow.
- What challenges did you meet along the way?

    When you have emerged from a public company like British Gas, then dealing with the exposure of that and the attendant media is certainly a challenge.
- What advice would you give to an aspiring manager?

    You need to have a great professional competence but alongside that you need to develop a capacity for management and a desire to expand your horizons.

Emotional coaching

Instilling wisdom is best carried out through a coaching process. Sporting analogies and heroes abound to help managers train their teams to be more proficient. The applicability can be suspect, so it was interesting to hear David Gower say at a dinner recently that he could find no parallels between cricket and business, but since he was paid handsomely to supply motivational speeches at conferences, he was happy to draw as many comparisons as it took. However, with or without sporting help, coaching is a vital management skill.

Of course the process of coaching new skills is made easier with motivated happy people. However employees often have problems and are not always willing and able. The test is how you handle the bad times and turn them into the good, and key to that is how you cope with the variety of emotions that are hurled at you.

Complete the emotional coaching questionnaire in Table 6.3. Be honest. Answer the questions according to what you actually do at the moment, not what you aspire to do.

Table 6.3 Emotional coaching questionnaire

1. People really have very little to be sad about	True	False	Don't Know
2. I think that anger is OK as long as it's under control	True	False	Don't Know
3. People acting sad are usually just trying to get you to feel sorry for them	True	False	Don't Know
4. If someone gets angry, they should be excluded	True	False	Don't Know
5. When people are acting unhappy they are real pests	True	False	Don't Know
6. Stress is good for you	True	False	Don't Know
7. When people are unhappy, I am expected to fix the world and make it perfect	True	False	Don't Know
8. I spend time helping staff sort out their stress problems	True	False	Don't Know
9. I really have no time for sadness in my life	True	False	Don't Know
10. Anger is a dangerous state	True	False	Don't Know
11. If you ignore someone's unhappiness it tends to go away and take care of itself	True	False	Don't Know
12. Everyone has to have some stress in their life	True	False	Don't Know
13. Anger usually means aggression	True	False	Don't Know
14. Feelings are private and not public	True	False	Don't Know
15. When you notice signs of stress you need to intervene quickly to help	True	False	Don't Know
16. I don't mind dealing with someone's unhappiness as long as it doesn't last too long	True	False	Don't Know
17. Helping staff cope with conflict is one of my			
18. managerial roles	True	False	Don't Know
19. I prefer a happy person to someone who is over-emotional	True	False	Don't Know
20. It's all right to show you're stressed	True	False	Don't Know
21. When someone is unhappy, it's time to problem solve	True	False	Don't Know

Table 6.3 (continued) Emotional coaching questionnaire

22. I help people get over unhappiness quickly so they can move on to better things	True False Don't Know
23. I don't see someone's unhappiness as an opportunity to learn much	True False Don't Know
24. I think when people are depressed they have over-emphasized the negative in life	True False Don't Know
25. In my view anger is natural like clearing your throat	True False Don't Know
26. When someone is acting angrily, they are very unpleasant	True False Don't Know
27. I set limits on people's anger	True False Don't Know
28. When someone acts stressed, it's to get attention	True False Don't Know
29. Anger is an emotion worth exploring	True False Don't Know
30. I try to change people's angry moods into cheerful ones	True False Don't Know
31. Getting angry is like blowing off steam, letting go of the pressure	True False Don't Know
32. When someone is unhappy it's a chance to get closer	True False Don't Know
33. People really have very little to be stressed about	True False Don't Know
34. When someone is unhappy, I try to help them explore what is causing it	True False Don't Know
35. People get over anxious spells if you leave them alone	True False Don't Know
36. The important thing is to find out why someone is unhappy	True False Don't Know
37. When people are depressed I'm worried they have negative personalities	True False Don't Know
38. If there's a lesson I've learned about unhappiness, it's that it's OK to express it	True False Don't Know
39. I'm not sure anything can be done to change unhappiness	True False Don't Know
40. When someone is unhappy, I'm not quite sure what they want me to do	True False Don't Know
41. Stress is such an overused word, people just use it is an excuse	True False Don't Know
42. If there's a lesson I have learned about anger, it's that it's OK to express it	True False Don't Know
43. When someone is angry, I try to be understanding of their mood	True False Don't Know
44. When someone is angry, I'm not quite sure what they want me to do	True False Don't Know
45. When someone is angry, I want to know what they are thinking	True False Don't Know
46. When someone is stressed and anxious I just feel they are not coping well	True False Don't Know
47. When someone is angry, I try to let them know I care no matter what	True False Don't Know
48. When someone is angry, I try to put myself in their shoes	True False Don't Know
49. It's important to help the person find out what caused the anger	True False Don't Know

Scoring

Dismissing: add up the number of times you said 'true' for the following items:

1, 2, 7, 9, 11, 16, 18, 21, 22, 23, 29, 32

If you responded 'don't know' more than four times, you may want to work at becoming more aware of emotion in yourself and others.

Disapproving: add up the number of times you said 'true' for the following items:

3, 4, 5, 10, 13, 14, 25, 26, 27, 32, 40, 45

If you responded 'don't know' more than four times, you may want to work at becoming more aware of emotion in yourself and others.

Laissez-faire: add up the number of times you said 'true' for the following items:

6, 12, 19, 24, 30, 34, 37, 38, 39, 41, 43, 46

If you responded 'don't know' more than four times, you may want to work at becoming more aware of emotion in yourself and others.

Emotional coaching: add up the number of times you said 'true' for the following items:

8, 15, 17, 20, 28, 31, 33, 35, 42, 44, 47, 48

If you responded 'don't know' more than four times, you may want to work at becoming more aware of emotion in yourself and others.

Emotional coaching analysis

Compare your four scores. The higher you scored in any one area, the more you tend to that style of managing. The perfect score is zero in the dismissing and disapproving categories, with high scores for emotional coaching and a peppering of scores in the laissez-faire category.

To dismiss or disapprove of another's upset or anger is to force the emotion to become subterranean. All sorts of strange behaviour ensues, with hidden agendas being pursued at meetings, and scapegoating others for our wrongs. Staff very swiftly determine whether it is sage to be emotionally honest, or whether they should simulate inscrutability.

High scores in laissez faire mean that you are happy to have emotion expressed around you, but don't necessarily feel you have to intervene to understand or sort it. A high score is fine but it should not be your highest. It should be coupled with an equally high, if not higher emotional coaching score.

When emotion is expressed at work, it means that people care. They may not express it well, and the language used may be aggressive, but where there's emotion there's life. Dealing with these feelings moves you, your group and the organization on.

You don't have to become a therapist to be an emotional coach. If the problem is beyond your expertise you can refer it to a professional. Most emotional coaching starts with the question 'Why?' Why do you feel that way? Why do you get stressed about deadlines? Why have you been feeling low?

Become an emotional coach for all emotions expressed, not just those you feel comfortable with. A head of education, when he came to this section, said that he could understand all emotions except depression. He expected anyone to be over their depression in three weeks. After that, he felt they were 'swinging the lead'. Awareness of this misconception was enough to change his coaching expectations and behaviour.

A managing director visited a development course as a participant called Tim was telling the tutor that all this emotional stuff was a 'load of crap'. He then turned on the managing director and criticized him in a very career-limiting way about his interest in personal development and the money he was wasting. A lesser man would have flinched and certainly placed Tim on the next redundancy list. This one stated that Tim's views were interesting and they should meet to talk. At 7am twice a week, Tim met with the managing director, first to discuss why he was so angry, then to be coached in his career. Tim went on to become a consultant and a great advocate of development programmes.

Handling difficult people

Even in the best of company cultures there are upset and difficult people: often, sadly, to be found clustered at middle management and more senior levels. If you want to rise to dizzier heights you must handle these people effectively.

Complete 'my experience with a difficult person'. Keep your situation with a difficult person in mind as we proceed through this section.

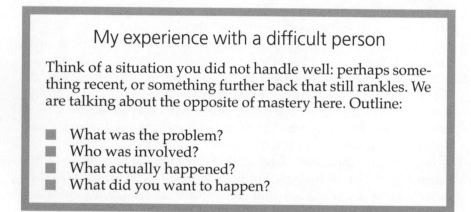

My experience with a difficult person

Think of a situation you did not handle well: perhaps something recent, or something further back that still rankles. We are talking about the opposite of mastery here. Outline:

■ What was the problem?
■ Who was involved?
■ What actually happened?
■ What did you want to happen?

Figure 6.1 provides an overview of the steps involved in handling difficult people, and indeed in influencing people generally. These skills are useful in any situation where you have to convince others of your point of view.

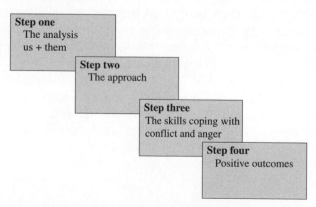

Step one
The analysis
us + them

Step two
The approach

Step three
The skills coping with conflict and anger

Step four
Positive outcomes

Figure 6.1 Overview of handling difficult people

Before plunging into skills and strategies, you must observe and analyse the behaviour of your protagonist and of course yourself. Ask yourself these questions:

- Is your difficult person difficult with other people too, or is it just you?
- If some people handle this person well, what do they do? Observe and learn the skills.
- What hot buttons do they press in you? In other words, what do they do to produce an angry or upset response?
- How do you respond? Are you sullen in your defiance, sharp with a riposte or do you gaze sphinx-like at them only to retaliate later?
- Could you be their difficult person? Perish the thought!

Peter, a consultant, was working on a company's development programme at one of its outposts abroad. He stayed at the same hotel as the managing director. This helped greatly as they often met over dinner and discussed the progress of the programme. After a few glasses of wine they both became creative, thinking of new ideas and fresh delivery concepts. The next day Peter would rush in to the training manager, Dennis, and enthusiastically expound what had been discussed at dinner the night before. Later he would wonder why Dennis was always negative and obstructive. One day Dennis told one of the other company consultants how much he disliked Peter. Peter's first response was to be dismissive. His next, on cooler reflection, was to try to see things from Dennis's point of view. Peter had the managing director's ear, something Dennis would have enjoyed. Peter had expected Dennis to adhere to his and the MD's enthusiasms, thereby undermining his position. Understanding that he had become Dennis's difficult person allowed him to begin to repair the damage.

TIPS FROM THE TOP

John Stuart, CEO, Woolwich plc

■ What were the principal things you had to learn to become successful?

I took on a wide variety of roles to give me breadth of experience. I was even a Union rep for a time.

I have learnt to question everything and everyone. If I finish work early I just go around and chat to people.

I love coaching staff. When they get more proficient, I get promoted. It's a win-win for all of us.

■ What challenges did you meet along the way?

I see work as fun. I set up an insurance business for the group and have started six or seven companies since. Changing the culture of a long established company has been an interesting challenge but not an insuperable one.

■ What advice would you give to an aspiring manager?

You need to be IT literate nowadays. But you also require the skills of dealing with people, especially your customers. You must also manage and influence upwards if you want to progress so that your ideas get taken on board.

Step one in dealing with difficult people: the analysis: them

Write a list of the irritating and anger-provoking behaviour your difficult person indulges in. For example, do they have to be right all the time? Do they never listen to a word you say even after having asked for your advice?

With the list in front of you, consider what that person wants out of behaving that way. All behaviour is purposeful, so they must want something as a result of the tremendous amount of energy they expend in behaving badly.

You may have listed things like 'they want their own way', or that they desire 'power', 'status', or even 'an easy life'. Whatever you have written, some of these motivations will be quite positive ones. So the motivation may be pure while the behaviour is not.

The major question that now must be asked is, **do we ever give our difficult people what they want?** For the most part the answer is no. In fact we often go out of our way to spike their guns and deprive them of their desires. If they want attention, we ignore them; if they want power, we undermine them; if they like status, we purposefully erode it. The trouble is, the more we ignore what they want, the more they want it because their needs are not being met, and so the bad behaviour continues.

To be successful in our negotiations we must consider giving them even a little of what they want. This is not as much of a sell-out as it sounds. We are just giving a little to get a little.

Mark was a lovely, earnest guy who had been recently promoted to manage a team of very challenging people in a manu-facturing organization. One woman in particular, a union rep renowned for her belligerence, gave him a hard time during team meetings. She would undermine his every idea, shouting out 'What a load of rubbish', and was an expert dodger of hard work. When her difficult behaviour was analysed, the list ran to three flipchart pages to capture all her bad habits, then another two to work out what she wanted. He decided she was desperate for power, status, her own way and probably his job to boot. Then came the million dollar question: did he ever give her what she wanted? He looked shocked at the mere notion of giving her anything at all, as he spent most of his time avoiding her. Eventually he agreed to try the approach as an experiment. He would give her a project to do when he was allocating tasks to others, as he did not want it to look as if he were rewarding her bad behaviour.

He was astonished to find her waiting by his door early the next morning. She had worked through most of the night to finish her project. She was there to ask for more and to make sure the rest of the team knew of her endeavours. Mark was even more astonished when this change lasted and she went on to become his greatest ally. She later explained to him that no one had ever given her a chance before, so she became subversive.

Step one in dealing with difficult people: the analysis: us

Dr Susan Dellinger has developed a very swift tool to analyse personality characteristics called psycho-geometrics. Complete the exercise below and suspend judgement till you have made your choices.

Exercise: Psycho-geometrics

Look at the shapes in Figure 6.2, and choose the one which best describes you. Choose a second shape which also describes you. Then turn to Table 6.4.

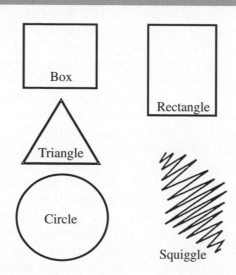

Figure 6.2 Psycho-geometrics shapes

Table 6.4 Quick indicators of shapes

Box	Triangle	Rectangle	Circle	Squiggle
Traits:				
Organized	Leader	In transition	Friendly	Creative
Detailed	Focused	Exciting	Nurturing	Conceptual
Knowledgeable	Decisive	Searching	Persuasive	Futuristic
Analytical	Ambitious	Inquisitive	Empathic	Intuitive
Determined	Competitive	Growing	Generous	Expressive
Persevering	Bottom line	Courageous	Stabilizing	Motivating
Patient	Athlete		Reflective	Witty/Sexy
Common words:				
Logistics	Interface	Unsure	Lovely	Experiment
Deadlines	Escalate	Consider	'Gut level'	Challenge
Allocate	Jargon	Maybe	Comfort	Create
Policy	Thrust	Delegate	Team	Develop
Efficiency	Return on Investment	Options	Cooperate	Conceive

Table 6.4 (continued) Quick indicators of shapes

Box	Triangle	Rectangle	Circle	Squiggle
Analysis	'Expletives'	Wait	Feelings	Begin
I did it!	You do it!	Why?	No problem!	What if?
Appearance – men:				
Conservative	Stylish	Erratic	Casual	Sloppy
Short hair	Appropriate	Changeable	No tie	Dramatic
No facial hair	Expensive	Facial hair	Youthful	Dirty
Appearance – women:				
Understated	Tailored	Erratic	Overweight	Varied
Navy, grey	Manicured	Extreme	Feminine	Artistic
Brown	Briefcase	Unusual	Faddish	Fat / Thin
Thin				
Office:				
Every pencil in	Status	'Mishmash'	Comfortable	Messy
place	symbols			
Computer	Awards	Imitator	Homelike	Bleak or
				dramatic
	Powerful	Disorganized	Plants	
Body language:				
Stiff	Composed	Clumsy	Relaxed	Animated
Controlled	Jaunty	Nervous	Smiling	Theatrical
Poker face	Piercing eyes	Fleeting eyes	Direct eyes	Mercurial
	Pursed mouth	Giggle	Full laugh	Sexual cues
High-pitched	Power voice	High-pitched	Mellow voice	Fast talk
voice		voice		
Twitches	Mesomorph	Silent	Talkative	Mannerisms
Slow movements	Smooth moves	Jerky moves	Head nods	Fast moves
Precise gestures	Large gestures	Flushed face	Excessive	No touch
Perspiration		Attractive	Touching	High energy
Personal habits:				
Loves routine	Interrupts	Forgetful	Easy going	Spontaneous
Put in writing	Game player	Nervous	Joiner	Disorganized
Always prompt	Early arriver	Late or early	Hobbies	Rebellious
Neat	Joke teller	Outbursts	Sloppy	Works alone
Planner	Power hand-	Avoids variety	Good cook	Life of party
Precise	shake	Blurts out	Patriotic	Daydreams
Collector	Fidgety		TV watcher	Interrupts
Social loner	Addictions		Socializer	Fickle

How can little shapes give you profound psychological insights? According to Susan Dellinger there is 85 per cent concordance between psycho-geometrics and other much more expensive and time-consuming psychometric tests. Also it is not so far-fetched when you think that the cars we choose, the houses, the wallpaper, the colours we prefer are all extensions of ourselves. Why not shapes? The results are also uncannily accurate: at least, our sample thought so.

Your second choice acts as a modifier of the first, so if you have chosen, for example, a circle first and a box second, then although you are very much a people person, you are an organized one. Not for you the distractions of socializing when work is to be done. Your social engagements are likely to be put in your diary just the same as other appointments. It is unusual but not impossible for a box also to be a squiggle. Perhaps you have had to modify your creative tendencies for a particular role at work. If you have that combination then prospective employers ought to know, as they will be delighted to have an organized innovator in their midst. I am sure creative people drive the more traditional ones batty with their unrealistic timescales and messy desks.

You can quickly see why conflicts arise. A squiggle working for a box or vice versa can be in for trouble. They both prize different ways of behaving at work – or at home for that matter. Who cares if your desk is heaped with papers and the occasional old sandwich, when you have just had a brilliant idea? A box, that's who.

Circles and triangles do not always see eye to eye either, as triangles can be irritated by a circle's perceived softness and wooliness. Some offshore medics from an oil company had for two years been trying to institute an employee assistance programme, and their proposals had all fallen on deaf ears. Eventually they succeeded mainly because every other oil company had one. Suddenly they realized that they had been extolling the virtues of the programme in humanitarian terms to those with access to the purse strings, who were all of course triangles and boxes who want to know the bottom-line difference. They had never provided these statistics.

Rectangles always fascinate because without fail they seem to be in a state of flux. The other descriptions hardly matter as the over-whelming attribute is a state of indecision and excitement as options are considered and paths explored.

For a team to operate successfully, different talents and types of people are needed. Can you imagine an entire team of circles? Great fun, lots of cups of tea but fewer targets reached. It is a case of 'vive la différence' for effective teamwork. This has to be accompanied by understanding of others around you. If you understand, then you can forgive and respect.

A journalist had read an article in *Interiors* magazine about the choice of interior design and different personality types. She wished to improve on this concept and was interested in psycho-geometrics as a tool. When asked what her choice would be, so that her choice of home interior could be predicted, she chose a rectangle and a circle. As a rectangle she was probably in rented accommodation. She also was perhaps thinking of changing jobs, so would not want roots and certainly not the financial commitment of a mortgage. As a circle, she would like comfort, but with little money to achieve it, she would add possibly a brightly covered throw over an aged sofa and add plants to cheer up worn wall-paper. Apparently, this was so accurate that she thought someone had cheated and had visited her home.

Table 6.5 Summary of psycho-geometrics results from sample of CEOs

2nd choice	1st choice					Totals (2nd choice)
	Box	Triangle	Rectangle	Circle	Squiggle	
Box		3	2	9	0	14
Triangle	1		4	9	2	16
Rectangle	2	2		1	2	7
Circle	7	10	2		3	22
Squiggle	0	6	1	10		17
Totals (1st choice)	10	21	9	29	7	76

Table 6.5 summarizes results from the sample of CEOs. The most frequent selections were circle (1st choice) and squiggle (2nd choice) and triangle (1st) and circle (2nd). Circle (1st) and box (2nd) or triangle (2nd) are also very popular. The combination of box and squiggle was not chosen at all. The circle was the most frequently picked shape: 51 people out of 80 chose the circle as either their first

or second choice. So our sample of successful people were primarily people-oriented with leadership and creativity combinations. How did you do?

Step two in dealing with difficult people: the approach

In San Francisco a number of years ago at a conference, we had the pleasure of meeting a diplomat who had participated in the SALT peace talks. He told a wonderful story about how these negotiations were concluded swiftly after all these years of cold war. After long tedious spells of arguing over the smallest details, manoeuvring to score an advantage for the Americans over the Russians and vice versa, both sides would take a break to discuss their next game plan. The two nations were positioned at either end of an internal garden in the centre of a hotel. Both had balconies and could view each other from a distance across this atrium. One day, at the end of a particularly enervating session, they retired to their rooms to plan the following day. One of the American party looked at the Russians on their side of the garden doing exactly the same as they were, brainstorming ideas, trying to outflank the opposition, beating them into submission. Tiredly he asked the group what they thought the Russians would want out of the next series of talks. They listed about 98 points on a flip chart. 'Why don't we work out what we will have to concede to them in the end and just give it to them now?' They felt they would have to give in on 96 of the 98 issues they had brainstormed, but there were two on which they couldn't concede.

You can imagine the Russians' faces when the Americans said they would capitulate on all but two of the issues. Negotiating these took considerably less time, and before we knew it Gorbachev and Reagan were on the White House lawn shaking hands and signing treaties, a sight unthinkable only a few years before.

This way of working is now called the Harvard Negotiation, and is used throughout the world in places like South Africa. Many books have been written about these high level talks but little about how we can use this technique in our more mundane but equally important dealings with others. **The balcony approach** is outlined for you more simply below.

The balcony approach

- Go to your balcony.
- Step to their side.
- Invite them to step to your side.
- Build a connecting bridge.

What does all this mean for us, and especially for the difficult people in our lives?

Firstly it means that in tackling anyone who is not being agreeable, we must look at what is going on and what part, if any, we play in their behaviour. So 'going to the balcony' is reminding us to assess and analyse both sides of the situation before jumping in with both feet. Then the approach recommends that we step to their side first, understand their story, even state verbally that we know where they are coming from. Because we are so tied up with our own agendas, we imagine that to win through we must stun them with our carefully honed arguments. We forget that to influence we must attend to the other person's motivation first. Why should they agree to anything we ask, if there is nothing in it for them?

TIPS FROM THE TOP

Lord Gordon of Strathclyde

- What were the principal things you had to learn to become successful?

  People are endlessly complex and if you hire the wrong people it gives you a barrel load of trouble. So I had to learn how to choose the right people for the job, then delegate effectively. I value the openness in relationships and realized that I can't work with anyone I dislike.

  I also discovered that financial direction is overrated. All it does is count past performance, not future ideas or thinking. And if I feel the financial statements are too complicated then I smell a rat. Something is being covered up. Cash flow is important; the rest is a lot of hoo hah.

> *I learnt that luck occurs when opportunity meets preparation.*
> ■ What challenges did you meet along the way?
> *No major challenges come to mind. I was in the right place at the right time with the right background and the right measure of enthusiasm.*
> ■ What advice would you give to an aspiring manager?
> *Management is a service not a promotion. You are there to serve your staff, to help them become more effective. You must gain satisfaction vicariously through the success of others.*

The **what's in it for them** or WIFT factor is crucial to this style of negotiation. The Russians would never have agreed to a speedy deal if, up front, there were not huge advantages for them. But you do not have to sell out your own principles to make this work, because once you have stepped to their side and got a handle on these WIFT factors you invite them to see things from your point of view. After that negotiate, negotiate.

Let's consider a practical example. You are out in the car for the day with three children in the back seat. You stop for petrol and when you have finished, three little voices proclaim 'I want to go to the toilet'. Unfortunately, you are told that this station's toilets are out of order but it is suggested you visit the garage across the road. There you meet that wonderful British institution, 'More than my job's worth'. This attendant says that the manager has told staff not to let anyone use the facilities who has not purchased petrol. He is intransigent. How do you convince him to let the children into the toilet as quickly as possible?

■ Would you be terribly nice and hope that the garage attendant was pleasant in return?
■ Would you threaten a letter to the manager?
■ Would you buy something small, say oil or sweets?

The balcony approach suggests that the WIFT factor for our garage attendant is to keep his job. Say something like, 'I don't want you to lose your job, of course, but I do have to get these children to the toilet. What do you suggest?' This approach allows you then to brainstorm solutions that suit both parties.

The other great advantage of having a strategy for these situations is that you can plan your interactions in advance. These contretemps can happen out of the blue, but even if you mess it up at the time you can plan the return match and then use a different tack.

Step three in dealing with people: skills for coping with conflict and anger

Sadly our relations with certain people may have become too entrenched for negotiation, or emotions may be running too high. Then it's time for another strategy, but first let's see how you handle negative emotion. Complete the 'What's the threat?' questionnaire, remembering to think of specific instances when you felt angry. You don't have to answer every question as it may not be your particular response.

Questionnaire: what's the threat?

How do you express and respond to anger?

- When do you usually keep quiet when you're angry?
- When do you usually walk away from the other person when you're angry?
- When have you simmered for days and then vented your anger in a big blow-up?
- When do you appear to be hurt when you're actually angry?
- When do you take your anger out on someone other than the person who caused the anger?
- When have you expressed your anger directly and firmly but without calling the other person names?
- When someone else is angry with you, when do you respond directly and effectively, with composure? Can you listen and try to understand their grievances?
- When do you feel hurt and withdrawn when someone is angry with you?

Anger is such a disruptive emotion, yet we all feel it at some time. How we handle anger is key to handling difficult people. Goleman talks about emotional hijacking, where anger takes over and rationality flies out the window. We keep quiet when we should talk, walk away when we should stay, simmer when we should ventilate and when we do let it out, it is usually at the wrong people. And when others are angry with us, do we handle that interaction any better? Possibly not!

Take a look at your answers to see what you should be working on. The ideal is an ability to talk about how you feel without raising your voice or losing the place. The DESC script below is wonderful for very clear communication without losing your temper. It looks deceptively simple but its use will lengthen your life, help you to communicate clearly and directly, and reduce the stress of handling difficult people.

The DESC script

Describe: the behaviour that is affecting you. Be clear and use any evidence that will support you argument.

Emotion: talk about how you feel, whether irritated, angry, enraged or unhappy.

Solutions: discuss what can be done or you would like to have to have done to improve the situation

Consequences: suggest what might result if the behaviour is not improved and the positives that could result if changes were made.

Often people have never been given feedback about their behaviour, and you may be the first to do so. Those who bully or use aggressive behaviour can get away with it for a long time. Working with the most difficult and challenging people shows that they do not plan to be obstructive. It's not as if they waken each day and wonder whom they can mess up or shout at. As often as not, they have no idea how they come across, and certainly no idea how much power they wield. If only they knew that if they just whispered most people would rush to their bidding. They really do need the feedback.

Describe

You must first describe your difficult person's behaviour precisely to them, face to face. A client was referred to us recently with the words, 'This man needs a personality transplant'. How helpful is that? It certainly did not enable him to change or provide any concrete objectives. If you have any evidence of bad or inappropriate behaviour, now is the time to produce it: time sheets if they have been late, reports of aggressive incidents, any feedback that that moves your discussion on from hearsay and gossip. Remember these people are very good at defending themselves and maintaining the status quo, so collect your ammunition well in advance.

Emotion

How you feel is powerful feedback, especially if you have been trying to effect change for a while. You may feel that it puts you in a vulnerable position to describe your feelings, but it does not. The majority of people do not wish to cause mayhem and upset, and this leverage can inspire change. A young woman on a training course talked about her sister who infuriated her. She would weekend in her flat, have wild parties to which the hostess was never invited, then leave the detritus for her to clear up. In the past the woman would swing from being silently martyred to having screaming arguments. This time she used the DESC script and talked about how her sister's behaviour made her feel: left out, exhausted and martyred, with an overwhelming desire never to invite her again. The sister was nonplussed to say the least. She had thought her sister hated her friends and so had never thought to include her. She had never helped with the cleaning because it was always completed by the time she and her friends surfaced the next day. Solutions were negotiated, and certainly when the woman was last contacted there was a lasting peace.

Solutions

If it is a work situation you may want your member of staff to write down their negotiated solutions. A lot of the compliance work carried out with GPs suggests that if they asked us to write down how to take our medication, there would be fewer half-empty bottles on shelves and less persistent infection around. However, we can make use of this research and have paper and pen handy for our protagonists to write down their actions. You can note them also, perhaps filing them for future meetings.

Consequences

Many people have little idea about the consequences of their behaviour. Perhaps they were just given things as children instead of earning them, or charmed their way constantly out of scrapes.

You may be the first person to talk about what will happen to them if they continue to behave in the same way. It is very positive to point out the good consequences that would ensue should their behaviour change in the desired direction.

The last essential is to provide a timescale for improvement and to monitor progress. If the practised difficult person knows that nothing will be followed up, he or she will not be motivated to change. It goes without saying that even the most minuscule movement in the right direction should be rewarded. If no one notices, why bother? If the right changes are not forthcoming, then retarget till they do.

The power of the DESC script lies in its directness. It is sharp, focused and you can remain relaxed as you communicate clearly how you feel. Why should your life be shortened by someone else's stupid behaviour?

Many managers have mentioned over the years how they are going to give a certain member of staff a 'flea in their ear' or 'a piece of their mind' or some other epithet. The reality is that if you ask the employee afterwards how the interview went, they tell you that they discussed holidays, football, and the manager talked vaguely about work. In other words, giving bad news is never easy and we often try to sugar-coat it. This process so dilutes the interaction that the core message is lost. We may think we have had the conversation while the recipient hasn't a clue. DESC allows you to be direct and stick to the point no matter what.

When someone is angry with you, it is so easy to become defensive and fight fire with fire. In this process we lose sight of our purpose, which is usually to get the other person to listen to us. If we want to be truly effective, instead of winning the point we must find a way of admitting to what is correct in our protagonist's argument. Have you ever tried arguing with someone who is agreeing with you? You just can't for any sustained period. Bob Sharpe, the psychologist who first introduced this concept, asked participants on his courses to role-play extreme anger with him. It was a cathartic moment. You are not often given carte blanche to be as nasty as you like, but people on that course managed very well. Then he cleverly started to agree with them, not with everything but selectively. They tried in vain to summon previous aggressive behaviour to no avail. They just could not do it.

One word of caution: be genuine in your agreement, as adversaries smell artifice at a hundred yards. That is why you must be selective: there's no need to agree with personal abuse.

Step four in dealing with people: positive outcomes

So often with difficult or challenging people we get into a mindset that allows nothing they do to be any good. They breathe and we are irritated. To improve the situation, we must envisage positive outcomes. If we visualize how we would like people to be, we can steer them in the right direction. You might want to share that vision with them so that you both have a goal to work towards.

The whole process of being positive has a relaxing effect so your hot button is less likely to be triggered. You may never love your difficult person but you *can* work with them.

Trying to understand your difficult person, even at this stage, can help you reach agreement. A taxi driver picked up a consultant from the airport and said he recognized her name. She said she had never seen him before. He explained that he picked her up each day from her flat (he named the street), took her into her office (he named the company) and waited for her at night, sometimes for an hour before taking her home. He had been doing this for some months. Suddenly she understood: a former employee, who had the same hair colour and could have been mistaken for her, now lived and worked at those addresses. Back at the office with the accountant, she reviewed the taxi account print-out. There was her name, but the former employee's telephone number. Of course the company immediately changed the password and the consultant made an appointment to see the other woman.

She was a very good actress and admitted to nothing for about half an hour. It must be a mistake, it wasn't her, the taxi company were at fault. She was impressive despite the consultant's best efforts with the DESC script. The consultant felt deflated and started to summarize the evidence, then said she could perhaps understand why it had happened. This woman had just bought a flat and so had possibly sold her car. She was sure she had not started out to use the taxi service every day, but when she had got away with it, her usage had escalated. Suddenly the woman burst into tears, admitted to everything, and handed over a cheque for the entire amount.

This incident teaches us a lot about human behaviour, and to quote Stephen Covey 'seek first to understand then to be understood'. Forming relationships and maintaining them is as important at work as it is at home.

Keys

- Daniel Goleman has helped us discover that emotional intelligence is a good thing.
- Part of emotional intelligence is the ability to express ourselves. Finding words to describe accurately how we feel even to ourselves communicates very directly and helps others take us seriously.
- Use FORE anywhere, bus stops, stations, airport lounges, to establish relationships. Good relationships ease our path through life.
- Invest in some emotional banking. When you become proactive in finding points of common interest it is difficult to be bored.
- Stroking is as essential to our lives as breathing. Positive strokes can include criticism. Negative strokes discount others.
- Revisit the stroking patterns exercise and start to stroke more those people at home and work you have taken for granted. Rewarding behaviour changes cultures.
- Become an emotional coach for all emotions and realize where there is emotion there is life.
- Handle difficult people elegantly by:
  - analysing that difficult person;
  - analysing yourself and what part you play;
  - adopting a more negotiative approach;
  - becoming skilled at dealing with anger and conflict;
  - focusing on positive outcomes.
  If this does not work, move on to the DESC script.

seven

The fifth commandment: trust the team

Success is not achieved in isolation. Our directors knew that they had neither the time nor the ability to do everything themselves, and were highly dependent on finding and keeping the right team. Finding business partners and then trusting them is a key business skill.

'Finding and keeping a good team' was, for our group overall, the fifth most highly rated characteristic of success. However it was more important for men, who rated it number two, than for women, where it ranked number six. Perhaps our men had, or thought they had, more deficiencies that had to be made up for by the skills of others.

For many people, relationships with their team were the key to job satisfaction. This was partly derived from the pleasure of seeing colleagues develop and the vicarious enjoyment from, in Christopher Rodrigues' words, 'being part of other people's success'. This also kept people going when times were tough, with many executives telling us that support from the team was the key to surviving the ups and downs of business life.

Not all team relationships were warm and comfortable. Speaking of their fellow board members, Harry Gould's description was 'irritating but useful', David Ure found something to 'admire and despise in all of them', Gwynneth Flower saw them as 'warring chicks', and Diana Parker found they could 'drive you batty'. This was often a result of a deliberate policy of not employing 'yes-men'. It seems that our directors had succeeded by associating with people who complemented their skills rather than those who would give them an easy life.

This chapter deals with the challenge of building and leading a team that has the necessary mix of skills to cope with the difficult task of running a business. In general, we will be assuming that the team comprises between four and eight people. This seems to emerge consistently as the ideal team size in most of the many studies of this subject.

Of course, the process has to start with *you*. Are you up to the challenge of leading a team? And are you clear about your own strengths and weaknesses so that you can identify the complementary characteristics you need to form a rounded team?

We start with a 10 point leadership checklist (see Table 7.1) then develop some of the key points.

Core leadership issues

Table 7.1 The 10 point leadership checklist

1. Agree strategy and vision with the team, but let individuals handle the detail and the implementation.
2. Be confident. If you're not, then look confident.
3. Be reliable and consistent.
4. Continually home in on the priorities.
5. Develop excellent listening and communication skills.
6. Radiate drive and urgency.
7. Respond flexibly to situations.
8. Sell, don't tell.
9. Take responsibility.
10. Use creative brainstorming techniques to develop new ideas and approaches.

Strategy and vision

A crucial test of an effective team is whether all its members have a clear vision of where they are going – and whether they all have the same vision! The leader's job is to set the strategic context for the organization, and to ensure understanding, support and enthusiasm for the strategy among all team members.

Confidence

Leaders simply have to radiate confidence, whether they are about to lead troops into battle, or their sales force into the latest campaign. Confidence is infectious, and individuals can be transformed by a strong and supportive leader who simply knows they will succeed. But lack of confidence is infectious too, so if you have doubts about a particular course of action it is wise not to let them show.

Reliability

While a few leaders have succeeded with an idiosyncratic style where no one could predict what they would do next, most of us look for consistency and reliability in our leaders. Many management gurus have noted the usefulness of adopting certain statements and phrases which reflect what the leader wants to achieve, and regularly introducing these into meetings and presentations. These become a consistent 'brand' with which the leader is always associated.

Prioritizing

In a lively business, there is never any shortage of things to do. However, as we discussed in the second commandment, it is easy to consume time with things that deliver little return. The leader's job is to keep the focus on the priorities, always asking 'What should we do next?' and ensuring that distractions are not allowed to interfere with the progression of the business.

Listening and communicating

In our interviews with business leaders, we were consistently struck by the brilliance of their communication skills. They listened attentively to what we had to say, and their responses were considered and articulate. We respect people who give us their single-minded attention, and explain their thoughts in ways that are clear and unambiguous. This is a key leadership skill.

Drive and urgency

In his work on sustaining business growth, Simon Phillips identified the importance of pace, or 'a sense of dynamism'. The leader needs to radiate energy and enthusiasm for moving forward. Of course, occasionally we have to fake it, and we need to remember to recharge the batteries in whatever way works for us.

Flexibility

Studies of failed businesses that were once successful invariably show that they were trying to maintain old approaches despite the fact that circumstances had changed. All of us, at least some of the time, resist change and try to settle for old and comfortable approaches. The leader's job is to remain sufficiently flexible to change old patterns when circumstances demand.

Sell, don't tell

Teams of intelligent, creative people do not take kindly to being instructed what to do, as if they were still at school. Leaders need to persuade, inspire and demonstrate – to 'sell' – their ideas, if they are to achieve real team commitment.

Responsibility

The management writer Charles Handy has described the tendency we all have to depend on 'them' to fix things for us. As we develop through our childhood, we rely on 'them' to feed and clothe us, to teach us survival skills and to tell us what to do. 'Them' may be our parents, our teachers or ultimately our employers. But leaders are people who recognize that they have become the 'them', and that they now have to take charge.

Creative brainstorming

All teams need creativity. They thrive and survive on new ideas and different approaches, in a framework of solid reliability that the leader provides. Studies have shown that the leader does not have to be the creative force, but does have to tap and cultivate the creative abilities within the team. The key is effective brainstorming to ensure that team members fully contribute to business innovation.

Assembling your team

If you can rise to the ten-point approach, how do you go about assembling your team? One option is to classify the requirements of your business and to find the best possible individual to fill each slot. A typical business might need someone for each of the following functions:

- finance;
- human resources;
- marketing;
- operational management;
- product development;
- sales.

You might, of course, not want this particular support mix. Perhaps you already *are*, or want to be, the finance director, in which case the list of support functions will be specific to your role.

However, this approach alone to building the team simply does not work. It does not guarantee either that you will have the skills you actually need for the business, or that the individuals will gel into a cohesive, co-operative group. The problem is that the mix of skills necessary for success cannot be described only in functional terms like marketing, but also requires a breakdown by behavioural characteristics.

Management consultant Rupert Eales-White provides four behavioural characteristics that are needed in teams to ensure success:

- analysis;
- creativity;
- drive;
- harmony.

How do you find those skills? And how do you know which category your existing people fit into, and therefore where your team strengths and shortcomings are likely to be?

The most significant work on this subject was undertaken by the management researcher Dr Meredith R Belbin. Working with the Cambridge Industrial Training Research Unit, he undertook more than nine years of study into the behaviour of business teams. The teams comprised every conceivable combination of individuals. They were scrutinized to see how well they performed when given a management game that required them to set up 'companies' and produce financial results.

Belbin's first result was startling. The experiment consisted of setting up eight teams, each of six people. Unbeknown to the subjects, one team, codenamed the Apollo team after the American lunar missions, consisted of the brightest and best business brains, as measured by a battery of mental and psychometric tests. The shock result was that the Apollo team came last. Naturally the experiment was repeated. In fact it was repeated 25 times with different groups, but always with the brightest and best forming the Apollo team. During these experiments, the Apollo team won only three times and typically came sixth out of eight. Overall, Apollo companies performed significantly worse than other companies, despite the apparent advantage of containing all the super-talent.

Observers of the Apollo teams noted that team members spent much of their time trying to persuade other members to their own well-stated point of view. However, no one seemed to ever convert anyone else, or be converted themselves. Everyone seemed to have a talent for spotting the others' weaknesses. There was no coherence in the decisions reached, and many pressing tasks were totally neglected. The eventual failure of the team was marked by mutual recriminations.

Belbin's work continued, dedicated to finding exactly what mix of individuals did make up a successful business team. Initially, he looked at the effectiveness of other 'pure' teams consisting of all the same type of people. He used the personality classifications of extrovert/introvert and stable/anxious developed by the psychologist Hans Eysenck. This gives four personality types which have been well studied in executive occupations (see Figure 7.1). Belbin and his team found that pure groupings of these four individual types had some merits and some drawbacks:

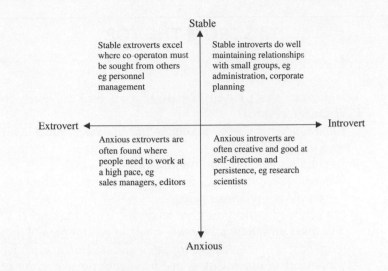

Figure 7.1 Eysenck's personality classification

▓ **Stable extrovert teams** were versatile and enjoyed group work, but were inclined to be euphoric and lazy.

▓ **Anxious extrovert teams** were dynamic and entrepreneurial. They were good at seizing opportunities but were easily distracted and liable to rush off at tangents.

▓ **Stable introvert teams** planned well and were strong in organization. However, they were slow moving and liable to neglect new factors in a situation.

▓ **Anxious introvert teams** were capable of good ideas but lacked team cohesion and had a tendency to be preoccupied.

Clearly, Belbin's work was leading to the observation that successful teams are not 'pure' teams with one particular type of person, even if that type is individually the brightest and best. But if the best team is some sort of hybrid, then what is the ideal mix, and what type of person is the model leader?

To resolve these questions, Belbin and his researchers noted that a number of different individual types had emerged in their team studies. This was a larger number that the four types given by the Eysenck categories and Belbin found it useful to describe the types by the sort of contribution they made to their business group. His classification of team members has become famous as the definitive itemizing of business personalities.

TIPS FROM THE TOP

Brian Larcombe CEO, 3i

- What were the principal things you had to learn to become successful?

    I had to learn to listen to others and to realize that I don't always get it right.
- What challenges did you meet along the way?

    When you become a CEO it dawns on you that nothing you say to people is any longer private.
- What advice would you give to an aspiring manager?

    You must articulate where you want to go and then obtain agreement from those managing you. The skills necessary for advancement in our business are teamworking with a bit of competitiveness and innovation.

Before we go into detail about the team types and their contribution to an organization, complete Belbin's 'self-perception inventory' so that you know your own particular team role. Allocate 10 points per section. You do not need to give points to every statement: however, each section must add up to 10, so answer (a) could have 10 points and the rest none, or five answers in the section could be allocated two points each. Do this for all seven sections, then transfer the allocated points per statement to the points table (Table 7.2). Then transcribe the scores to the analysis sheet (Table 7.3) and add the totals to give a distribution of your team-role characteristics.

Self-perception inventory

1. **What I believe I can contribute to a team:**
   a. I think I can quickly see and take advantage of new opportunities.
   b. I can work well with a very wide range of people.
   c. Producing ideas is one of my natural assets.
   d. My ability rests in being able to draw people out whenever I detect they have something of value to contribute to group objectives.
   e. My capability to follow through has much to do with my personal effectiveness.
   f. I am ready to face temporary unpopularity if it leads to worthwhile results in the end.
   g. I can usually sense what is realistic and likely to work.
   h. I can offer a reasoned case for alternative courses of action without introducing bias or prejudice.

2. **If I have a possible shortcoming in teamwork, it could be that:**
   a. I am not at ease unless meetings are well structured, controlled and generally well conducted.
   b. I am inclined to be too generous towards others who have a valid viewpoint that has not been given a proper airing.
   c. I have a tendency to talk too much once the group gets on to new ideas.
   d. My objective outlook makes it difficult for me to join in readily and enthusiastically with colleagues.
   e. I am sometimes seen as forceful and authoritarian if there is a need to get something done.
   f. I find it difficult to lead from the front, perhaps because I am over-responsive to group atmosphere.
   g. I am apt to get caught up on ideas that occur to me and so lose track of what is happening.
   h. My colleagues tend to see me as worrying unnecessarily over detail and the possibility that things may go wrong.

3. **When involved in a project with other people:**
   a. I have an aptitude for influencing people without pressurizing them.

b. My general vigilance prevents careless mistakes and omissions being made.

c. I am ready to press for action to make sure that a meeting does not waste time or lose sight of the main objective.

d. I can be counted on to contribute something original.

e. I am always ready to back a good suggestion in the common interest.

f. I am keen to look for the latest in new ideas and developments.

g. I believe my capacity for judgement can help to bring about the right decisions.

h. I can be relied upon to see that all essential work is organized.

4. **My characteristic approach to group work is that:**
   a. I have a quiet interest in getting to know colleagues better.
   b. I am not reluctant to challenge the views of others or to hold a minority view myself.
   c. I can usually find a line of argument to refute unsound propositions.
   d. I think I have a talent for making things work once a plan has to be put into operation.
   e. I have a tendency to avoid the obvious and to come out with the unexpected.
   f. I bring a touch of perfectionism to any job I undertake.
   g. I am ready to make use of contacts outside the group itself.
   h. While I am interested in all views I have no hesitation in making up my mind once a decision has to be made.

5. **I gain satisfaction in a job because:**
   a. I enjoy analysing situations and weighing up all the possible choices.
   b. I am interested in finding practical solutions to problems.
   c. I like to feel I am fostering good working relationships.
   d. I can have a strong influence on decisions.
   e. I can meet people who may have something new to offer.

f. I can get people to agree on a necessary course of action.

g. I feel in my element where I can give a task my full attention.

h. I like to find a field that stretches my imagination.

6. **If I am suddenly given a difficult task with limited time and unfamiliar people:**

a. I would feel like retiring to a corner to devise a way out of the difficulty before developing a solution.

b. I would be ready to work with the person who showed the most positive approach.

c. I would find some way of reducing the size of the task by establishing what individuals might best contribute.

d. My natural sense of urgency would help to ensure that we did not fall behind schedule.

e. I believe I would keep cool and maintain my capacity to think straight.

f. I would retain a steadiness of purpose in spite of the pressures.

g. I would be prepared to take a positive lead if I felt the group were making no progress.

h. I would open up discussions with a view to stimulating new thoughts and getting something moving.

7. **With reference to the problems to which I am subject in working in groups:**

a. I am apt to show my impatience with those who are obstructing my progress.

b. Others may criticize me for being too analytical and insufficiently intuitive.

c. My desire to ensure that work is properly done can hold up proceedings.

d. I tend to get bored rather easily and rely on one or two stimulating people to spark me off.

e. I find it difficult to get started unless goals are clear.

f. I am sometimes poor at explaining and clarifying complex points that occur to me.

g. I am conscious of demanding from others the things I cannot do myself.

h. I hesitate to get points across when I run up against real opposition.

Table 7.2 Points table

Section	Scores							
	a	b	c	d	e	f	g	h
1								
2								
3								
4								
5								
6								
7								

Table 7.3 Self-perception inventory analysis sheet

Section	IMP	CO	SH	PL	RI	ME	TW	CF
1	g	d	f	c	a	b	b	e
2	a	b	e	g	c	d	f	h
3	h	a	c	d	f	g	e	b
4	d	h	b	e	g	c	a	f
5	b	f	d	h	e	a	c	g
6	f	c	g	a	h	e	b	d
7	e	g	a	f	d	b	h	c
Total								

Key:

IMP– Implementer
CO – Co-ordinator
SH – Shaper
PL – Plant
RI – Resource investigator
ME – Monitor-evaluator
TW – Teamworker
CF – Completer-finisher

Table 7.4   A summary of team types

Type	Typical features	Positive qualities	Possible weaknesses
Implementer	Conservative, dutiful, predictable	Reliable, organizing ability, self-disciplined, hard-working, common sense, turns ideas to action	Inflexible, unresponsive to new ideas
Co-ordinator	Calm, self-confident, mature	Good chairperson, delegates well, sense of objectives, welcomes contributors without prejudice	Can be seen as manipulative, delegates personal work, ordinary in intellect and creative ability
Shaper	Highly strung, outgoing, dynamic	Drive and readiness to challenge inertia, courage to overcome obstacles	Prone to provocation, irritation, impatience, hurts people's feelings
Plant	Creative, individualistic, serious minded, unorthodox	Genius, imagination, intellect, knowledge	Up in the clouds, ignores details, too preoccupied to communicate
Resource investigator	Extroverted, enthusiastic, curious, communicative	Develops contacts, explores anything new, responds to challenge	Loses interest once initial enthusiasm has passed, over-optimistic
Monitor-evaluator	Sober, unemotional, prudent	Good judgement, discretion, hard-headed	Limited drive, lacks inspiration, doesn't inspire others, overly critical
Teamworker	Socially oriented, rather mild, sensitive, listener, averts friction	Can respond to people and situations, perceptive and diplomatic, calms the waters	Indecisive at moments of crisis, easily influenced
Completer-finisher	Painstaking, orderly, conscientious, anxious	Capacity for follow-through, perfectionism, delivers on time, finds errors and omissions	Worries about small things, reluctant to let go, poor at delegating, can nit-pick

Table 7.4 summarizes the characteristics of Belbin's nine team types. It is worth noting that Belbin later added an additional 'type', not evaluated by the self-perception inventory. That was the 'specialist', the single-minded, dedicated individual. Specialists can contribute vital skills in rare supply, but typically contribute only on a narrow front without an interest in the big picture.

The mix for a successful team

Belbin and his researchers used their knowledge of business types to observe what mix comprised a successful team. Their conclusions fell into six main categories:

The right person in the chair

The successful chairperson is someone who is trusting by nature, accepting people without jealousy or suspicion. However, this acceptance is counterbalanced by a strong basic dominance and a powerful commitment to delivering on goals and objectives. The good chairperson is calm and unflappable in the face of controversy, realistic and naturally self-disciplined. He or she is an enthusiast with a capacity for excitement that motivates others, but is not a pure extrovert since they are prone to detachment in social relations.

Interestingly, successful chairpersons were not, on average, more mentally able or more creative than the others. In general the successful chair was up to the mental ability of colleagues, but not very far ahead of them. People who were slightly cleverer than their teams were slightly less successful in the chair, and people who were much cleverer were much less successful. However, you can't continue that graph in both directions: those who were much less clever were also much less successful!

A member of the research group who analysed the chairperson scores summarized the successful chairman as 'someone tolerant enough always to listen to others but strong enough to reject their advice'.

One strong plant in the group

Winning companies were characterized by the inclusion of a 'plant'. The plant is the Belbin team type who is creative, imaginative and unorthodox. So a successful company needs at least one very creative and clever member.

Belbin found that if you couldn't have creativity *and* cleverness, then creativity was the more important characteristic, but if both were combined at high level in a single person this was a great advantage. The difficulty for a creative plant with only average cleverness was that of establishing team-role credibility in the company. In fact the failure of the plant to fulfil a team role was the most distinguishing mark of companies which looked as though they were destined for success, but which actually failed.

Another occasional problem, to which Belbin drew attention, was that of including a plant who was creative in an inappropriate way. For example, he or she was literate when numeracy was really needed.

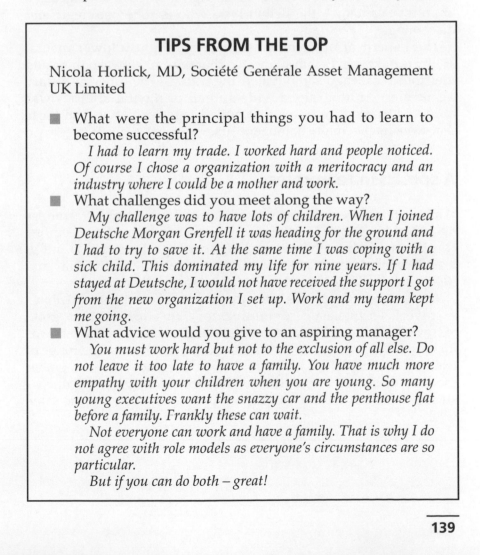

TIPS FROM THE TOP

Nicola Horlick, MD, Société Genérale Asset Management UK Limited

■ What were the principal things you had to learn to become successful?

I had to learn my trade. I worked hard and people noticed. Of course I chose a organization with a meritocracy and an industry where I could be a mother and work.

■ What challenges did you meet along the way?

My challenge was to have lots of children. When I joined Deutsche Morgan Grenfell it was heading for the ground and I had to try to save it. At the same time I was coping with a sick child. This dominated my life for nine years. If I had stayed at Deutsche, I would not have received the support I got from the new organization I set up. Work and my team kept me going.

■ What advice would you give to an aspiring manager?

You must work hard but not to the exclusion of all else. Do not leave it too late to have a family. You have much more empathy with your children when you are young. So many young executives want the snazzy car and the penthouse flat before a family. Frankly these can wait.

Not everyone can work and have a family. That is why I do not agree with role models as everyone's circumstances are so particular.

But if you can do both – great!

A spread of mental abilities

Belbin found that the best-performing companies had a spread of mental abilities. The absolutely perfect formula was to have one very clever plant, another clever member, a chairman with slightly higher than average mental ability, and other company members with slightly below average mental ability.

The reasoning behind this formula is that the brilliantly clever and creative plant is a huge asset to the company *provided* ultimate responsibility lies with the chairperson. For this to succeed, the company needs someone with the mental ability to find the flaw in imaginative but possibly unsound propositions, with the chair acting as ultimate arbiter. The ideal high-intellect challenger is a 'monitor-evaluator', the Belbin type who is sober, strategic and discerning.

The benefit of other members having slightly lower mental ability is puzzling. Belbin suggested that the gap between them and their other colleagues motivated them to fill the other necessary team roles. At any rate, a wide spread of mental abilities was observed to produce teams that pulled together better than those that were intellectually homogeneous.

A spread in teamroles

Winning teams were characterized by a good spread in the teamroles described by Belbin. In particular, companies seemed to need one completer-finisher (the painstaking, conscientious type), and at least one implementer (the disciplined, reliable individual that Belbin originally described as the 'company worker').

Another key player was often the resource investigator (Belbin's extrovert, enthusiastic communicator). In addition to a good extrovert, additional balance was given if a distinct introvert was included. The key was that a winning company has a wide range of team-role strengths on which to draw. Different types of member increase the range of the team while also minimizing the unconstructive friction when two or more people compete for the same role.

A match between the attributes of members and their responsibilities

A particular mark of winning teams was the way in which individuals took on jobs that fitted their personal abilities. This involved finding methods of fitting the right person for the right job and *not* assuming that past experience with a particular activity was sufficient justification for continuing with that role.

An effective method of avoiding a mismatch between person and role was to give assignments to small groups or pairs of people rather than a single individual. An example is the way in which finance was handled in the team games. Sometimes the finance role was given to the individual claiming the most finance experience. However, in winning teams finance was often given to two people, one used to dealing with figures and a sharp-minded person as a check on the process. Flexible pairings of this sort allowed informal arrangements to develop, with individuals settling into roles which properly matched their skills to their jobs.

A recognition of shortcomings

Weakness can be compensated for by self-knowledge. This is as true for companies as for individuals. Belbin gives some impressive examples of teams that, on the face of it, looked like no-hopers but which triumphed when they acted on knowledge of their deficiencies.

An example was a deliberately constructed group consisting entirely of shapers, mostly of low mental ability. Belbin's shaper is the challenging, dynamic type. When the group met, they openly confronted their problems and recognized the risk that they would, one, not come up with any good ideas, and two, argue over every issue. They responded by appointing their brightest member as the official 'plant' and, knowing the importance of the plant/chairperson relationship, allowed the plant to choose the chairperson as the individual with whom he would most comfortably work. To avoid endless fruitless argument, they decided to vote on every issue. This gave the team a flow of ideas and the ability to make quick decisions and seize opportunities. The result was that a team was deliberately constructed so that it would finish last not only won, but won handsomely.

Utilizing and developing team types

The rest of this chapter looks in more detail at the characteristics of the various team types and the ways in which they should be utilized and developed. From this you should be able to identify your team's strengths and weaknesses. You can then develop plans either to fill gaps with the right people or, like the shaper team above, to develop an approach that overcomes shortcomings.

First, the quick and simple approach. You might not have the time or opportunity to undertake detailed analysis, or might want to make a preliminary judgement about individuals before approaching them. Belbin provides a useful list of phrases and slogans which indicate individuals' likely team type. Use this to make a preliminary assessment of your team mix.

Implementer

- If it can be done, we will do it.
- An ounce of action is worth a pound of theory.
- Hard work never killed anybody.
- If it's difficult, we do it immediately. If it's impossible it takes a little longer.
- To err is human, to forgive is not company policy.
- Let's get down to the task in hand.

Co-ordinator

- Let's keep the main objective in sight.
- Has anyone else got anything to add to this?
- We like to reach a consensus before we move forward.
- Never assume that silence means approval.
- I think we should give someone else a chance.
- Good delegation is an art.
- Management is the art of getting other people to do all the work.

Shaper

- Just do it!
- Say 'no', then negotiate.
- If you say 'yes I will do it', I expect it to be done.
- I'm not satisfied we are achieving all we can.
- I may be blunt, but at least I'm to the point.
- I'll get things moving.
- When the going gets tough, the tough get going.

Plant

- When a problem is baffling, think laterally.
- Where there's a problem, there's a solution.
- The greater the problem, the greater the challenge.
- Do not disturb, genius at work.
- Good ideas always sound strange at first.
- Ideas start with dreaming.
- Without continuous innovation, there is no survival.

Resource investigator

- We could make a fortune out of that.
- Ideas should be stolen with pride.
- Never reinvent the wheel.
- Opportunities arise from other people's mistakes.
- Surely we can exploit that?
- You can always telephone to find out.
- Time spent in reconnaissance is seldom wasted.

Monitor-evaluator

- I'll think it over and give you a firm decision tomorrow.
- Have we exhausted all the options?
- If it does not stand up to logic, it's not worth doing!
- Better to make the right decision slowly than the wrong one quickly.
- This looks like the best option on balance.

- Let's weigh up the alternatives.
- Decisions should not be based purely on enthusiasm.

Teamworker

- Courtesy costs nothing.
- I was very interested in your point of view.
- If it's all right with you, it's all right with me.
- Everybody has a good side worth appealing to.
- If people listened to themselves more, they would talk less.
- You can always sense a good atmosphere at work.
- I try to be versatile.

Completer-finisher

- This is something that demands our undivided attention.
- The small print is always worth reading.
- 'If anything can go wrong it will', and as O'Toole said on Murphy's law, 'Murphy was an optimist'.
- There is no excuse for not being perfect.
- Perfection is only just good enough.
- A stitch in time saves nine.
- Has it been checked?

Specialist

- In this job you never stop learning.
- Choose a job you love, and you'll never have to work a day in your life.
- True professionalism is its own reward.
- My subject is fascinating to me.
- The more you know, the more you find to discover.
- It is better to know a lot about something, than a little about everything.
- A committee is twelve people doing the work of one.

To help plan your team structure, here are some notes giving more information about the ideal roles for the different types, and the behaviours that need to be avoided.

The implementer

Objective: to turn general concepts into a practical working brief; to carry out that brief in a systematic fashion.

Methods to be cultivated:
- Helping ensure that the team's tasks have been structured and the objectives clearly outlined.
- Sorting out the practical details from the broad brief, and attending to them.
- Maintaining a steady, systematic approach whatever the pressure or lack of pressure.
- Persevering in the face of difficulty and striving to meet targets.
- Providing practical support and back-up to other team members.

Behaviour to be avoided:
- Unconstructive criticism of team members' ideas and suggestions.
- Lack of flexibility: an implementer's contribution is greatest when they can strike a balance between perseverance and adaptability.
- Competing for status within the team through their strong sense of personal identity.

Additional points: as managers, implementers' strengths lie in their concern for clarifying objectives in practical terms, and introducing and maintaining structure in a team. As team members, their qualities of conscientiousness and perseverance will help ensure that projects are completed to standard and to schedule. Their sense of duty prevents their concern for personal status interfering with their work towards helping all team members achieve their objectives.

The co-ordinator

Objective: to control and organize the activities of their team, making best use of the resources available.

Methods to be cultivated:
- Preparing the ground so that each meeting is structured and organized to enable all its business to be transacted efficiently within the time allotted.

- Encouraging each individual to play his or her part in pursuit of the team's objectives by identifying both the objectives of the exercise and the way in which each team member can best help.
- Being on the look out for weaknesses in the team's make-up and working to correct them, either by making changes in team membership or by calling for and expanding certain teamroles amongst existing team members.
- Co-ordinating the use of the resources available both within and outside the team, and keeping people's efforts orientated in the direction of obtaining the team's goals.
- Exercising personal self-discipline and perseverance in acting as a focal point for group effort, especially when things get difficult.
- Proper and appropriate delegation. Choosing the moment at which to move from consultation and discussion to decision-making.

Behaviour to be avoided:
- Taking advantage of a formal role to hog the stage.
- Rigidity and obstinacy posing as grit and determination.
- Failure to recognize individual abilities and merits in the team so that poor use is made of team resources.
- Competing with major team resources, particularly the plant or monitor-evaluator, and refusing to admit superior ability in other team members.
- Abdicating leadership role in the face of opposition or apathy.

Additional points: as managers, co-ordinators are in a position to employ their talents overtly. In a more junior role, they should support harmony, co-ordination and structure in the team without making their contributions in any way a threat to the more senior members of the group. Always, co-ordinators should remember that while they have many of the qualities that underlie other team roles, they must be prepared to play the role or roles that ensure the most effective team performance. They may have to shift between disguising their talents and taking a leading role according to their resources and the situation, and despite their strong ego, they must know which part to play and when.

The shaper

Objective: to give shape and form to the team's activities.

Methods to be cultivated:
- Directing the team's attention to the need to set objectives and establish priorities, and helping establish these clearly.
- Taking a wide perspective of the team's purpose and helping members perceive their role and contribution within the overall scheme.
- Exerting a directive influence on group discussions, and summing up the outcomes in terms of the objectives and targets set.
- Giving the team's activities generally an appropriate shape or pattern by co-ordinating the various contributions.
- Keeping a constant objective and detached view of the team's progress and achievements, and intervening when they seem to veer from a relevant and appropriate path.
- Intervening when the group is in danger of moving too far from its brief, or another member is 'getting away' with an inappropriate idea or suggestion.

Behaviour to be avoided:
- Steamrolling team members when in a position of authority.
- Assuming more authority and status than the group would warrant.
- Competing with other team members, particularly the plant and the monitor-evaluator.

Additional points: shapers can develop a sense of direction in a group that is leaderless, but they should do so in a subtle way rather than intensively. If they find themselves in a more formal leadership position, they will need to consider the co-ordinator role, and adopt a more positive controlling co-ordinating position. Such a role, with its greater emphasis on routine activities and duties, will entail some additional self-discipline.

When shapers have only junior status in a group, they need to time their contributions and interventions diplomatically, possibly putting them in the form of leading questions.

The plant

Objective: to act as a prime source of ideas and innovation for their team.

Methods to be cultivated:
■ Concentrating their attention on basic strategies and major issues.
■ Formulating new ideas relevant to the team's objectives.
■ Looking for possible breaks in approach to a problem with which the group has been confronted for some time.
■ Timing their contributions; presenting their proposals at appropriate moments to assist their positive reception.

Behaviour to be avoided:
■ Attempting to exhibit their capabilities over too wide a field.
■ Devoting their efforts and creative capability along lines of their personal interests rather than their team's needs.
■ Taking umbrage when their ideas are monitored, evaluated and possibly rejected.
■ Getting too inhibited about putting their ideas forward, especially in a dominant, extrovert or over-critical group.

Additional points: plants as managers must exercise considerable self-discipline and be prepared to listen to their teams' comments on their proposals (particularly their monitor-evaluator colleagues). On the other hand they must not let the stresses of controlling the team stifle their creative input. It will take all their ingenuity to combine the roles successfully. In a less senior role, plants can hope to be used as a resource, but if this does not turn out, they should devote some of their energies and talents towards establishing themselves as the person to whom the team turns for ideas, solutions, and a fresh viewpoint.

The resource investigator

Objective: to explore outside resources and develop contacts that may be useful to their team.

Methods to be cultivated:

■ Making good use of their ability to get on with people quickly and easily to extend the range of the team's contacts and useful friendships.

■ Using their interest in new ideas and methods to explore possibilities outside the immediate working environment and introducing them to the team.

■ Expanding their role as the team's point of contact with outside bodies, keeping up to date with all developments that may be relevant to the team's work.

■ Assisting in maintaining good relationships and harmony within their team, and in encouraging fellow team members to make best use of their talents, especially in times of pressure and crisis.

Behaviour to be avoided:

■ Getting too involved with their own ideas at the expense of exploring others'.

■ Rejecting ideas or information before submitting them to the team for their opinion.

■ Relaxing too much when the pressure of work eases.

■ Allowing their liking for talking and sociability to lead them into unproductive use of time.

Additional points: the resource investigator when working well can broaden the scope and vision of the team. At worst, the team may feel abandoned by them as they investigate elsewhere.

The monitor-evaluator

Objective: to analyse ideas and suggestions both from within and from outside the team, and to evaluate their feasibility and practical value in terms of the team's objectives.

Methods to be cultivated:

■ Using their critical thinking ability constructively in the team's interests.

■ Achieving a judicious blend of experimenting outlook and critical appraisal.

■ Building on their colleagues' suggestions; helping to develop their ideas to relevant and practical fruition.

■ Making a firm but tactful case against their team adopting unsound approaches to their problems and choosing the appropriate moment for doing that.

■ Developing a close working relationship with the team's plant, if there is one.

Behaviour to be avoided:

■ Using critical thinking ability for their own advance at the expense of their team's objectives.

■ Tactless and destructive debunking of colleagues' suggestions.

■ Negative thinking allowing their critical powers to outweigh their open-minded receptivity to new ideas.

■ Competitive behaviour, particularly with the co-ordinator or plant.

■ Lowering the team's morale by being rather too critical, objective and damning at an inappropriate moment.

Additional points: a successful monitor-evaluator combines high critical thinking with personal qualities of fair-mindedness, practicality and receptivity to change. The role is often combined with another team role. When monitor-evaluators are also team leaders, they must take extra care that they do not over-dominate the other members of the team, and stifle their contributions. The art of feeding other people your lines is particularly relevant in their case.

At a less senior level, monitor-evaluators have the problem of making their point heard, and not appearing a threat to their colleagues. If they can avoid becoming unduly sceptical and cynical in the process, their experience at this stage will stand them in good stead as they rise in the hierarchy.

The team worker

Objective: to help individual members to achieve and maintain team effectiveness.

Methods to be cultivated:

■ Observing the strengths and weaknesses of members.

■ Supporting members in their strengths, for example by building on suggestions.

- Underpinning team members in their shortcomings by personal assistance or by finding appropriate resources.
- Improving communication between members.
- Fostering a sense of team spirit by setting an example in team member behaviour.

Behaviour to be avoided:
- Competition for status or dominance in the group.
- Siding with one member against another.
- Behaviour which might give the group a negative image both to the members themselves and to outsiders.
- Any conspicuous or ostentatious behaviour in the exercise of the team worker function.

Additional points: the team worker role can be exercised at different levels of status within the group. As managers, team workers should interpret their role as developers of others and delegators. At a junior level they may act as behind-the-scenes helpers. Their status, however, should not affect their basic objectives in serving the team.

The completer-finisher

Objective: to ensure all the teams efforts are as near perfect as possible and that nothing is overlooked.

Methods to be cultivated:
- Generally keeping an eye open for mistakes, of omission or commission, especially those that may fall between the responsibilities of two people.
- Choosing an area of work in which finishing qualities are important.
- Looking for mistakes in detail that may spoil the finished product.
- Actively searching for aspects of the work which need a more than usual degree of attention.
- Constantly endeavouring to raise the standard of all the team's activities by vigilance and help as required.
- Maintaining a sense of urgency within the team.

Behaviour to be avoided:
■ Unnecessary emphasis on detail at the expense of the overall plan and direction.
■ Negative thinking or destructive criticism. Lowering team morale by excessive worrying.

Additional points: the completer-finisher in a team has to work hard at being chosen to review work and check for errors rather than being seen as a nitpicker. As leaders, they should look for another completer-finisher in the team or coach someone else, as they will not have time to be so detail conscious.

Finally, a reminder that in revisiting his studies, Belbin introduced a ninth team-role type, the specialist. These are not included in the inventory scoring but do represent another role of importance in some teams. Specialists are valuable when a particular form of professional expertise is needed. Belbin notes that the importance of distinguishing the valued specialist from the valued generalist has come increasingly to the fore as an important issue with which management needs to grapple when handling talented personnel.

In a nutshell, specialists are single-minded, self-starting and dedicated. They provide knowledge and skills in rare supply. On the debit side, they may contribute only on a narrow front, dwelling on technicalities and ignoring the big picture.

Finally, in reviewing the value of the many years of study of himself and his team, Belbin made many recommendations to the executive. We will close this review of team relationships with a summary of six key points.

■ Establish which team-role styles you can deploy yourself, bearing in mind the observations of others. Perfect these styles so they can be enacted with skill and professionalism. Develop phrases and sayings to declare your claim on these roles.
■ Outlaw team roles that are foreign to you. Do not incorporate them into your habits or allow them to form part of the expectations of others. Failure to do this will place you in a weak position.
■ Identify the needs of your business and assess where you are lacking in crucial team roles. In particular ensure you have a

capable creative plant within the team structure.

■ Endeavour to have a mix of team-role characteristics and mental capabilities within your team.

■ When you have projects that demand skills not available within the immediate team, use working parties that co-opt the appropriate resources to fulfil the task in hand.

■ Recognize that genius is sometimes more critical than management. Recognize and foster genius and, if necessary, organize the management around it.

TIPS FROM THE TOP

Charles Allen, CEO, Granada Group

■ What were the principal things you had to learn to become successful?

I had to learn to manage honestly and directly. Also to understand what would motivate other people to make changes for me and the organization. If you do not tap into what is in it for them then you are on a hiding to nothing.

■ What challenges did you meet along the way?

I have survived two hostile bids for the company from LWT and Forte Hotels and lived to tell the tale.

■ What advice would you give to an aspiring manager?

Young executives need to follow their instincts rather than slavishly following what others tell them. Achieving an individual way of doing things increases confidence and decision making.

Always think ahead. Work out what to do within the next year, constantly clarifying priorities and reviewing these monthly.

Keys

■ Understand the team characteristics of yourself and your colleagues.

■ Assemble a mix of people with the right blend of personal, as well as technical, attributes.
■ Ensure the team has at least one creative member.
■ Reinforce your personal team roles with consistent behaviour, supported by appropriate phrases and sayings.
■ Do not allow yourself to take up team roles for which you are not suited.

The **sixth commandment: de-stress**

Our board directors consistently gave a high rating to their ability to cope with stress and recognized that managing stress is now a business essential. There are many approaches to stress management, but the key is awareness and doing something about it. In this as in other aspects of business, successful people take control, and various techniques to become stress free will be presented and demonstrated.

A boardroom is not a place for the stressed out, according to our sample of chief executives and managing directors. They rated the ability to manage their stress as the sixth most important skill in our 10 commandments for success. They are certainly a healthy group. Only eight of them had experienced a serious illness, operation or accident. Only one, an American, had the heart problems traditionally associated with executive stress. Is it by chance that he was also the only one to take telephone calls during our interview, and seemed to be more harassed than the rest of our sample?

It is unimaginable that these board directors had no stressful events to deal with. They mentioned difficult people, financial challenges, press hounding, bureaucratic and government interference. So it must be how they handle these events that allows them to be stress free. As Bertrand Russell said, 'It's not the experience that happens to you: it's what you do with the experience that happens to you.'

This chapter looks at what stresses might be in your life, your idiosyncratic response to that stress and really simple techniques to become more relaxed and in control. We start with a list of potential stresses in the workplace, which serves to remind us that stress is an umbrella concept. It covers a multitude of areas with myriad effects and many outcomes. The idea is that this chapter should simplify and shed light on recent research in the area and what you can do personally.

Look at the list below and note anything which puts pressure on you, irritates you or creates what you might feel as stress.

Stress in your work environment

Noise

Open-plan offices were hailed as the way forward for better office communication. Everyone would work together as a team and there would be no 'them and us' between management and employees. What they did not reckon on was the noise. Desks are often packed into every available space, which means overhearing calls from the next desk and being constantly interrupted. Taking written work home to complete in peace and quiet has become the norm.

Of course, the further up the corporate ladder you go, the more carpet you see. A great example of this was James Cullen's office. As you ascend in the lift you pass floors of tightly packed desks and very little visible carpeting. Reaching the Bell Atlantic inner sanctum that is the CEO's office, there are expanses of green carpet, a whisper of voices, and a slight whirr of muted technology. It is worth getting to the top just to achieve the peace and quiet.

Lighting and temperature

Sick building syndrome described a cluster of working conditions which led employees to feel unwell. For years these were ignored because they emanated from 'hysterical' women. When researchers came to analyse these issues they found that administrative staff, the major complainers and predominantly women, were often clustered in the centre of a building away from natural light and with no control over temperature.

Their bosses, mostly men, were on the periphery where they could open a window to cool themselves or control the lighting.

Having control over your environment is something we will return to throughout this chapter.

Natural light is very important for our well-being. We need at least two hours of natural light a day to function in an energetic way. Of course companies could invest in lighting that replicates natural light, but in the absence of this investment, getting outside during breaks becomes essential.

Office layout

Packed offices, no designated meeting rooms, managers distanced from staff by being together on the top floor, dingy surroundings with no art on the walls or plants to enliven the place, can create an environment that demotivates rather than inspires.

Management style

This is probably the most crucial ingredient. When Compaq started in Scotland the first tranche of staff worked in a marquee in the field where they would later build the plant. The conditions were appalling but the employees look back at that time as one of tremendous motivation, as everyone participated and problem solved in an equal way. Later when they had a state-of-the-art building staff began to complain about stress. New managers had been added who were less participative, managers in general were distanced from staff as their offices left the shop floor, and the camaraderie of the start-up was lost.

An authoritarian style is generally agreed to be outmoded, but many managers, while paying lip service to egalitarian philosophies and empowerment, still bark out orders like tinpot dictators. This destroys any desire by staff to offer up ideas for improvement, and they tend to hide any mistakes.

Working hours

Cary Cooper's research at the University of Manchester into the effect of long working hours on stress discovered that the average British employee worked longer hours than those in other European countries. Long hours at work, while not a necessary cause of stress, lead people to have less free time with no room for hobbies. Weekends are used to catch up on the previous week's sleep deprivation. The result is very circumscribed lives which only revolve round work. Long hours were found by Cooper to correlate significantly with ill health.

Appraisal systems

The whole concept of appraisals was to provide employees with feedback about their work performance and help them to improve. In the hands of a skilful manager this can provide focus and direction, but in the hands of the untrained it is destructive, partisan and stressful.

Staff turnover

One of the signs of an unhappy company is high staff turnover. People vote with their feet if they feel unappreciated or abused. Of course, as they leave, the rest of the team have to work even harder to cope. Exit interviews are essential for companies to know what is going on.

Stress in your job

Lack of training

Employees are often promoted at work to become managers because of their technical brilliance. What they are not trained to do is to manage. The ensuing mayhem is the stuff of litigation.

Work underload or overload

Too much or too little, both are a source of stress. An open and participative company would notice the ensuing lack of motivation or exhaustion and would intervene. Mostly people refuse to speak up as they are frightened they will lose their jobs. Stress is still viewed as vulnerability.

A large high street bank made all of the staff in one department redundant except for one man. He thought they had made a mistake, so arrived really early in the morning and left late at night so he would not be seen. He also tried to complete the work previously carried out by six people. This subterfuge came to an end as he collapsed with exhaustion three months later and had to be admitted to hospital. The bank was lucky he was a fair man and not litigious. Senior management realized their error in leaving him single handed, hired new staff and put him in charge. It was no error that they had not made him redundant: they had always wanted him to stay.

Equipment

Tesco was carrying out some research into sales of pharmaceutical drugs. They noticed that in one supermarket the sales of paracetamol had increased disproportionately. When they investigated the reason they discovered that at the time of the increase the company next door had problems with the server for their computers.

Equipment going wrong is a major headache. Journalists have coined the term 'computer rage' to describe cases where computers have been kicked and punched in anger. When we were writing this chapter the computer lost an entire day's input. Hitting it or dropping it from a great height was very tempting.

Stress factors in yourself

Gender

Our research revealed an increased number of women at the top of companies, although some were in non-executive director positions, but many still feel excluded from the promotional ladder owing to their gender. If that discrimination were not bad enough, the workplace can also be a hotbed of sexual harassment. Perhaps that was why Sir Ian McAllister said during his interview that the Ford board was no place for a woman.

Cultural background

Being different, whether in colour, accent or sex, can lead to problems. Diversity can bring such riches to the workplace but to some it is a threat. Humiliation ensues from this kind of discrimination and contributes to stress.

Colleagues, staff and bosses

How we relate to these three working groups will determine the joy or absence of joy we get from work. We are often selective about which group we relate to best. Some people get on well with their team and colleagues but they find managing their boss impossible. They may become aggressive when refused permission for something they feel is essential. Or they may think that their boss is incompetent – and let them know it. Some feel very competitive with colleagues and would trample over anyone to win. Others ignore their teams as they schmooze their way to the top. Whichever group is ignored will probably provide problems later in a career.

Fitness and health

If we are fit and healthy then we are more likely to withstand the rigours of a stressful job. The trouble is that if we spend all our time working, no time is left to exercise or indeed eat a healthy diet.

Family ties

Human beings can cope effectively with a number of pressures, especially if there is some island of tranquillity in their lives. Our board directors viewed their homes and families as just such an escape from their work life. However if there are tensions at home as well as work, any pressure is more likely to turn into stress.

All of the above create a potential for stress. Taken individually they might merely add up to minor irritations. Cumulatively they pose more of a problem.

To explore this concept further, complete the stress value of life events list in Table 8.1. If any of these life events have occurred in

Table 8.1 Stress value of life events

Death of a spouse	100
Divorce	73
Marital separation	65
Jail term	63
Death of close member of family	63
Personal injury or illness	53
Marriage	50
Fired from job	41
Marital reconciliation	45
Retirement	45
Change in health of family member	44
Pregnancy	40
Sex difficulties	39
Gain of new family member	39
Change in financial state	38
Death of close friend	37
Change to different type of work	36
Change in number of arguments with spouse	35
Mortgage over £50,000	31
Foreclosure of mortgage or loan	30
Change of responsibility at work	29
Son or daughter leaves home	29
Trouble with in-laws	29
Partner beginning or stopping work	29
Outstanding personal achievement	28
Beginning or ending school	26
Revision of personal habits	24
Trouble with boss	23
Change in hours or conditions of work	20
Change in residence	20
Change in education	20
Change in recreation	19
Change in social activities	18
Mortgage or loan less than £50,000	17
Change in sleeping habits	16
Change in number of family get-togethers	15
Change in eating habits	15
Vacation	13
Minor violations of the law	11
Total	

your life in the last 18 months to two years, circle the numbers that relate to them. Then total your scores and compare them to Table 8.2 The potential outcomes should not be viewed as absolutes, but the concept of a number of life events increasing your chances of becoming ill or having an accident is important.

Table 8.2   Potential outcome of stressful life events

Score	Increased chance of accident or illness
Around 150	30%
150–300	50%
300 and over	80%

TIPS FROM THE TOP

John Spence, CEO, Lloyds TSB Scotland

■ What were the principal things you had to learn to become successful?

Having the discipline to do the paper work.

■ What challenges did you meet along the way?

Since my sight has deteriorated, Gary, my PA, reads management books to me and keeps my ideas register. He even comes with me as I walk the dog.

■ What advice would you give to an aspiring manager?

It is important to handle the many strands of a business to move it forward.

You must also strive to be even tempered. Colleagues need constancy. You must lift those around you by being consistently upbeat.

Background to the stress value of life list

This list of life changes was researched by Holmes and Rahe when they questioned a number of hospital admissions and discovered that major life events had preceded their admission as a result of accident or illness. All major life events, good as well as bad, involve some change and these have a potential for causing stress. For example marriage, promotion and moving house will be less pressurizing than bad events, but still involve disruption of the status quo. It takes at least two years to recover from major changes like bereavement or divorce.

Too little change can lead to boredom and depression.

Reachback and afterburn

The concept of 'reachback' and 'afterburn' explains that it is often not just the event itself, but what goes before and after, that contribute to stress. Using an example highlighted in the Figure 8.1, marriage does not happen as a spontaneous event unless you elope. There is usually a lot of organization before a wedding, including potential disagreements over guest lists, catering and flowers. Then, as comedians like to point out, the afterburn is for life. Each life event has overlapping anticipatory anxiety and a tail-off of tension thereafter, so at some point with all this layering of anxiety, the chance of reaching a breaking point increases.

A number of years ago when the *Herald* newspaper was called the *Glasgow Herald*, they held a conference to look at stress at work. They issued the stress value of life events list to the audience. Five people scored over 300 points, with some reaching 500 or 600. All had had some kind of accident that week, such as falling off a ladder or crashing a car.

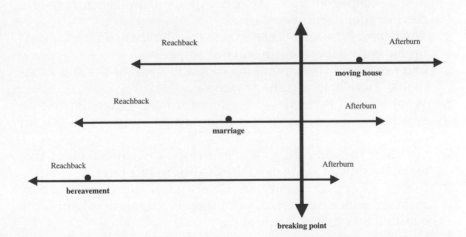

Figure 8.1 Reachback and afterburn

The short-term effects of stress

Imagine it is night and you thought everyone was tucked up in bed. You hear a window sliding open and soon after, the sound of footsteps on the stairs. Make a list of the things you might experience physiologically.

You may have noted symptoms such as faster heartbeat, faster breathing and being hyper-vigilant. This happens preparatory to a 'flight or fight' response which enabled the species to survive when under threat.

Nowadays, unless we are mugged or robbed, threats come in the form of job interviews, presentations or redundancy. Unfortunately, fighting or running away are not very socialized options, so we are often left with all the pent-up energy from this stress response. If this continues, our bodies habituate so we cease to notice how stressed we are. This is the danger time. However, let us get back to short-term stress and understanding its impact. Figure 8.2 shows how wonderfully we are designed for this kind of stress:

- *All our senses* become more acute. We hear more distinctly, see more sharply, and the hairs on our body stand up so we feel anyone or thing brushing past us.
- *Endorphins* are released from the hypothalamus in the brain to provide us with that 'high'. They also act as a painkiller so that mothers in labour can keep going and runners finish the race despite damaged limbs. We certainly have more energy to face this intruder or run away.
- The *thyroid hormone* is secreted into the bloodstream, and speeds up the body's metabolism and our responses.
- Our *heart beats faster*, pumping blood to the muscles and lungs to make us a better fighting machine.
- What we call *butterflies in the stomach* is an adrenalin release which also speeds us up and gears up the nervous system for action.
- *Cortisone* is produced so that we resist any infections if that assailant should injure us or throw dust in our faces.
- *Sweaty palms*, or sweaty anywhere else, are a homeostatic measure which means that our body temperature is kept fairly constant by cooling perspiration.
- Our *blood clots more readily* so that if the intruder assaults us we will not bleed to death.

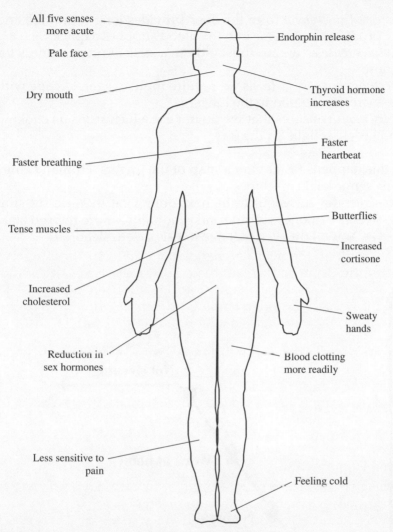

All five senses more acute

Endorphin release

Pale face

Dry mouth

Thyroid hormone increases

Faster heartbeat

Faster breathing

Butterflies

Tense muscles

Increased cortisone

Increased cholesterol

Sweaty hands

Reduction in sex hormones

Blood clotting more readily

Less sensitive to pain

Feeling cold

Figure 8.2   Short-term physiological responses to stress

■ *Peripheral parts of the body feel cold* as the blood drains from these to the more vital organs for survival: the heart lungs and brain. Warm hands tend not to be important for survival.

■ *Sensitivity to pain* is decreased so our fight or flight response is not impeded. Games like rugby would be unplayable without this stress reaction.

■ *Sex hormones are reduced,* as fighting or running for our lives are not the right time for lovemaking, despite what moviemakers would have us believe.

■ *Increased cholesterol* from the liver provides long-term fuel, and the production of sugar into the blood supplies a quick fix.

■ *Muscles tense* as we are constantly in a state of preparedness for action.

■ *Breathing becomes faster* as we require more oxygen to cope with the increase of blood to the lungs.

■ *A dry mouth* ensures that we do not eat which stops us choking and keeps us light for the fray.

All of this happens faster than a snap of the fingers. Human beings are truly remarkable machines.

If the intruder turns out to be next door's cat then pulses stop racing, stress hormones subside and gradually a more relaxed state takes over. You might even manage to get back to sleep.

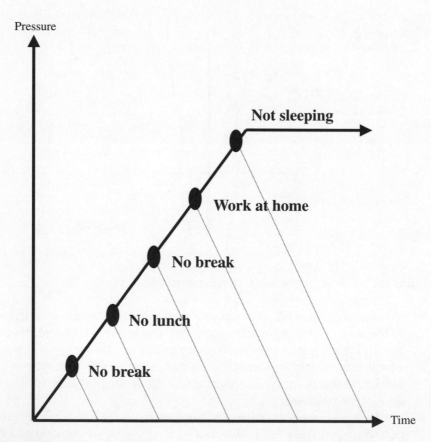

Figure 8.3 Pressure build-up

The pressure build-up

Since we are so honed to perfection for short-term stress, it would seem sensible to keep stress to short bursts. However the nature of stress has changed. It has been replaced by a more insidious modern variety. Figure 8.3 shows one way in which the short term becomes long term, sometimes without our awareness. Let's put you in that example.

Arriving at work you may discover that all you have planned has been hijacked by a proposal needed urgently for the following day. You work through all your breaks, coffee and lunch, hoping to finish at a reasonable hour, but as six o'clock comes and goes you are still working. Deciding to take the rest of your work home, you set out to clear your desk. Have you noticed how many people carry pilot's cases (and you know they are not pilots)? Multiple plastic bags are the alternative. This is presumably in case the train or bus is a few minutes late and a desk full of papers can be whipped out at a moment's notice.

When you arrive home you are so exhausted by the day's events and your lack of nutrition that all you really want to do is eat and watch TV. You are not relaxing as you are aware of the bundle of papers which you must finish by tomorrow for inclusion in the proposal. By 10.30 pm you have to get started and you carry on working well after midnight. You eventually get to bed. With arguments and figures competing for attention in your mind, you are wide awake till the early hours of the morning. It seems that on the hour every hour you look at the clock, becoming more agitated as you cannot imagine functioning adequately with no sleep. Just before dawn you fall into a deep sleep, to be rudely awakened by the alarm.

When you arrive at work your baseline for stress has risen. Nothing you did on the previous day reduced your stress levels and induced relaxation. Hans Selye, the French-Canadian researcher, stated that it takes about three weeks to habituate to a stressful lifestyle of this sort, and become a victim of long-term stress. The danger is that you are unaware of your high stress levels. There are plenty of jobs around which require the commitment of working long hours and taking work home, or at least people think that is what they have to do to keep up.

The long-term effects of stress

What is good for our functioning in the short term is a different matter in the long. The human race still has the same nervous system as prehistoric man. Catch or be caught was the rule of the jungle. Life today is less absolute, with many people subjecting themselves to the stress of the wrong job, being bullied by a superior or being married to the wrong person. This long-term stuff lowers self-esteem and limits our ability to tackle the issues.

When stress has persisted for a while the symptoms shown in Figure 8.4 tend to appear:

- *Headaches* can occur when muscle tension has persisted. Sitting at a desk clutching a phone, or driving long distances every day, can produce postural strain which can lead to headaches. Treatment with analgesics can work but does not tackle the real issues.
- *Insomnia* can be a real problem as all the stress hormones are mobilizing the body for action rather than sleep. The knock-on effect of not sleeping is to increase stress levels.
- *Weight loss* often happens during the acute phase of stress. In the long term eating relaxes and weight gain then takes over.
- There is an increased risk of *heart disease* as the heart is beating at a greater rate over a long period of time, and if you have cholesterol deposits in your coronary arteries any additional stress could lead to a heart attack.
- As the blood is also being pumped faster round the body there is an increased chance of hypertension or *high blood pressure*. This can lead to strokes or aneurisms.
- Over a period of time stress hormones become depleted. There is not an endless supply. If cortisone is absent, you may experience allergic reactions to food or the environment. *Skin conditions* become more common.
- *Indigestion and ulcers* appear as the acid secreted during stress eats into the stomach.
- *Poor circulation* can be the result of long-term stress, as we are never sufficiently relaxed to have warm extremities.
- *Sexual problems* can ensue if we are so stressed that we never feel like making love. The effect on a relationship can be devastating.

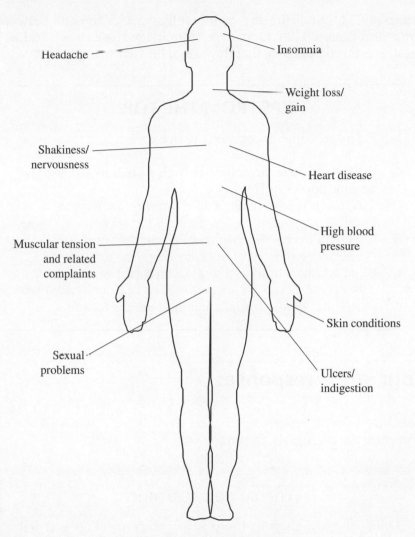

Figure 8.4   Long-term physiological responses to stress

▨ Because we are constantly in a state of preparedness for a crisis
   we experience *muscular tension* and related complaints such as
   lower-back pain and repetitive strain injury.
▨ *Shakiness and nervousness* are the end products of long-term
   stress and the depletion of stress hormones.

You can begin to see how you can suffer quite severe physical
ailments if stress in your life is not controlled and managed. Our

group of CEOs and directors were well aware of the link between stress and illness. They took steps to manage their stress, and as a result it is no coincidence that they are a healthy group.

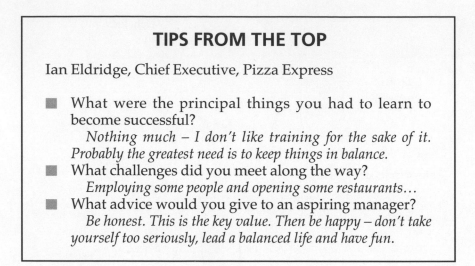

TIPS FROM THE TOP

Ian Eldridge, Chief Executive, Pizza Express

■ What were the principal things you had to learn to become successful?
   Nothing much – I don't like training for the sake of it. Probably the greatest need is to keep things in balance.
■ What challenges did you meet along the way?
   Employing some people and opening some restaurants…
■ What advice would you give to an aspiring manager?
   Be honest. This is the key value. Then be happy – don't take yourself too seriously, lead a balanced life and have fun.

Your stress responses

Consider what happens when you are hit by a stressful event. Complete the exercise in the box.

When it gets too much

Think of a situation in the past or present when you felt everything had got on top of you.
What is/was the situation and its impact on you?
What thoughts did you experience?
What emotions or feelings did you have?
What actual behaviour did you show?
What bodily symptoms or reactions were you aware of?

Many people are unaware that it is a thought or thoughts that trigger a stress response, closely followed by feelings. Identifying these allows us to intervene with more effective coping strategies and earlier in the stress chain. If thoughts and feelings are ignored, behaviour and bodily reactions of the kind noted earlier can provide clues as to our stress levels.

All of us have idiosyncratic responses to stress. Complete Table 8.3 and discover the pattern of your reactions to stress.

Table 8.3 Your stress signature

Do you experience any of the following:

	Often	*Occasionally*	*Never*
Physical Signs Chest pain Diarrhoea Headache Indigestion Sleep problems Palpitations Tiredness Allergies Colds			
Psychological Signs Negative thinking Inability to relax Irritability Poor memory Reduced concentration Intolerance eg of noise Mood swings Sexual problems			
Behavioural signs Awkward positions of body Poor posture Fidgeting Pacing up and down Restless Always rushed Drinking too much Disorganization			

Obviously the more scores you have in the 'often' and 'occasionally' categories, the more you are showing signs of stress. It is also worth looking at the pattern of the scores. Are they all in one section, or spread over two or three? It is important to recognize the pattern of your particular signs and symptoms.

At the same time it is worth being aware of these *ineffective coping strategies* and whether you indulge in any of them:

- increased drinking;
- increased smoking;
- working longer hours;
- skipping lunch;
- withdrawal;
- rushing about;
- sleeping more;
- denying there is a problem.

Some people who become stressed adopt a whole plethora of unhelpful responses. We know we should relax, take exercise, eat vitamin-rich food, but not everyone does it. However, many of our sample of chief executives and directors were very aware of their stress levels, and a large majority did some kind of exercise. Despite being such a hard-working group, they also pursued a variety of hobbies. Making time for other pursuits is not only stimulating, but relaxes as you focus on something completely different.

Many of this sample did not find what they did stressful, despite their long hours. They simply loved work, viewed it as therapeutic or felt, as James Cullen of Bell Atlantic said, 'It is only a game'. Putting work in its place also highlighted home life for this group. Returning to a happy home environment allowed a healthy distancing and objectifying to happen. The ability to form lasting supportive relationships in all areas of life is the subject of the fourth commandment: relate.

One of the first signs of stress is the loss of a sense of humour. Work as fun was a philosophy espoused by almost all this group. So if work is a drag, the chances are you will not be successful, no matter how hard you try. Finding an area of work that is stimulating is of prime importance in achieving a fast track to the top.

Solutions to stress at work

The rest of the chapter will concentrate on simple solutions to stress at work. These are things you can do immediately, which take very little time out of your already stretched schedule.

Relaxation

Figure 8.5 shows three simple relaxation techniques. It takes about three weeks to learn how to relax when you practise every day. The advantages are:

- better concentration and memory;
- increased creativity;
- faster problem solving;
- deeper sleep;
- calm attitude to people issues;
- more effective immune system.

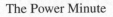

The Power Minute

The 5 Minute Break

The 15 Minute Lunch

Figure 8.5 Simple relaxation techniques

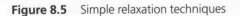

The power minute
We all breathe, yet the majority of us do it badly. The trouble is we don't notice this until a stressful situation occurs. Give yourself the one-minute breathing test: breathe normally for one minute and count the number of breaths you take (in and out counts as one).

Between 10 and 12 is an average number of breaths. More than that, and you are breathing too rapidly and your breaths are too shallow. It is not so much that you are not taking in enough oxygen, but that you are not breathing out sufficient carbon dioxide. Breathing out is the important part of the process as it rids the lungs of stale air, stops us feeling dizzy and makes muscles less cramped and sore.

When we are tense our breathing tends to speed up automatically. By slowing it down you also decrease your heart rate and pulse rate. The more relaxed we are, the more effectively we work. Stress on the other hand makes us worried about ourselves and distracts us from the surrounding environment.

Do the one minute breathing test again, but this time consciously breathe in and out more slowly. This relaxed breathing is the 'power minute' and it will energize you. Even the most stressed of you can make time for it. If you are working late, the power minute will help you identify priorities and increase concentration, so that the time spent at your desk is halved. Sleeping is good relaxation, but on waking it takes about an hour to an hour and a half to become fully alert. With relaxation your alertness is instantly enhanced.

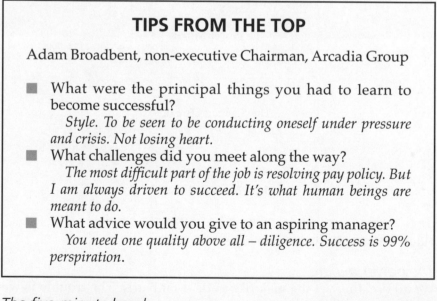

TIPS FROM THE TOP

Adam Broadbent, non-executive Chairman, Arcadia Group

■ What were the principal things you had to learn to become successful?
   Style. To be seen to be conducting oneself under pressure and crisis. Not losing heart.
■ What challenges did you meet along the way?
   The most difficult part of the job is resolving pay policy. But I am always driven to succeed. It's what human beings are meant to do.
■ What advice would you give to an aspiring manager?
   You need one quality above all – diligence. Success is 99% perspiration.

The five-minute break
Unions fought hard to get breaks for employees during the working day, but today a tea or coffee break away from your desk

is frowned upon or seen as career-limiting in some companies. This is foolishness: human beings have an average concentration span of about one and a half to two hours. This can be stretched if there is a crisis or a deadline to be met, but you cannot work continuously in crisis mode. If you do not take a pause your brain takes little 'micro sleeps': you catch yourself looking out of the window then wondering where you were in that document, or even worse when driving, how you got there. Your productivity is reduced if you are in micro-sleep mode. It's much better to take a five-minute break and return to your desk refreshed and focused.

The 15-minute lunch

The 'lunch is for wimps' attitude prevalent in the 1990s did everyone at work a great disservice. Taking a 15-minute lunch is similar in philosophy to the five-minute break. Your lunch does not have to take an hour: life is life and crises do happen, and then an hour is too much to be away. But you still need a break. Getting out for a walk or even just eating your lunch on the other side of your desk will break your concentration and revitalize you.

Sleep

If you are working hard you do not want to be burdened with insomnia, yet that is when it is most likely to happen, as we explained earlier in the chapter. Insomniacs often surround themselves with books, magazines, music, TV and videos, or going to bed too early. Bed must be associated with relaxation, not stimulation, for a sleeping pattern to be established. A major factor in overcoming insomnia is to understand that we need less sleep than we think. What stresses insomniacs is the fear of not functioning the following day.

Here are some guidelines for getting a good night's sleep. Mark any that you think might be useful to you.

- Move your alarm clock so you can't see the time when you're in bed. Thinking 'Oh no, it's 3.00 am, that's only four hours before I get up' is counter-productive to relaxation.
- Limit tea, coffee, chocolate and cola drinks to before 6.00 pm. They act as stimulants and can induce insomnia. Have no more than three or four caffeine-containing drinks during the day.

■ One to two hours before retiring to bed should be winding-down time. Do not imagine you can follow a high rate of activity with immediate sleep.

■ If you are tossing and turning in bed for more than 15–20 minutes, get up. Sit in a chair and read, doze or use a relaxation tape. Bed must be associated with sleep and relaxation, not restlessness.

■ Even if you slept fitfully, do not nap during the day. This will disrupt your sleep pattern.

■ Try to get up at the same time every day regardless of when you went to bed, even at weekends. This allows a good sleep pattern to become established.

■ Use the power minute, a relaxation tape or exercises before sleeping. This will induce not only a greater quantity but also a better quality of sleep.

■ If your mind is active, keep a notepad by your bed to jot ideas down. You will then relax and sleep with a clear mind. There is always something gloriously therapeutic about writing things down: getting it out of your head and down on paper objectifies and clarifies.

Eat well

At times of stress we often want food fast, so fast food is what we eat. This is as often as not devoid of any nutritional value. It is important to acquire the right vitamins and nutrients without becoming quirky in your dietary habits.

Vitamin robbers

■ Stress
■ Smoking
■ Alcohol
■ Dieting
■ Medication

The 'vitamin robbers' list is a reminder of the things that can deplete us of vitamins. They include medications such as analgesics and antibiotics. If your lifestyle includes these, consider taking some vitamin supplements: these are not as good as getting vitamins naturally from food, but in times of stress they can help. It goes without saying that you should cut out smoking and cut down on drinking.

Figure 8.6 provides a reminder of the foods you should eat daily.

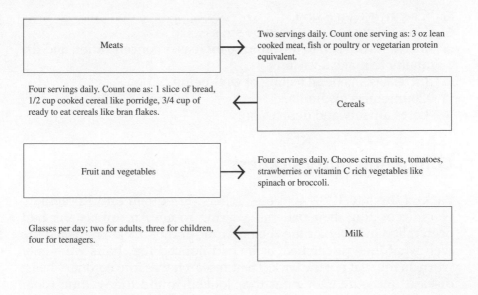

Figure 8.6 A daily food guide

Exercise

We all know we should do it, and regularly, but at times of stress we do not always manage to find the time. If that describes you, make sure you find someone to go to the gym or pool with you: it can act as an incentive and also turns exercise into a pleasurable social event.

Some advantages of regular exercise are:

Physiological:

- Increases muscle girth and a reduced proportion of fatty tissue. Better shape and increased agility.
- More efficient lungs and less laboured breathing.
- A lowered pulse rate. The heart can do its job with less effort.
- Reduced blood pressure.
- Suppression of appetite – useful for losing weight.
- Increases the metabolic rate.

Psychological:

- Channels aggression.
- Uses up energy produced by stress.
- Increases oxygen to the brain so increases concentration and the ability to make decisions.
- Increases a general feeling of well-being.
- Counteracts insomnia.
- Eases anxiety and depression.

Combating hurry sickness

Back in the late 1970s two researchers, Friedman and Rosenman, were decorating their patients' waiting room. An upholsterer had been called in to repair the chairs. At the end of the job he asked the men what they researched, as he had noticed the chairs were only worn on the seat not the back. Their research was into coronary heart disease, and sure enough as they looked round the waiting room next day, all their patients were sitting on the edges of their seats.

That upholsterer changed the direction of their research. They had been concentrating on diet and a sedentary lifestyle, but now they realized they had to look at the stress factors that might correlate with coronary heart disease. They found a cluster of characteristics

Figure 8.7 Hurry sickness

which they named Type A and Type B. You can benchmark yourself using the stress-prone scale in Table 8.4.

Table 8.4   The stress-prone scale

	Yes	No
1. I feel there are not enough hours in the day to do all the things I must do	☐	☐
2. I always move, walk, talk and eat rapidly	☐	☐
3. I frequently feel impatient with the rate at which events take place	☐	☐
4. I unconsciously urge other people to 'get on with it'	☐	☐
5. I have a tendency to finish sentences for other people	☐	☐
6. I become unnecessarily irritated when the car in front of me goes at a pace which I consider too slow	☐	☐
7. I find it frustrating to wait in a queue, for example at a filling station or restaurant	☐	☐
8. I can't tolerate watching others perform tasks I know I can do faster	☐	☐
9. I think about and often do more than one task at the same time (for example, listen to colleagues while phoning or writing notes)	☐	☐
10. I still think about business/professional problems when I am engaged in recreation	☐	☐
11. I become impatient when I have to do repetitive tasks (such as writing cheques, washing dishes, writing bank deposit slips)	☐	☐
12. I often rush through reading anything. If possible I obtain condensed summaries	☐	☐
13. I have a tendency to emphasize key words vigorously in ordinary speech when there is no real need	☐	☐
14. I have a habit of expressing the last few words of my sentences more rapidly than those at the beginning	☐	☐
15. I find it difficult not to bring the conversation round to my work and interests	☐	☐
16. I pretend to listen to other people and their views. (I am really preoccupied with my own thoughts.)	☐	☐
17. I frequently feel vaguely guilty when I relax and do nothing for a few hours or days	☐	☐
18. I attempt to fit in more and more in less and less time and as a result make few allowances for unforeseen circumstances	☐	☐
19. I frequently clench my fist or bang on the table or pound one fist into the palm of my hand when I am making a conversational point	☐	☐
20. I find there are many deadlines in my job that are difficult to meet	☐	☐
21. I frequently clench my jaw	☐	☐
22. I find there are times when I grind my teeth	☐	☐
23. I frequently bring work home with me	☐	☐
24. I find I evaluate myself, other people and their activities more by numbers than before	☐	☐
25. I am not satisfied with my present job	☐	☐
Total scores	☐	☐

Add all your 'yes' scores. Use these categories to place your total:

Category 1   3 points or less
Category 2   4–8 points
Category 3   9–13 points
Category 4   14 points or more

A person in category 4 is most stress-prone, showing Type A behaviour, and is significantly more at risk of heart disease, requiring stress management and counselling. People in category 3, although less likely to have heart disease than category 4, are still stress-prone and would benefit from stress management training. Category 2 people are more relaxed but should be aware of the risk of creeping towards category 3. A category 1 person, described also as Type B, is least likely of all to have a heart attack and need not worry about being stress-prone.

Much research has been carried out into Type A and the key component to emerge is the tendency of As to hostility. A predisposition to tension and rushing about contribute to a short fuse.

Figure 8.8   Type A behaviour

To beat hurry sickness:

At work

- Stop trying to think of, or do, more than one thing at a time.
- If you see someone doing a job more slowly than you would, do not interfere.

Figure 8.9   Type B behaviour

- Before you tackle a task ask yourself:
  - will it matter five years from now?
  - must it be done right away?
  - can it be delegated to someone else?
- Interrupt long sessions of work with relaxation.
- Try to hear out people without interrupting.

Socially

- Before you speak ask yourself:
  - do I really have anything to say?
  - does anyone want to hear it?
  - is this the right time to say it?
- Go without a watch.
- Walk, talk and eat more slowly.
- Visit an art gallery, museum, park or zoo.
- Refrain from projecting your own sense of time urgency on others.
- Listen to people rather than planning what you are going to say next.

On your own

- Start reading books that have nothing to do with your job.
- Start driving in the slow lane – don't overtake for at least 10 minutes per 30 minutes of travel.

- Choose the longest queue at a bank or supermarket.
- Do absolutely nothing but listen to music for 15 minutes.
- Contact or write to an old friend who has a different job from you.
- Don't cut things fine: give yourself an extra five minutes to get from A to B.

Men especially seem to find it difficult to cope with driving in the slow lane or choosing the longest queue. They often feel these are extreme measures. However, is it essential to be the fastest thing on two wheels or legs? Competitiveness can be destructive, and if every aspect of a life involves competition, this constant striving can lead to health problems – and a boring person.

Paul Martin in *The Sickening Mind* cites the compelling results from a coronary prevention project in America which carried out a long-term survey on over 1,000 men who had already suffered a heart attack. A random group received counselling to reduce all aspects of Type A behaviour. It was successful especially in curbing their hostility and sense of urgency, and it also halved their risk of suffering another heart attack.

Tackle time wasters

Instead of dealing with time wasters we often try to avoid them or keep working when they speak to us. Review the examples of common time wasters in Table 8.5, and note which occur in your working life.

Table 8.5 Examples of common time wasters

Self-generated	*Environmental*
Disorganization	Visitors
Procrastination	Telephone calls
Inability to say no	Junk mail
Lack of interest (attitude)	Waiting for someone
Burnout	Unproductive meetings
Gossip	Crises
Unnecessary perfectionism	Coffee time conversations
	Unused reports

How to control interruptions

These interventions are useful ways to educate interrupters about their behaviour, control your time and help you give single-minded attention when necessary. Planning, diarizing and controlling time all help to alleviate hurry sickness.

- Set a time and stick to it.
- Set the stage in advance. Tell the other person how much time is available.
- With casual droppers in, remain standing.
- Meet in the other person's office.
- Avoid small talk when you are busy.
- Get them to the point by always focusing on the priorities.
- Have a clock available for both parties to see.
- Use a call back system.
- Be ruthless with time but gracious with people.

Recognizing stress in others

Once you have tackled your own stress, as a good manager and aspiring director you must be aware of other peoples' stress. Using the recognition exercise below, focus on one team member. This exercise reveals how analytical you need to be to ascertain another's stress levels. You then must think about how you want to intervene.

Stress recognition exercise

- Who is most likely to suffer from stress in your team?
- Choose one person at random for this exercise.
- Review at the stress value of life changes list and estimate your chosen person's score.
- Review the stress signature exercise and identify any signs and symptoms they show.

Now consider the following:

- Are they Type A or B? Look at the stress-prone scale.
- Did they meet all their objectives in their last appraisal?
- Do they use ineffective coping strategies?
- Do they have an understanding of stress management techniques?
- Are they on the list of people vulnerable to stress?

Ten categories of people vulnerable to stress

- Negative thinkers and worriers
- People with low self-esteem and self-worth
- Lots of change going on in their lives
- People who live alone
- One of 'those' birthdays coming up
- Anyone over 40 in an organization which is downsizing
- Competitive and aggressive
- Not trained for the job
- Middle management
- The right-brained person in a left-brained environment and vice versa (someone who is creative or artistic in a very routine environment, or a logical person in an artistic setting)

If you decide this person is suffering from stress, you could take any of these actions to help reduce it:

- Mention that you have noticed a change in their behaviour. Ask why.
- Suggest they speak to a business counsellor who you know is good.
- Offer stress management training.
- Suggest a course of relaxation.
- Act directly as an arbiter in any dispute.
- Check if stress is being caused by something or someone in their department.

Pressure is dynamic and self-developing, whereas stress is destructive. Somehow, what we must do is keep the pressure going, but acquire the skills to be stress free.

Keys

- Be aware of all the potential stresses in your life, at work and at home.
- If going through a time of change involving many life events, make sure you take time out to relax.
- Monitor any pressure build-up at work and know your own stress signature.
- Reduce ineffective coping strategies and replace them with relaxation, eating well, exercising, combating hurry sickness and tackling time wasters.
- Recognize the signs of stress in others, intervene and offer to help.

nine

The **seventh commandment: love change**

When we asked our sample of leaders whether they liked change – most people don't – they told us they not only loved change, but saw their ability to initiate change as crucial to their success. Embracing change, and recognizing that it is now a necessary part of business life, is an essential.

The seventh most highly rated characteristic of success was 'skill at initiating change'. This was more highly rated by women than men, with women placing it on average in fourth place. Enthusiasm for change permeated the thinking of our subjects. It seems that the drive and urgency that successful people bring to their businesses is essentially based on a need always to be changing the way things are.

When asked directly about change, our group almost unanimously said that they were not only comfortable with change, but actively expected and encouraged it. Some coupled this enthusiasm with a warning note. Clive Thompson stressed that the 'CEO doesn't have to change things, but can progress through evolution not revolution'. But most swept aside even these cautions and admitted that change was the fuel that kept them going. Many acknowledged that they suffered from a low boredom threshold and that change kept things interesting.

In reality, most of us are obliged to live with change in business. We may look back on the old days when things seemed to be settled and constant with nostalgia, but now we either have to embrace and lead change, or have change thrust upon us. A survey by

Bulletpoint Communications showed that 62 per cent of all UK managers were affected by organizational change in any year. In manufacturing and financial services the rate of change was 75 per cent per year, and in utilities it was 90 per cent.

Change comes from all directions. These are common triggers:

■ the need to respond to the Internet and e-commerce;
■ introduction of new technology;
■ changes of business ownership and structure through mergers and acquisitions;
■ implementation of business re-engineering programmes;
■ major quality initiatives;
■ downsizing the workforce;
■ new management deciding to do it their way;
■ pressure from competition;
■ patent protection running out;
■ legal or professional changes demanding a response;
■ new demands from customers.

Issues like these mean there is no longer any breathing space. According to Wayne Calloway, 'The worst rule of management is "if it ain't broke, don't fix it". In today's economy, if it ain't broke, you might as well break it yourself, because it soon will be.'

We start with a look at some of the reasons why change efforts can fail, then build a plan to ensure that change programmes have the best possible chance of success. Finally, some exercises highlight particular needs and develop key skills.

Things that can go wrong with change initiatives

Misunderstanding the nature of change

To succeed, change needs to be embraced as a way of life. This section is about making real, fundamental and permanent alterations to the way things are done. It is not about one-off initiatives like poster campaigns, training courses or new advertising slogans. Change is a journey rather than a destination. Planning for change is not the same as planning for an event. It is about altering perceptions, creating new visions, and carrying the hearts and minds of others with you.

Changing for the sake of it

In the first century AD, the Roman writer Titus Petronius recorded the problems with making changes just for the sake of it. 'We trained hard; but it seems that every time we were beginning to form into a team we would be reorganized. I was to learn later in life that we tend to meet any new situation by reorganizing, and a wonderful method it can be for creating the illusion of progress while producing confusion, inefficiency and demoralization.' The danger revealed by Petronius is that we perceive the need for change but press on without the groundwork of establishing the purpose, setting the goals and persuading and motivating others.

Lack of planning

The transformation of a business takes time, and risks losing momentum if there is a lack of planning of the process and a failure to identify the markers by which success will be judged. This chapter aims to identify the elements of a change programme so that the plan can be thought through in advance. It is particularly important to spot any likely obstacles along the road that would derail the programme if not fully anticipated.

Failure to achieve a sense of urgency

As we discussed in the second commandment, there is an important distinction between things that are important and things that are, or seem to be, urgent. The important things are those that really must be done for the survival of the business, but the urgent things are those that tend actually to get done, whether they are important or not. The leader's challenge is to create a sense of urgency around the important things. This requires unflagging energy and a sustained commitment to the process, in ways which everyone understands and shares.

Absence of vision

Vision is a much-used word in management texts these days, but for good reason. To avoid purposeless change for the sake of change, and to ensure that everyone is driving in the same direction, a clearly articulated vision is a must. The requirements of the vision are that it should be explainable in few sentences, that it clearly demonstrates the direction in which the business should be going, and that it is supported by most of the people involved. If the future of the business is buried away in procedure manuals, or depends on 'things turning up', lack of vision could be the problem.

Unrealistic goals

A common management assertion used to be that goals, whether personal or corporate, should be 'challenging but attainable'. Nowadays that aim seems somewhat feeble, but it does make a point: visions and the goals do need to be reality tested. It is no good just plucking a splendid aim out of the air, like 'to be the biggest company in the world', if it fails to understand the real capabilities and opportunities of the business. A similar problem is setting goals too far in the future. A 30-year vision is fine, but there have to be some tangible landmarks which everyone can support – and celebrate when they are reached.

A desire to cling to the past

People resist change because they fear the unknown and become anxious about departing from their area of comfort. The science writer Kathryn Brown, in reviewing psychological studies of this phenomenon, suggested that resistance to change is programmed into the brain as an aid to survival. The mind exaggerates the pain of possible future events to ensure that we proceed with caution. The job of the leader is therefore to guide the fainthearted, to ensure that the positive advantages of change are understood, and to demonstrate that the changes are practical and within the capabilities of the people involved.

Lack of organizational support

Like people, organizations tend to resist change. The larger the organization, the more it is likely to have bureaucracies that will mobilize to stifle change. The structure of a business, with its HR departments, legal advisers, quality controllers and all, has developed around the way things used to be, not necessarily the way things ought to be. This powerful infrastructure will see change as an alien invader threatening comfortable lifestyles, and can make life very difficult for the entrepreneur with vision. This is a real test of leadership, and of the ability to persuade those with influence that change is really in the interests of everyone.

A risk-averse culture

Businesses differ in their risk aversion but most, quite properly, will not be willing to gamble recklessly their stakeholders' investments. The downside of risk aversion is the fear of failure that leads to a sceptical questioning of every new initiative. Will the share price fall? Will employees support us? Will we get the blame if it goes wrong? The solution is enough careful thought and research to ensure the maximum chance of success and, if necessary, proper protection in the event of failure.

Failure to communicate

Perhaps the most common reason for the failure of change initiatives is inadequate communication. The challenge is that, like the change process itself, communication has to be part of the new way of life, not a one-off event. Communication is not 'done' once the staff briefing is issued or the article written for the company magazine. It is a never-ending requirement, it has to be interesting, and it has to use all available media. Needless to say, the content of the communication has to be consistent with the behaviour of the leaders of the business.

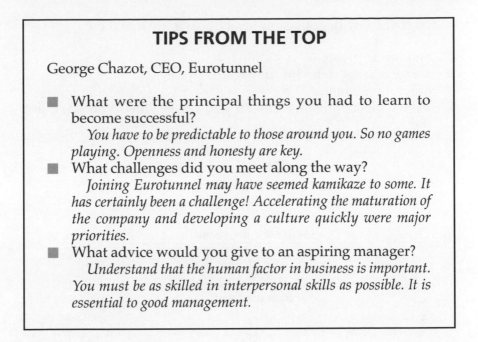

TIPS FROM THE TOP

George Chazot, CEO, Eurotunnel

■ What were the principal things you had to learn to become successful?

You have to be predictable to those around you. So no games playing. Openness and honesty are key.

■ What challenges did you meet along the way?

Joining Eurotunnel may have seemed kamikaze to some. It has certainly been a challenge! Accelerating the maturation of the company and developing a culture quickly were major priorities.

■ What advice would you give to an aspiring manager?

Understand that the human factor in business is important. You must be as skilled in interpersonal skills as possible. It is essential to good management.

A plan for change

This review of the pitfalls now enables us to build a positive plan for change, designed to give the best possible chance of success with the least pain along the way. The successful change process is summarized in Figure 9.1.

Articulate the vision

This, the start of the process, is the fundamental questioning time: the time to avoid change for the sake of it, balance ambition against realism, and find the message which will rally the troops. Management researchers James Collins and Jerry Porras coined the acronym BHAG (big hairy audacious goal) to describe the vitality of a vision that excites and energizes successful companies.

The characteristics of vision-level BHAGs are that they:

- are easy to grasp;
- are seen to be 'right' for the organization;
- are truly exciting;
- have a clear finishing line so you know when you have got there.

Articulate the vision

⇓

Pick the team

⇓

Develop the programme

⇓

Lobby the doubters

⇓

Communicate with enthusiasm

⇓

Monitor progress

⇓

Tackle the culture

Figure 9.1   The successful change process

Sometimes the vision that meets those requirements comes easily. NASA's vision in the 1960s was to put a man on the moon, indisputably meeting the above tests. But for modern, complex businesses, the reality is that developing the vision will take months of debate and refinement before the statement emerges in a form that everyone knows is right.

Collins and Porras give examples of successful vision statements in a number of different categories.

Category one is the 'target' which can be quantitative:

Become a $125 billion company by the year 2000. (Walmart, 1990)

or qualitative:

Become the dominant player in commercial aircraft and bring the world into the jet age. (Boeing, 1950)

Category two is the 'common enemy':

Crush Adidas. (Nike, 1960s)

Category three is the 'role model':

Become the Harvard of the West (Stanford University, 1940s).

Category four is the 'internal transformation':

Transform this company from a defence contractor into the best diversified high-technology company in the world. (Rockwell, 1995)

These categories are not exclusive and are given to spark the process rather than limit the options. The challenge is to avoid a boring mish-mash of uninspiring words and to find the key to unlocking the real potential of the business in a way that will gain enthusiastic acceptance throughout the organization.

Pick the team

The fifth commandment dealt with the process of assembling a team with the necessary blend of skills to see a task through to completion. The change process requires the right team, and the individual roles described by Meredith Belbin, and set out in Chapter 7 will help in establishing the right mix. The Professor of Leadership at Harvard Business School, John Kotter, has suggested four particular characteristics of a team that can direct a change effort:

■ *Position power*: are enough key players on board, especially the main line managers, so that those left out cannot easily block progress?
■ *Expertise*: are the various points of view – in terms of discipline, work experience, nationality and so on – relevant to the task at hand adequately represented so that informed, intelligent decisions will be made?
■ *Credibility*: does the group have enough people with good reputations in the firm so that its pronouncements will be taken seriously by other employees?
■ *Leadership*: does the group include enough proven leaders to be able to drive the change process?

John Kotter also suggests that two sorts of individual should be avoided at all costs when putting together the team to guide change. The first is the type with enough ego to fill a room, leaving no space for anyone else: in other words, a non-team player whose selfishness excludes others from participating in the process. The second is described by Kotter as the 'snake'. Snakes are disruptive individuals who spread mistrust. They undermine individuals and their relationships by spreading doubt about people and unsettling the harmony and trust which is essential for a team to function happily and effectively.

This may be a good time to consider organized approaches to team building. Team building used to be an essentially social process: drinks after work, golf days and Christmas parties. Nowadays much more demanding options are available. These are often structured events in which a group of people set off for several days with the objective of climbing a mountain, walking over hot coals or whatever. The team faces the challenge together, plans the approach, gives moral support to the waverers and celebrates ultimate success. The outcome is an increased level of trust and intimacy within the group, an understanding of each other's strengths and weaknesses, and the knowledge that together they can face a difficult challenge and succeed.

Develop the programme

The declaration by NASA that they would reach the moon was not enough to get there. The devil has always been in the detail, and the programme that has to deliver the vision is the hard part.

The detailed implementation programme is the subject of the feasibility studies, market research, marketing plans, financial plans, business plans, project specifications and product designs which now have to emerge as the business moves forward. However, assuming that the leadership team has the right mix of skills, the detailed planning is essentially a matter of professionals plying their trades.

This stage can easily meet some of the pitfalls described earlier, in particular the risk of losing support because everything is delivered too far in the future. Most new businesses fail because they anticipate results too soon. Natural enthusiasm, the need to impress the investors, and a failure to spot the complication of some steps, result in a business plan that is simply too optimistic. The managers lose heart, the investors lose confidence and the whole enterprise folds. This is tragic, since success may have been just round the corner, and the up-front money is lost.

The solution is to ensure that at least something is delivered within suitably short timescales. The 'something' will depend on the business and the objectives of the change exercise. It might be a customer satisfaction survey showing significant improvements, a new product that excites the bosses, or a sharp reduction in costs. Whatever, it should be designed to keep the project moving, maintain momentum and demonstrate that the effort is achieving something.

John Kotter describes this requirement as the achievement of 'short-term wins', and suggests six reasons for their importance:

- *Provide evidence that sacrifices are worth it*: wins greatly help justify the short-term costs involved.
- *Reward change agents with a pat on the back*: after a lot of hard work, positive feedback builds morale and motivation.
- *Help fine-tune vision and strategies*: short-term wins give the guiding coalition concrete data on the viability of their ideas.
- *Undermine cynics and self-serving resisters*: clear improvements in performance make it difficult for people to block needed change.

- *Keep bosses on board*: provides those higher in the hierarchy with evidence that the transformation is on track.
- *Build momentum*: turn neutrals into supporters, reluctant supporters into active helpers.

It is important to plan for these interim achievements, not just hope they will happen. The change team needs to review areas in which gains can quickly be made, set up the monitoring and measurement necessary to identify them, and be ready to publicize the achievements so they deliver maximum mileage.

Lobby the doubters

Doubters are a problem in all organizations, but to some extent they are valuable. Their challenges, provided they are intelligent, reveal missed detail and areas where further work is needed. This sort of input helps ensure the robustness of a project, and eliminates any danger that an opportunity might be viewed too optimistically.

TIPS FROM THE TOP

Brian Davis, CEO, Nationwide Building Society

- What were the principal things you had to learn to become successful?
  I had to develop helicopter vision to propel the society forward into the future. I also came to realize I have my best ideas in the bath!
- What challenges did you meet along the way?
  I have a low threshold for boredom and so the challenge for me is coping with the tedium of regular meetings. I like work to be fun.
- What advice would you give to an aspiring manager?
  You must demonstrate your capabilities so that you are noticed by someone like me. Get yourself a supportive boss and then acquire a broad range of experience.

On the downside, doubters can spread anxiety when you need confidence and commitment, and undermine team spirit. Doubters don't require a democratic vote to gain representation. One active doubter can easily persuade ten others, so their influence needs to be addressed carefully. Let's consider the problems with change that the doubters might be having:

■ The changes might not be compatible with their own personal objectives.
■ They might feel unable to deliver their part of the change programme.
■ They might have genuine disagreement with all or part of the planned changes.
■ They might be pathological pessimists who always disagree with everything.

Influential or active doubters need to be picked off one by one, but the approach should depend on which type of doubter they are. It will also depend on your relationship with them. Do you know them personally, and where are your relative positions in the pecking order?

Type one is George, a bright young graduate who early on in his job was given the task of putting the organization's policy manuals into computer-based training (CBT) format, CBT is high-tech and exciting, and George's early efforts have been widely praised for their competence and innovation. George has gone to great lengths to train up in CBT and is beginning to feel that, with or without the company, that is where his future will probably lie. However, the change programme involves a new client-focused service area for which CBT is not an appropriate tool. George is muttering that the investment in CBT will be wasted, and suggesting that the new approach is too risky.

George needs to be treated with sensitivity and creativity: a heart to heart is called for, and the outcome must be a mutual commitment to the way ahead. There are three possible options: for him to drop CBT and join the new project wholeheartedly, to incorporate CBT into the new initiative, or for him to leave the company so he can pursue CBT elsewhere. Any of these would be acceptable, but nothing else would. If CBT is to be dropped, George needs to be persuaded that the alternative offers just as much status, interest and opportunity. It might be worth finding out George's team type (the fifth commandment) and ensuring that the new role plays to his strengths.

Sylvia is type number two, outwardly confident because for many years she has maintained records of engineers' work for clients with great competence. This gives her status and importance, since the client records are the cornerstone of the billing system. However, the intended changes involve engineers inputting their client details directly into a computer. Sylvia's new job will be to analyse the information using spreadsheets and databases, and produce a profitability analysis of each month's performance.

Sylvia is too proud to admit it, but she is scared. She has never really felt comfortable with computers, and doubts whether she can learn the new skills. At 55, she was hoping she could get away with the old systems until her retirement. She is complaining loudly about the proposed changes to anyone who will listen. She has developed a range of themes: lack of consultation, clients won't like it, engineers won't like it, results will be meaningless. But in reality, she just doesn't think she can do it.

Another earnest meeting is called for. This time the challenge is to demonstrate to Sylvia that not only can she do it, but she will enjoy it. She needs time and training. Above all, she needs the motivation that comes from sharing the vision and understanding that she will still be important.

Marcia, the number three type, presents a serious challenge. She is the finance director, and doesn't believe the cash flow projections for the change programme. She is in danger of creating anxiety at the highest level. Indeed, without her support, the programme is unlikely to proceed.

Marcia must be converted. There are no real alternatives here, but it is extraordinary how powerful a simple personal approach can be. In recently reviewing a real-life Marcia, we found that all her objections had been indirect: a refusal to sign off authorizations and so on. Almost as a last resort, we arranged a meeting and carefully planned the points to be made. We found Marcia was easily persuaded that the new direction was right for the business, but had a real problem with the way we were proposing to invoice. She had a good point, we agreed the necessary changes, and the programme went ahead with her full support.

The final problem is with Derek who opposes for the sake of it. He sees the downside in everything and enjoys complaining loudly. Derek is a destructive force, acting as the nucleus for all other doubters to combine together to inhibit progress.

Tactic number one for Derek is to give him responsibility, and specifically charge him with a part of the change programme. Derek is often a useful committee member. He is unlikely to have the courage to oppose the programme in a committee full of enthusiasts, and will have no option but to buy in and do his bit. If he won't go for the responsibility, he must be moved out of the way. Doubting Derek and the change programme are simply not compatible.

Communicate with enthusiasm

'Communication' is the word you can guarantee to find in the index of any management textbook. It is axiomatic that, for any business initiative to succeed, it must be properly communicated. Yet communication is not the natural skill of all business leaders, and it is often the weak link in implementing a programme for change. As noted earlier, effective communication has to be a way of working, not a one-off exercise. Here is a five stage checklist to test the communication of change:

1. Keep it simple.
2. Use all available media.
3. Walk the talk.
4. Have a campaigning approach.
5. Keep going.

Einstein said 'everything should be made as simple as possible, but not simpler'. The balance is to make sure that the language of communication is straightforward and accessible, but the messages remain intact. This takes work, as Pascal noted when he apologized for writing a long letter, saying he 'had not had time to make it shorter'.

Here is Neil Kinnock announcing a change programme for European Commission reforms:

The Reform Strategy proposals identify the ways to efficiently integrate assessment of resources with decisions on positive and crucially negative priorities. A system of Activity Based Management will be introduced, facilitated by Strategic Planning and Programming arrangements under the authority of the President, and by the use of targeting, evaluation and accountability operations overseen by the Budget.

Does this pass any real test of effective communication? Is it clear what is going to happen? Is it exciting and motivating? This initiative falls the simplicity test, and even creates a suspicion that the reforms have no real content, but just consist of some politically constructed words.

The second item in the checklist is to use all available media. The practice of NLP (neuro-linguistic programming) teaches that individuals differ in the ways they receive information. Some people are primarily auditory, others visual and others rely on feeling. A communication directed at a group will need to use all the styles, or the message will penetrate only to a minority. The problem is that we tend to assume other people receive information the same way that we do, and so construct communications that would be right for us but go over the heads of the majority.

For these reasons, the communication programme needs to be devised by a mixed team. They will assess all the options available which could include videos, staff magazines, notice boards, computer-based intranet sites, and staff meetings, and marshal them to present a consistent, motivating message with which everyone can feel involved.

Action point three, 'walk the talk', is to lead by example. The leader of a campaign to reduce car usage is hardly going to carry the day if he or she drives everywhere. According to John Kotter, 'Nothing undermines the communication of a change vision more than behaviour on the part of key players that seems inconsistent with the vision.' We saw a very powerful example of this when a client's chairman insisted everyone answer telephone calls courteously and within three rings. When he was walking around the building, which was often, he would personally run over to a persistently ringing telephone and answer. He would then politely take a message, which was always delivered. Telephone answering quickly became a serious business, and the whole organization became sharper and more customer focused.

The fourth point, to take a campaigning approach, addresses the need for enthusiasm and commitment. Some years ago, research was undertaken into the effectiveness of posters to improve workplace safety. They typically displayed messages to encourage people to wear their protective clothing, report accidents and near-misses and so on. In most cases they had no effect on safety whatsoever. However, there was an exception when the posters were used as part of a sustained campaign. For a workplace communication to succeed, the battle plan should be drawn up so there is no escaping the message.

Finally, keep going. Communication, like training, never ends.

This is not only a matter of keeping up the major initiatives like presentations and publications, it is also about introducing the message into everyday behaviour. In our interviews, Tom Hamilton, told us he could make any issue he chose the company priority just by referring to it at every opportunity. If the issue is sufficiently important, then keep at it, and the message will become rooted in the psyche of the organization.

Monitor progress

In looking at the development of the programme, we considered the importance of having interim stages that acted as 'landings' to demonstrate progress and create opportunities for celebration. In any significant change exercise, these landing stages are key moments for assessment and should be anticipated and planned for.

To monitor progress there needs to be clarity about what the incremental steps are and how they are to be measured. It may be that the incremental steps are obvious. If the change is designed to drive sales, the achievement of sales targets will be the monitoring mechanism. This, after all, is the purpose of the budget and business plan. However, a major re-engineering exercise could take some time to drive bottom-line results, and it may be necessary to construct some other progress indicators.

Try asking, 'Where would we like to have got to in six months, and how will we know we are there?' The answer might be something like, 'We will have rewritten the software, recruited and trained the additional sales team and commenced the press publicity programme.' These answers are fine, but are rather soft in their measurability. So the next question has to be, 'What were these stages supposed to accomplish?' If the press publicity was designed to achieve coverage in national newspapers, what would be a measure of this? Five references in the major broadsheets? Eventually some testable yardsticks will emerge, and you will have the means to monitor the programme.

Project management is a complex skill, often requiring the toughest, cleverest managers in the business. Many projects will need planning techniques and specialist software, with endless references to Gantt charts and progress graphs. However, the essence is to anchor the project in steps that can be unambiguously measured or tested, and then to not tolerate vagueness or slippage from the schedule.

Tackle the culture

The culture of an organization is sometimes described as 'the way we do things around here'. It describes the values employees share and the behaviours they have in common. When new employees arrive, they are very likely to adopt the same values and behaviours so as to fit in. Indeed they were probably recruited, at least in part, because they felt like a comfortable cultural fit. The culture of an organization, like the culture of a region or a religion, is not dependent on any individual member and is very slow to change.

Cultural characteristics take many forms. There may be a macho culture, or a 'doing it by the book' culture, or a safety-first culture. There are organizations where the culture is to start as early and finish as late as possible, as well as organizations where working beyond 5 pm is regarded as eccentric. Cultures might accept, even encourage, drinking alcohol at lunchtime, or view it as a disciplinary offence. Cultures may regard pinstriped suits as the working uniform, or think of jeans and a sweater as smart dress. Cultures can be cautious and slow to embrace change, or fall upon the latest fad with passion and enthusiasm.

The problem with culture in a fast-moving business environment is that the cultural norms may be resistant to the new requirements: sometimes with good reason, since the changes will effectively destroy the old culture. This happened to large sections of the print industry when the established 'hot metal' processes were swept away by computer typesetting. You are probably not planning anything quite so dramatic or confrontational, but you still need to ensure that the culture shifts in an accommodating way.

A starting point might be to take stock of the current organizational culture. This is difficult to spot from the inside, but specialist consultants can undertake a culture audit and give an objective analysis. This will reveal the extent to which you have a reward culture, a blame culture, a change culture or whatever. It may well reveal the particular challenges you will face in introducing change.

The cultural changes then need to be addressed bit by bit. The keys are to tackle the organization's processes by which behaviour is rewarded or sanctioned. These are likely to include:

■ promotion guidelines;
■ bonus and salary arrangements;
■ appraisal assessments;
■ disciplinary procedures.

Adjustments to these processes, as well as addressing recruitment criteria and, as always, setting the example, can slowly but surely change an organization's culture. It won't be easy. Implementing culture change is one of the most difficult challenges facing any manager. It is the ultimate test of leadership.

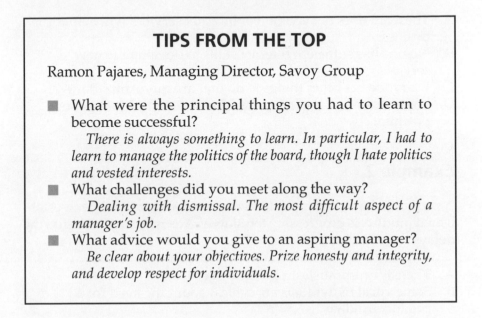

TIPS FROM THE TOP

Ramon Pajares, Managing Director, Savoy Group

- What were the principal things you had to learn to become successful?

  There is always something to learn. In particular, I had to learn to manage the politics of the board, though I hate politics and vested interests.
- What challenges did you meet along the way?

  Dealing with dismissal. The most difficult aspect of a manager's job.
- What advice would you give to an aspiring manager?

  Be clear about your objectives. Prize honesty and integrity, and develop respect for individuals.

Exercise: rate your change skills

This exercise is designed to home in on your strengths and weaknesses as a manager of change. It should help identify those elements of the change process where you might have difficulties. Read each business example and then choose the response that is closest to your particular situation. Choose more than one response if appropriate, and do not choose any if none apply.

Example 1

You have realized your competitors are introducing Internet-based services, and call a team together to develop electronic products for your own business. The meeting does not go well because:

A. The team does not accept that Internet services will help the business
B. No-one has sufficient Internet skills to develop the new services
C. Everyone has other things to do that are more important
D. Wasting time on the Internet will reduce individuals' bonus potential

Example 2

A project to launch an updated version of a successful, well-established product is progressing too slowly. At a meeting to discuss the delays the main feedback is:

A. There is no enthusiasm for the project
B. Some vocal individuals are cynical about the need for a product up-date
C. People are uncertain about what exactly they are supposed to be doing
D. Company procedures are unsuited to product development projects

Example 3

You appointed an external research company to assess your clients' perceptions of your business. They report that you are seen to be lacking in innovation. Management reactions to the report are:

A. The research team is incompetent and has got it wrong
B. The company simply doesn't have the ability to be innovative
C. If only the products on the drawing board could be actually produced, all would be well
D. They are doing what they have been told to do, so it must be someone else's problem

Example 4

Business has suddenly slumped as a result of fierce competition. You ask your team for ideas to turn the business around. Responses are:

A. Scattered, unrealistic and inconsistent
B. Critical and unhelpful, blaming others for the problems
C. Concerned, but people simply don't know what they are supposed to do
D. Insistence that the company should simply continue as it has always done

Example 5

You believe there may be opportunity for developing your products for overseas markets. Your colleagues' reactions are:

A. The staff wouldn't support such developments
B. The company does not have the expertise for overseas trading
C. There is no spare resource to start developing an overseas market
D. We don't understand the overseas requirements and should stick with what we know

Example 6

Your company has merged with a similar business and staff are anxious about the changes this will bring. You arrange a meeting to review their concerns. The main feedback is:

A. The other company is much clearer about where it is going, and there won't be a place for us in the new organization
B. Our skills will not be required, considering all the new whiz-kids who will be coming
C. We do not have the flexibility to integrate with a new team
D. Our people will be dominated by the management style and clear procedures of the new business

Example 7

You have employees who are suffering from extreme stress. You meet with them to try to understand their problems. The finding is:

A. They do not really see where they or the company is going and can't find the motivation to keep working
B. Their colleagues are not supportive and often undermine new initiatives
C. There never seems to be any achievement to celebrate or enthuse about
D. It is never quite clear exactly what they are supposed to do on any particular day

Example 8

A new quality programme has identified the need to respect the 'internal customer' and to encourage more collaboration and support amongst staff. At a meeting to progress this, the feedback you receive is:

A. Different staff have different jobs to do so there is no need to increase internal co-ordination
B. There is suspicion and rivalry amongst staff and no enthusiasm for closer co-operation
C. People are unsure about their own roles, so it will not help to seek the support of others
D. Collaboration is alien to the way the organization operates. Individuals are judged only on their own performance and won't help others

Example 9

A new chairman decrees that business teams will be restructured around client sectors, rather than the old geographic network. The main reaction is:

A. Grudging resistance, with people asking what the point is
B. This is like moving deckchairs on the Titanic and will not address fundamental skill weaknesses

C. Weary resignation, and a failure to understand what will be accomplished
D. A discomfort with the change process and unease about the need to work with new colleagues

Example 10

Two of your best managers have resigned in the same week. You meet with them informally to try to understand why they are leaving. The messages are:

A. The company is not inspirational and visionary, and there is no excitement in thinking about a long-term future with the business
B. They just cannot get along with others in the business who seem negative, cynical and out of place
C. There is no sense of achievement or celebration and business progress seems slow
D. The business is no fun and the personal development and appraisal processes fail to generate enthusiasm or commitment

Scoring

This exercise is designed to highlight the sort of issues that might be limiting the effectiveness of a change programme. Count up your A, B, C and D scores and review them against the following guidelines:

Mostly As
This suggests a lack of understanding of a vision in the business. This may result from the absence of a vision in the first place, or from the existence of a vision that is not being communicated. As a result, staff are not buying in to the direction of the company and do not see a long-term future for themselves.

Mostly Bs
This indicates some fundamental team weaknesses. The team has the wrong mix of skills, or includes individuals who are undermining the overall aims of the business.

Mostly Cs

The programme for progress has not been developed adequately. People are not clear about what they are supposed to be doing and there may be a lack of project management skills. There is an absence of short-term wins and progress is so far in the future that day to day job satisfaction is lacking.

Mostly Ds

The organizational culture is not suited to change. It may be that the business is rooted in the past since managers are not committed to change. As a result, the company's processes, such as staff appraisals, do not support the changes that the business now needs to introduce.

If the exercise has revealed areas for attention, review the 'successful change process' described earlier and home in on the elements that address the greatest weaknesses.

TIPS FROM THE TOP

Dawn Airey, Director of Programmes, Channel Five

■ What were the principal things you had to learn to become successful?

Managing creative people can be difficult at times. I also had to learn how to collaborate, as you are only as good as the people around you.

When you are running things, I discovered that how you react to a situation really influences people. You can't just shoot from the hip.

■ What challenges did you meet along the way?

You do not get anything more challenging than starting a new television channel. I have to manage a budget of £120 million and I had to develop the experience to handle that.

■ What advice would you give to an aspiring manager?

You have to understand the whole of the business if you desire promotion.

You need to know about strategic imperatives, but also knowing everyone and taking the team with you are equally important.

Keys

- Recognize that change is now a permanent characteristic of business life.
- Develop an impressive, deliverable goal.
- Create a sense of urgency around important changes.
- Establish tangible landmarks to chart progress and to celebrate.
- Communicate the need for change, a vision of the future, and what is expected from staff.

ten

The **eighth commandment: know yourself**

> We were consistently impressed with the responses when we asked our directors what they saw as their strengths and weaknesses. Without hesitation they listed their talents, and then their failings. Confident self-knowledge is the building block for progressing in business.

The eighth characteristic of success, rated similarly by men and women, was 'knowing your strengths and limitations'. Our interviewees demonstrated their own abilities here by answering questions on their personal strengths and weaknesses. They typically answered quickly and decisively with an apparent objectivity, as though they were talking about someone else. This dispassionate self-knowledge seems to be a key success characteristic, enabling individuals to play to their strengths and to avoid being lured into their areas of weakness.

For the record, the most commonly named strengths of our leaders were leadership, communication skills, delegation, ability to get on with people, team player, enthusiasm, strategic, fair, hard working, analytical, clarity of vision, loyal, tough, straightforward and honest. Their weaknesses were impatience, low boredom threshold, too attentive to detail, not sufficiently attentive to detail, not suffering fools gladly, too blunt or abrupt, and sometimes too soft.

'Know thyself' was the inscription on the temple of Apollo at Delphi and has been advised by the subsequent observers and philosophers from Shakespeare's 'this above all: to thine own self be true' to Robbie Burns's 'O wad some Pow'r the giftie gie us, to see oursels as others see us!' However, Thomas Carlyle thought that self-knowledge was an 'impossible precept' and recommended that we should settle for 'know what thou canst work at'. This chapter will develop an approach for gaining some insights into what we are really like, and for separating the things we have to live with from those 'thou canst work at'.

Knowing ourselves is crucial to achieving a happy and successful life. Unfortunately many people, perhaps even the vast majority, are steered into lifestyles and careers that are not suited to their true aptitudes and desires. When we are impressionable and under the control of others, notably our parents and teachers, we are likely to be directed where *they* want us to go, not into the things that match our skills and truly excite us. Indeed, a part of our culture is an acceptance that work is not meant to be enjoyed but is a means to an end, a way of spending 48 weeks of the year earning sufficient money to enjoy the remaining four.

In the fifth commandment, we noted the advice of Meredith Belbin to 'Outlaw team roles that are foreign to you. Do not incorporate them into your habits or allow them to form part of the expectations of others.' Your team-type exercise should already have revealed something about yourself. You will recall from Chapter 7 that there are eight types:

- *The implementer*: reliable, practical and systematic.
- *The co-ordinator*: decisive, confident, controlling and motivating.
- *The shaper*: dynamic, courageous and provocative.
- *The plant*: creative, individualistic and imaginative.
- *The resource investigator*: curious, enthusiastic and optimistic.
- *The monitor-evaluator*: unemotional, prudent and hard headed.
- *The team worker*: sociable, perceptive and diplomatic.
- *The completer-finisher*: painstaking, conscientious and perfectionist.

Check your own scores. Do you emerge strongly as a particular type, or do you have a mix of characteristics? What types are you *least* like? Then the key question: does your current role play to your strengths? To have the greatest chance of succeeding in business we should attempt to develop our jobs in directions where we can excel, and strenuously avoid allowing the expectations of us to be in areas where we are weak. If we have the luxury of being able to employ a team, then the priorities are people who fill our skill gaps – not clones of ourselves.

We do not have to despair that we are not the 'right type' to succeed on a company board. A board is a team and needs the 'biodiversity' of a mixture of skills to succeed, especially in these fast-moving times. This was the central finding of Belbin's early research work. However, if our aim is not just to be a successful board member, but to be the chairperson of the board, then there may be a challenge. The most likely type to succeed as chairperson is the Belbin 'co-ordinator'. This type was originally named the 'chairman', but was re-named to avoid an implication that it was more important than other types. If we want to be the chairperson, but are not the calm, self-confident, mature individual that typically fits the bill, then we have to face the facts. We have to decide whether these are things we can work at, or whether we will have a happier, more successful business life settling for a board role where we are within our comfort zone. We all know people who are brilliant 'number twos' and who achieve great success by providing the support skills to their leader, like Sir Bernard Ingham, former chief press secretary to Prime Minister Margaret Thatcher. In recognizing that he was an outstanding communicator and publicist, Ingham found success in ways that would probably have been impossible had he aspired to be the leader.

TIPS FROM THE TOP

Sir Bryan Nicholson, Chairman, BUPA

- What were the principal things you had to learn to become successful?

    I'm an assiduous learner and, although never trained in senior management, have always thoroughly researched the businesses I have been involved with. I often have to exercise self-restraint (but still over-bid in bridge).

- What challenges did you meet along the way?

    Overcoming a fear of failure. Seeing beyond the detail and developing a strategic picture.

- What advice would you give to an aspiring manager?

    Bring values to your work. Strive for betterment. Consult widely. Don't discriminate – help those who are down and don't nanny those who are up.

Modes of self-understanding

In seeking to understand ourselves, Belbin's team roles are far from the only classifications of individual types. Let's consider some of the other approaches.

Personality

This loosely defined psychological term describes the attitudes and behaviours by which individuals view the world and the way in which they relate to others. Personality is remarkably stable throughout life. A colleague recently attended a reunion of some old university friends who had not met for thirty years. He wondered if he would recognize them, and found that in many cases he did not. Typically, they had acquired fat and lost hair (they were all male!). However, their personalities were strikingly familiar. Their attitudes, tone of voice, sense of humour and so on seemed to have been fixed in time, and the fact that they had known each other as young students, and were re-meeting as middle-aged men, made little difference.

Many so-called 'theories' of personality have been developed to assist psychologists in predicting, and sometimes modifying, behaviour. We introduced one approach in the Chapter 7, the personality type classification developed by Hans Eysenck. Eysenck used complex statistical analysis to group hundreds of traits, such as reliability, optimism, anxiety, aggression and laziness, shown by large numbers of people. He presented these initially on two 'dimensions' of personality, introversion-extroversion and stability-anxiety (or neuroticism). Later he added a third dimension based on the level of psychoticism.

Figure 10.1 shows the basic two-dimensional Eysenck model with some of the main traits illustrated. The four quadrants created by this two-dimensional classification relate to age-old observations about personality. Eysenck himself pointed out the relationship between his own work and the proposals of the ancient Greek physician Hippocrates (400 BC). Hippocrates suggested there were four human temperaments: *sanguine* (cheerful and active, relating to the stable/extrovert type), *melancholic* (gloomy, relating to anxious/introvert), *choleric* (angry and violent, relating to anxious/extrovert), and *phlegmatic* (calm and passive, relating to stable/introvert).

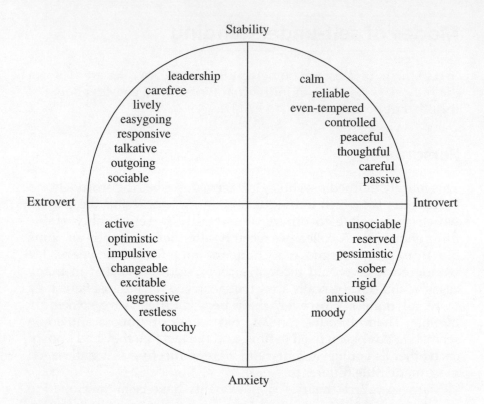

Figure 10.1 Eysenck's personality classification

Ancient Greek theory suggested that a particular individual could only be counted as a member of one personality category. It also created the 'four humours' to account for them: choleric individuals had an excess of yellow bile, the sanguine personality resulted from too much blood, melancholia was caused by an excess of black bile, and the phlegmatic person had an excess of phlegm. However, Eysenck's dimensions are continuums along which everyone can be placed.

To help you place yourself on the personality matrix, here is a summary of Eysenck's description of the extreme types at the ends of the scales. Consider where you are on the two dimensions, and this should give you a point inside the personality circle:

Dimension one: anxious/stable

The extreme anxious (or unstable or neurotic) type: an anxious, worrying individual, moody and frequently depressed. Likely to sleep badly and to suffer from various psychosomatic disorders. Overly emotional, reacting too strongly to all sorts of stimuli and finds it difficult to get back on an even keel after each emotionally arousing experience.

The extreme stable type: tends to respond emotionally only slowly and generally weakly, and to return to baseline quickly after emotional arousal. Usually calm, even-tempered, controlled and unworried.

Dimension two: introvert/extrovert

The extreme introvert: quiet and retiring, fond of books rather than people. Reserved and distant except to intimate friends. Plans ahead and distrusts the impulse of the moment. Dislikes excitement and likes order. Keeps feelings under close control, seldom aggressive. Reliable, somewhat pessimistic and places great importance on ethical standards.

The extreme extrovert: sociable, likes parties, has many friends, needs people to talk to. Craves excitement, takes chances, generally impulsive. Fond of practical jokes, always has a ready answer, likes change, carefree, easy-going and optimistic. Tends to be aggressive and loses temper quickly. Not always reliable.

Eysenck's third dimension based on psychoticism is less relevant here since high scorers are unlikely to be boardroom aspirants. Extreme psychotics are solitary, troublesome individuals, not fitting in anywhere. They may be cruel and inhuman, lacking in feelings and altogether insensitive. They display hostility, even to loved ones. They have a liking for odd and unusual things, a disregard for danger and take pleasure in upsetting other people.

Here is a summary of the types of executive position in which the various types particularly succeed.

Stable extroverts are particularly effective in jobs that involve liaison with others. They are leaders in business with interpersonal skills that are persuasive and motivating. They are trusted and can persuade others to co-operate with them. Good roles include hands-on sales and personnel management.

Anxious extroverts are restless and succeed where there is a need to keep up the pace and exert pressure on others. They can cope with a rapidly-changing environment and their positive, optimistic approach is well suited to today's dynamic business environment. Anxious extroverts succeed in jobs including sales management, production management and jobs with deadlines such as editing.

Stable introverts succeed where there is a need to form good relationships with a small group of people over a sustained period of time. They are effective in local and central government, as planners in business, and in professions such as solicitors where effective professional relationships with colleagues and clients are critical to success.

Anxious introverts are the group in which some of the most creative people belong. They are effective in jobs demanding dedication and persistence such as research scientists and other specialists committed to long-term projects. They are self-motivating and feel a commitment to the effective completion of their tasks.

What if you spot a mismatch between your personality and the job you are doing? Do you change your job or your personality? This is a challenging question, and raises issues about the extent to which personality can be changed at all. Freud believed that personality develops during the first five years of life and is pretty well fixed thereafter. On the other hand, some aspects of an individual's personality, for example moodiness or indecision, might be associated with factors such as environment or personal relationships that can be changed. The issue of personality changes has been much debated following the development of antidepressant drugs such as Prozac. By inhibiting the absorption of serotonin, Prozac can prevent a person from worrying needlessly and give them a more cheerful outlook on life. This has given rise to suggestions that personality is chemically influenced, and therefore potentially changeable.

However the reality is that, unless aspects of our life or health affect our behaviour, personality is something we are more or less stuck with. We might well want to tackle aspects of our behaviour that are limiting, such as the introvert's dislike of joining in with a party, but we will probably find that the easiest route to success and happiness is to mould the job to the personality, rather than the other way round. This is not to suggest that we settle for second best, in fact quite the opposite. We need to understand ourselves and the way we react to the world, and to use that information to find the best possible outlet for our talents.

Intelligence

Intelligence is just as elusive to define and measure as personality, and can also be changed only to a limited extent. We should not be too beguiled by tests and measures. The psychologist Stephen Ceci of Cornell University tells the story of a man looking into a pram. 'What a lovely baby' he says. The mother replies, 'Oh, don't go by that, you should see her photographs!' He is warning us not to regard intelligence test scores as more important than the attainments they are supposed to predict (but in fact tend not to).

There is another good, and rather surprising, reason for not including intelligence tests in this book. Our conventional view of intelligence (measured by intelligence quotient or an equivalent scoring system) does not seem to correlate with success in the boardroom. Belbin monitored this using an intelligence score called Critical Thinking Appraisal (CTA). He found that a high CTA score in a team leader seemed almost to get in the way of good performance. Teams with chairpeople who had very high mental ability tended to perform badly, even if their personalities were well suited to the chairperson role. High mental ability seemed to 'overshadow the effects of personality'. On the other hand, teams with chairpeople with low mental ability did better than expected, provided the chairperson possessed the appropriate personality. So a less than ideal mental ability for a job can be overcome, at least to some extent, through character attributes. Strangely, extremely high intelligence may be more of a barrier to boardroom success than relatively lower intelligence.

TIPS FROM THE TOP

Sir Bob Reid, formerly CEO of Sears, non-executive director, Bank of Scotland

■ What were the principal things you had to learn to become successful?

I had to learn patience when I became a chief executive and of course people skills.

I believe that everybody deserves respect and should be allowed an individual identity at work. Debate should never be allowed to become corrosive.

> *An organization should enjoy what it is doing.*
> ■ What challenges did you meet along the way?
> *Few challenges have occurred except that of retail busi-*
> *nesses trying to make money.*
>
> *I have loved every job I have ever had and had no desire to*
> *move on. I just got offered things. Oh I did ask to go to the*
> *railways. That seemed an interesting challenge.*
> ■ What advice would you give to an aspiring manager?
> *You need to get as broad a business experience as possible.*
> *You can't just rely on technical expertise alone.*
>
> *I notice that some young people lead very complex*
> *emotional lives. You need to keep it simple. You don't want to*
> *get confused. Stay with one partner and do what you want to*
> *do with them.*
>
> *I was lucky to get my wife at the right time. Now she would*
> *want a career!*

All this suggests some problems with the whole concept of intelligence. The psychology researcher Howard Gardner suggested that intelligence was the 'ability to solve problems or fashion products that are of consequence in a particular setting or community'. Clearly, simple measures of mental reasoning ability do not meet this requirement in a business setting, since they seem not to be 'of consequence' in the boardroom. Gardner himself suggested the solution by observing that there is not just one underlying mental capacity but several, and that it is the fact that there are multiple intelligences that enables human beings to take on diverse roles. Gardner suggested seven intelligences:

■ **Linguistic intelligence**: the capacity for speech and the use of language.
■ **Musical intelligence**: the ability to create, communicate and understand meanings made up of the quality of sound.
■ **Logical-mathematical intelligence**: the ability to use and appreciate relationships in the absence of objects – abstract thought.
■ **Spatial intelligence**: the ability to perceive and construct visual or spatial information.
■ **Bodily-kinesthetic intelligence**: the ability to use the body to solve problems or fashion products.

■ **Intrapersonal intelligence**: the ability to distinguish among one's own feelings, intentions and motivations.

■ **Interpersonal intelligence**: the ability to recognize and make distinctions among other people's feelings, beliefs and intentions.

This perhaps starts to home in on why conventional measures of mental intelligence, which tend to focus on linguistic, logical-mathematical and spatial intelligence, do not totally predict ability in the boardroom. Boardroom success will sometimes demand other intelligences, particularly interpersonal, that are likely to be missed by straightforward IQ tests.

The limitations of orthodox intelligence tests were developed further by the Harvard University professor Daniel Goleman. In his best-selling book *Emotional Intelligence*, Goleman argued that the conventional view of intelligence is far too narrow, and that human emotion plays a much greater role in thought, decision making and individual success than is generally acknowledged. Goleman coined the term 'emotional intelligence', sometimes called 'EQ', to describe the characteristics of people who excel, both at work and in their personal relationships. EQ includes self-awareness, self-motivation, impulse control, persistence, compassion, empathy and sociability. Goleman noted that these qualities could also be described by the old-fashioned word 'character'.

A crucial difference between EQ and IQ is that EQ can be developed. Goleman particularly urged that emotional skills should be taught to children. However, improving emotional intelligence is not beyond the reach of adults. The starting point is awareness of your emotional responses, and this suggests another dimension of behaviour, ranging from a passive lack of feelings and reactions at one extreme, through to a continual, over-excitable response to even minor events. In developing EQ, Goleman listed some areas that could be worked on:

■ *Emotional self-awareness*, including the ability to recognize one's emotions, and to understand the causes of feelings.
■ *Managing emotions* such as anger and frustration, resisting verbal put-downs and expressing feelings constructively and without fighting.
■ *Harnessing emotions productively* by being more responsible and controlled, attentive to the task in hand and less impulsive.
■ *Reading emotions*, or developing empathy, by taking other people's perspective and becoming better at listening.

■ *Handling relationships*, including resolving conflicts, improving communication skills, becoming more concerned and considerate, and being more democratic in dealing with others.

The fit between your personality and your job

A central question is whether there is a match between our skills and desires, and the job we are doing. Many authors have addressed this issue. A real leader is John Clark, who writes of his own experiences in *The Money or Your Life*. Clark was a successful lawyer, a partner in a prominent law firm, with two degrees in law. However, he realized that law was not his vocation and would not deliver personal fulfilment. He left the legal profession and found satisfaction in management, writing, consulting and volunteer work. In a way, John Clark's book is the opposite to this one, since he threw away the notion of career success when he realized he was not fulfilled. His advice is 'follow your bliss', and not to pursue a career for the sake of it: good advice, and we would be alarmed if our book was taken to be an endorsement of boardroom life for those to whom it is not suited.

The questionnaire in Table 10.1, developed by Mensa, addresses your job/personality fit. Answer all the questions, and be honest in your responses – only you will ever see them.

Table 10.1 Mensa's career and personality questionnaire

Career or vocation?	Yes	No
1. I am a very logical rational person	☐	☐
2. People are always asking me to help with practical tasks	☐	☐
3. I would examine a set of accounts to discover a small error even if it took all day	☐	☐
4. I like tinkering with cars	☐	☐
5. At school I preferred art and literature to chemistry and physics	☐	☐
6. I am good at coping with crises	☐	☐
7. Being a leader is tiresome and difficult	☐	☐
8. I was always good at science at school	☐	☐
9. The life of a school teacher would suit me	☐	☐
10. I have never done anything dangerous just for fun	☐	☐
11. If you want things done properly, you must do them yourself	☐	☐
12. I have always been good at maths	☐	☐
13. I am quite quiet and reserved	☐	☐
14. Office systems and procedures bore me to tears	☐	☐
15. I never mind speaking in public	☐	☐
16. Music is an important part of my life	☐	☐
17. I normally feel able to cope with life	☐	☐
18. The problems of artificial intelligence fascinate me	☐	☐
19. Managing staff would be a pain in the neck	☐	☐
20. I have always been mechanically minded	☐	☐
21. I like computer games	☐	☐
22. I can't understand what makes people want to gamble	☐	☐
23. It must be fun being an actor	☐	☐
24. People ask me to take charge because I am good at what I do	☐	☐
25. Variety is the spice of life	☐	☐
26. A career in sales would excite me	☐	☐
27. I have read books which changed my life	☐	☐
28. Helping problem families would be an interesting and useful thing to do	☐	☐
29. I like to be in charge	☐	☐
30. Computer games distract children from more useful pastimes	☐	☐
31. I hate being on my own	☐	☐
32. Noise often distracts me from the task in hand	☐	☐
33. I like anything involving figures	☐	☐
34. Government sponsorship of the arts is a waste of money	☐	☐
35. I would prefer to look at a great car than a great painting	☐	☐
36. I would like to explore far-off places	☐	☐
37. Every day should present a different challenge	☐	☐
38. I dislike crowds	☐	☐
39. Filing and clerical work may not be glamorous, but they have to be done and I am good at them	☐	☐
40. I feel depressed without people around me	☐	☐
41. I take a great interest in other people's problems	☐	☐
42. Music can move me deeply	☐	☐

Table 10.1 (continued)   Mensa's career and personality
questionnaire

Career or vocation?	Yes	No
43. I often feel vaguely unwell for no good reason	☐	☐
44. I don't like being told what to do	☐	☐
45. I hate routine tasks	☐	☐
46. A visit to a nuclear power station would make an interesting day out	☐	☐
47. I enjoy trying to make people accept my views	☐	☐
48. Caring for the mentally handicapped would be too distressing	☐	☐
49. I like to be surrounded by people	☐	☐
50. A little danger adds spice to life	☐	☐
51. I should like to live for some months in a space laboratory	☐	☐
52. I have often wanted to write a novel	☐	☐
53. I am a natural leader	☐	☐
54. It irritates me when people bungle simple tasks like putting in a screw	☐	☐
55. I could not work in an office all day	☐	☐
56. Machines are more reliable than people	☐	☐
57. People regard me as level headed and capable	☐	☐
58. I dislike criticism from others	☐	☐
59. I would rather get on with a practical task than waste time writing or painting	☐	☐
60. I find changes in my routine unsettling	☐	☐
61. I would enjoy the work of a research scientist	☐	☐
62. I can usually persuade people to my point of view	☐	☐
63. I get pleasure from making things	☐	☐
64. A career in advertising would suit me	☐	☐
65. I would be attracted to a job which involves a lot of travel	☐	☐
66. I dislike parties where I don't know anyone	☐	☐
67. I would rather let others take responsibility	☐	☐
68. Computers are too complicated for me to understand	☐	☐
69. The life of a travelling salesperson appeals to me	☐	☐
70. I understand which laws of physics govern the working of an engine	☐	☐
71. I often suffer from an upset stomach for no reason	☐	☐
72. I enjoy designing systems to make things more efficient	☐	☐
73. I tend to organize people	☐	☐
74. I would much rather people did not bring their problems to me	☐	☐
75. I am attracted to thrilling sports such as skiing or hang-gliding	☐	☐
76. I should like to be a contestant on a TV game show	☐	☐
77. Science will enable humanity to achieve feats our grand-parents could not have dreamed of	☐	☐
78. I find computers fascinating	☐	☐
79. I have a good eye for detail	☐	☐
80. Most people would describe me as the life and soul of the party	☐	☐
81. I would enjoy the life of an artist	☐	☐
82. I would rather take a job which promised substantial but uncertain rewards than work steadily for a fixed salary	☐	☐

Table 10.1 (continued)   Mensa's career and personality questionnaire

Career or vocation?	Yes	No
83. I prefer to get on with a job of my own	☐	☐
84. I really enjoy understanding how machines work	☐	☐
85. I like to be with people	☐	☐
86. I can understand the fascination of gambling	☐	☐
87. People who waste time on the arts never achieve anything	☐	☐
88. I like the security of a set routine	☐	☐
89. I find it very hard to work in messy surroundings	☐	☐
90. Practical people are more valuable to society than academics	☐	☐
91. Looking after disabled children would interest me	☐	☐
92. I enjoy solving puzzles and crosswords	☐	☐
93. I find I am able to cope in most circumstances	☐	☐
94. Social events are more fun if you go in a crowd	☐	☐
95. I like to know what I will be doing each day	☐	☐
96. It is important for someone to cross the Ts and dot the Is	☐	☐
97. I can usually get my own way in the end	☐	☐
98. The work of a nurse would be rewarding	☐	☐
99. I have often been asked to speak in public	☐	☐
100. It annoys me that some people can't change a light bulb for themselves	☐	☐
101. People should sort out their own lives	☐	☐
102. Logic problems present an interesting challenge	☐	☐
103. Being a police officer would be a good way of helping the community	☐	☐
104. I can talk persuasively on almost any topic	☐	☐
105. It gives me great satisfaction to mend things	☐	☐
106. People who fuss about the adverse effects of scientific research fail to understand its great importance	☐	☐
107. Social workers should spend less time meddling in other people's affairs	☐	☐
108. I would enjoy training as an accountant	☐	☐
109. I would like to be a politician	☐	☐
110. I sometimes lose my temper for no good reason	☐	☐
111. I could never work in a boring job just because the money was good	☐	☐
112. I hate problems involving maths	☐	☐
113. Science has made a greater contribution to human progress than all of the arts put together	☐	☐
114. Clerical work is boring and trivial	☐	☐
115. I get fits of depression for no real reason	☐	☐
116. I would find bookkeeping an interesting career	☐	☐
117. I find it easy to contribute to meetings and group discussions	☐	☐
118. Being a clerical assistant would be too boring for me	☐	☐
119. I would be interested in studying viruses under a microscope	☐	☐
120. I would enjoy freelance work which involved constant changes and new challenges	☐	☐

Scoring

The test is divided into 12 dimensions and each answer is marked as either positive or negative. If you have answered 'yes' to a positive question, give yourself 1 point. If you have answered 'no' to a negative question also give yourself one point. If you answer a positive question with a 'no' or a negative question with a 'yes', give yourself no points. The maximum number of points you can score on each dimension is 10.

Artistic/creative dimension: 5+ 16+ 27+ 34+ 42+ 52+ 59– 63+ 81+ 87–
Practical/mechanical dimension: 2+ 4+ 20+ 35+ 54+ 56+ 84+ 90+ 100+ 105+
Scientific dimension: 8+ 18+ 46+ 51+ 61+ 70+ 77+ 106+ 113+ 119+
Administrative/clerical dimension: 3+ 14– 39+ 72+ 79+ 96+ 108+ 114– 116+ 118–
Caring/helping dimension: 9+ 28+ 41+ 48– 74– 91+ 98+ 101– 103+ 107–
Logical/computational dimension: 1+ 12+ 21+ 30– 33+ 68– 78+ 92+ 102+ 112–
Persuasive dimension: 15+ 26+ 47+ 62+ 64+ 97+ 99+ 104+ 109+ 117+
Need for excitement: 10– 22– 36+ 50+ 65+ 75+ 76+ 82+ 86+ 111+
Stability: 6+ 17+ 32– 43– 57+ 71– 89– 93+ 110– 116–
Need for change: 23+ 25+ 37+ 45+ 55+ 60– 69+ 88– 95– 120+
Need for people: 13– 31– 38– 40+ 49+ 66– 80+ 83– 85+ 94+
Need for control: 7– 11+ 19– 24+ 29+ 44+ 53+ 58+ 67– 73+

You should now be able to see how you rate on each of the dimensions and what that means for your career. For example, if you have high scores on artistic/creative, need for excitement, need for people and need for change, but you actually work as a cashier in a bank, the need for change would be strongly indicated. On the other hand, someone who had high scores on practical/mechanical, stability and need for control might well be looking at an engineering career.

TIPS FROM THE TOP

James Cullen, President and CEO of Bell Atlantic

- What were the principal things you had to learn to become successful?

    Work is just a game. You must understand that you are going to look stupid to at least one person every day. If you take yourself too seriously you lose it!

- What challenges did you meet along the way?

    Dealing with illogical, backward thinking regulations is a vexing but necessary part of the job.

- What advice would you give to an aspiring manager?

    Becoming less compartmentalized is essential. An ability to see the bigger picture is the major skill of the good director. But retaining that youthful sense of candour is good.

Exercise: personal feedback

The final exercise in this chapter is a practical one. It takes us back to Robbie Burns' desire to 'see ourselves as others see us'. How do we find out whether our self-image, perhaps of being balanced, perceptive and inspirational, is actually shared by our friends and colleagues? The answer is simple, but rarely exercised: we ask them.

In many workshops over many years, we have explored a range of ways in which personal feedback can be obtained. These include detailed questionnaires and elaborate role-play exercises. However, consistently the most useful and revealing has been one of the simplest. It is to ask a representative range of people – bosses, subordinates and other colleagues – to answer three questions:

- What should I start doing?
- What should I stop doing?
- What should I continue doing?

The easiest way to set up this exercise is within the context of an overall review process: perhaps during the annual appraisal round, or as a prelude to a business review exercise. This way, everyone is in on the act, everyone gets feedback, and there is no singling-out of any individual for particular attention. The responses should be brief but in writing, and the way in which they will be used should be agreed in advance: probably as a basis for a one-to-one review between an individual and their manager.

The structure of the questions ensures that the feedback will not simply be anodyne and polite. With luck, it also means that the answers will be succinct and to the point. However, the tricky bit is to take on board the messages. It is easy to accept the nice bits and ignore, or even deny, the tough parts where change is desirable. But remember that we are all less than perfect, and that we are all on a continual journey of change and development. Honest feedback means we can fine-tune the process, and progress in ways that will make a real difference to our business performance.

Keys

- Develop a good understanding of your personality, types of intelligence, and individual skills.
- Be receptive to feedback from colleagues to obtain an objective understanding of yourself.
- Settle for what can't be changed, but practise new habits to address improvable areas of weakness.
- Develop job aspirations that are well matched to your particular characteristics.
- Avoid allowing those in authority to steer you in directions that do not suit you.

The **ninth commandment: strike a deal**

> Our ninth commandment relates to the ability to negotiate. Leaders need to achieve 'win-win' outcomes with partners and providers. They have the creativity to construct a proposition from which everyone will gain, the toughness not to relinquish more than they can afford, and the charisma to steer the encounter to a successful conclusion.

The ninth characteristic of success was 'the ability to deal and negotiate'. This was closely linked to another quality we asked about: 'a willingness to take risks'. So this chapter is about the process of negotiating to the most successful outcome, and the risks you might have to take along the way.

From the outset, we should stress that our executives were *cautious* risk takers. Risk taking was a subject we explored in detail in our interviews, and very few people felt that 'risk taker' was a good general description of them. Not many of them gambled as a recreation, and perhaps this reveals a key distinction. Our interviewees knew that progress could sometimes not be made without risk, and they had the vision to see when a risk was necessary, and the nerve to then take it. However, they would not gamble casually with their or their stakeholders' money, and they would not take any risk without fully understanding what was at stake and what the odds really were. Christopher Rodrigues described this as 'thinking several steps ahead – it's the difference between a manager's job and the CEO's'.

The business of negotiation permeates the life of a successful executive. It influences everyday relationships where the challenge is to motivate people to give their best performance. It dominates the sales process – many of our executives found that involvement in sales was one of the most enjoyable parts of their job, described by Christopher Castleman as 'hustling for business'. And it is the key to agreeing the big strategic issues that ultimately lead to success or failure.

Interestingly, the area of our questioning in which the word 'negotiation' came up most often was when we asked 'What are the most important things you have had to learn?' The most common answer to that question was 'patience'! But after that, the team felt that negotiating skills were the most important of all skills to learn – and believed that they could be learned. Some added that such skills were partly intuitive, David Barnes commenting that he had a 'nose for a deal'. Others felt that they had started early in life: Ros Wilton had 'started trading with my father when I was four'.

Several executives had particular views on the nature of risk. They all saw that risk was central to their jobs and recognized that they were taking risks all the time. But they all wanted to proceed with their eyes open, knowing what was at risk, and what would be the worst possible consequence of failure. Sir Bob Reid said that 'Everything is a risk – calculate it'. Peter Jacobs wanted to encourage more informed risk taking by establishing 'a failure culture' in which failure was recognized and sometimes applauded as a consequence of courageous risk taking.

So when should you negotiate, when should you take a risk, and how is it done? This chapter is based on 13 key principles of negotiation. This may seem a daunting list of things to keep in mind round a negotiating table, but you will find that many are things you do already, and others are a reminder of points that will come in useful at a crucial moment. Here's the list:

- Know what you want.
- Listen actively.
- Be informed.
- Don't concede, bargain.
- Don't get stuck over positions.
- Learn to re-frame.
- Don't be dominated by price.
- Look for win-win.
- Don't be put off by tactics.

- Take risks.
- Manage the relationship.
- Prepare for last minute problems.
- Stay in control.

Know what you want

Rita has been asked to arrange the company's annual conference, and to negotiate the 'best deal' with a suitable hotel. After phoning around Rita discovers, to her alarm, that only one hotel has the right space on the right date in the right area. She prepares for her meeting with Toby, the hotel manager.

Toby has a problem. On the week Rita wants to book her conference, parts of the hotel are being redecorated. This will limit the areas guests can use, and involve some inconvenience and noise. However, hotel bookings are down, and Toby really needs more guests during the decoration week. He will settle for any reasonable deal that keeps the hotel occupied.

The meeting is unsatisfactory and inconclusive. Toby explains the decorating problem, but stresses that most of the hotel will be functioning normally and that the staff will bend over backwards to minimize the inconvenience to guests. Rita asks what, in the circumstances, is the 'best deal' that Toby can offer. Toby volunteers a 15 per cent discount on the usual rates. Rita now has a dilemma. She doesn't know whether this is a good rate, and is reluctant to press on asking for further discounts since this could commit her to a deal – and she can't really decide whether she should make a booking at all in view of the likely disruption. Rita feels she has to consult with others (weakening her personal standing) and the meeting ends without a conclusion.

How could this unsatisfactory outcome have been avoided, enabling Rita to complete a satisfactory negotiation during the meeting? Rita's problem was that she didn't really know what she wanted. When it came to it, she did not know whether to press on and do a deal. This is a common dilemma and is discussed in the best-selling book on negotiating, *Getting to Yes* by Roger Fisher and William Ury. Fisher and Ury created the concept of the 'BATNA' (best alternative to a negotiated agreement). You must know the BATNA before you can negotiate with confidence. What Rita needed to know was what her company would do if she failed to negotiate a deal with a hotel. Would this be an unmitigated disaster because the dates had been agreed with a lot of very busy people, or would they easily find other places and other dates?

It is important not to commence a negotiation just to see where it leads. It will lead you to a place where you are not equipped to make a decision unless you know your BATNA. Knowledge of what is really important will ensure that you are not unnecessarily committed to coming to an agreement at all costs, and that you know what absolutely must be achieved because the alternative is unacceptable. The key question to ask is, 'what will happen if this negotiation fails?' That way you will understand your true negotiating power and will establish an objective understanding of the value of the other party's proposition.

Listen actively

If you have used the BATNA approach to understand your own negotiating priorities and limits, it would clearly be extremely helpful to know the importance of a deal to the other side. Can they afford to let the negotiation fail? Are there particular things they need? Or things they can easily concede? Do they need the deal to be structured in a particular way to save face? These questions can be answered by actively listening to (and watching the behaviour of) the other party.

We have all been in a situation where we have embarked on a 'negotiation' to purchase something, but were actually desperate to buy. A friend recalled purchasing her first car. It was a clapped-out old wreck but she had decided it was exactly the car for her. She would probably have bought it even if the price had gone up during the negotiation. The salesman was experienced enough to let her talk, and he listened carefully to what she was saying. She didn't challenge the price at all, but merely sought his endorsement for things she liked about the car. She wanted him to tell her it was a great deal. He, of course, was happy to do this, and she became the enthusiastic owner of her first car.

The value of listening is obvious, but is easier said than done when you are in the throes of a complicated negotiation. However, it is vital. The other party's words, and the frequency with which they raise particular points, will reveal their priorities. The title of this principle is 'active listening', which means that you need to manage the process. This involves seeking clarification and asking 'why?' and 'why not?' to encourage them to reveal their perceptions and their priorities. This approach is also satisfying to the other side, who will appreciate being taken seriously rather than simply going through a ritual.

The principle of active listening may seem to be in conflict with a tough negotiating approach in which you do not take any account of the needs of the other side, but good negotiating is the reverse of this. It demands a real understanding of the issues in play, the sensitivities involved, and the things that have to be satisfied for everyone to believe they have a good deal.

Be informed

William was involved in negotiations with a big prospective client to sell a wide range of services. William's company was on the short list, having progressed through a complicated tendering process, but they were still up against their major competitor. The client had made it clear that their services seemed fine but the price was too high. William wanted the business, but to deliver at a lower price would mean wiping out most of the margin.

Then William met one of his sales colleagues. He had been talking with one of the client's production managers, who had mentioned that they had had slow response times and poor documentation in past dealings with the competitor. Naturally, this information was extremely valuable to William. He stressed that, despite the higher prices, his services were responsive, better-documented and better value for money. His knowledge had increased his bargaining confidence and homed in on the area of real importance to the client.

Information is vital in effective negotiation. The more you know about your own product, the competition's offerings, and the buyer's organization, the stronger your negotiating position. Acquiring information involves having the right contacts and applying the principle of active listening.

TIPS FROM THE TOP

Sir Patrick Sargeant, non-executive director, Euromoney

- What were the principal things you had to learn to become successful?

  You must be honest in your dealings in business. Your word is your bond and you will only succeed if a good reputation precedes you.

- What challenges did you meet along the way?

  I have loved every bit of my job, but what challenges the most is the time it take to persuade people to your point of view.

- What advice would you give to an aspiring manager?

  Develop the humility to realize that you are not infallible. Others have answers too.

Another aspect of information is discussed by the vice president of the Centre for Effective Negotiating, Gary Karrass, in his book *Negotiate to Close*. It is the 'power of legitimacy'. Karrass notes that many transactions can be associated with some sort of formality which makes them much easier to progress. Examples of things that bestow 'legitimacy' are printed price lists, guidelines from professional bodies, quality standard documents, trade union procedures, legal requirements and contract conditions. It is much harder for a negotiator to raise objections when a 'legitimate' third party factor is introduced, and in the words of Karrass, 'its effect can be almost magical'. Being informed about external procedures and documents that add legitimacy is a key aspect of this principle.

Don't concede, bargain

A casual view of a negotiation might be that it resembles the purchase of souvenirs in a middle-Eastern market. The seller proposes a ludicrously high price and the buyer a correspondingly ludicrous low price. Slowly the two prices are nudged together until they settle somewhere in the middle.

This model suggests that negotiating consists entirely of conceding, probably on price. Indeed, this probably is the way many negotiations proceed. However, the experienced negotiator will always try to ensure that concessions are reluctantly traded, and always in exchange for something. Fortunately, in business deals, there is more in play than haggling over T-shirt prices in the market.

Let's go back to William's situations. Suppose he has been asked to drop the price by £100,000. but he knows that his position is quite strong and that the poor response times of the competition are an issue for the buyer. Firstly William should not react too quickly; any concessions need to be hard fought. A reasonable response could then be, 'Frankly, I can't see scope for more than a £20,000 reduction, and that would be on the basis of reducing response times from 24 hours to three days.' There is now a bargaining proposition on the table. William has demonstrated why he is more expensive than the competition (better response times), and he has blocked any attempt to get the price further down. If the new proposal is accepted, he has gained something in exchange. Even if he ultimately has to concede the £20,000 and maintain his response times, he has moved the £100,000 proposal out of the way.

Now that William is trading rather than conceding, we should consider one additional rule of bargaining: to concede in diminishing increments. Perhaps William has settled for a £20,000 price reduction and obtained some concessions on response times, but the client's buyer is still pressing on price. William must resist offering another £20,000 (or worse still, £30,000), no matter what the trade. This would imply that there might be lots of other price reductions available, and that the buyer just needs to keep pressing to find them. A response now (after an even longer thinking period) could be, 'There isn't much scope now, but if price is still an issue we could perhaps reduce it by £8,000 if we phase the documentation over two years.' Again, William is trading and would perhaps like the two-year commitment this proposal would bring, but he is now introducing diminishing returns for applying any further pressure on price.

A real trap is to concede on things that look free but actually are not, such as delivery times, payment times or instalments, or price freezes. It can seem so desirable to conclude the central aspect of the deal that peripheral issues are treated lightly. The problem is that something like extended payment times represents real money. It deprives you of cash flow and gives your buyer the interest on the money instead of you. You may have closed the deal on the price you wanted, but you have damaged the margin that price was intended to deliver. You must calculate the actual cash value of the proposal and again, trade it rather than concede it.

One way to find opportunities for trading is to ask a question starting with 'if'. In his book *101 Ways to Negotiate More Effectively*, David Oliver describes this as 'the magic if'. The use of 'if' is Oliver's 56th 'way'. The frequent use of the word 'if' makes it clear that a trade is expected. If they want something from you it will cost them. 'If' questions also allow for exploration of the scope for negotiation. They include:

> If you can agree … we can commit to …
> If we can reduce … then we can adjust …
> If you arrange … I will agree …

In summary, the approach is to trade rather than concede, to take your time so that any concession is not seen to come too easily, to move in small and diminishing increments, and continually to use 'if' questions to explore the scope for negotiating.

Don't get stuck over positions

There is a tendency for negotiations to get deadlocked, with both sides stuck in a position from which they find it hard to move. Fisher and Ury illustrate this with an account of the breakdown of negotiations between the United States and the Soviet Union for a ban on nuclear testing. The issue on which talks collapsed was how many times per year each country should be allowed to investigate suspicious events on the other's territory. The Soviet Union agreed to three inspections, but the United States insisted on at least ten.

By focusing on the numbers, both countries were backed into a position from which there was little scope for movement, despite the fact that no one had defined what was meant by an 'inspection'. Instead of attempting to design an inspection procedure that would meet the United States' interest in verification as well as the Soviet Union's desire for minimum intrusion, the parties were stuck with extreme positions from which there was no obvious opportunity for movement.

At the time of writing a similar impasse exists between Nationalists and Republicans in Northern Ireland. With both parties apparently wanting an end to violence, the discussions are locked over the issue of the destruction of IRA weapons. The only hope of a satisfactory negotiated solution is for the parties to focus on ways of guaranteeing peace, but they are stuck over the positions they have taken on weapons.

The problem with bargaining over positions is that they are likely to miss the real purpose of the negotiations and can easily lead to extreme positions from which movement is very difficult. They encourage stubbornness, increase the time and cost of getting to agreement, and introduce a risk that no agreement will be reached at all.

Positional bargaining really amounts to arguing over some detail, not the general principle. It is common in domestic encounters. 'I'm not going to Spain under any circumstances.' 'I won't go out with my sister.' The only hope is to change the game, and the key requirement is to concentrate on interests, not positions.

If you can home in on the underlying interests of the participants then a much wider range of options is likely to emerge. Perhaps your partner's objection to a holiday in Spain is based on a desire for a quiet holiday, in which case the discussion can focus on ways of guaranteeing quietness. Maybe a boy's refusal to be with his sister results from a belief that this will prevent a ride on the Big Dipper. A skilled negotiator will always seek to understand the real needs of all parties, to resist allowing a drift into immovable positions, and to keep a creative range of options available so that a good outcome for everyone can be achieved.

TIPS FROM THE TOP

Tom Hamilton, Hamilton Private Equity Partners

- What were the principal things you had to learn to become successful?

    Nothing in particular, although I have benefited from experience and a range of high-level management training courses.
- What challenges did you meet along the way?

    The most difficult thing is to fire someone you know. It is the ultimate admission of failure.
- What advice would you give to an aspiring manager?

    Be honest, be tenacious. Don't waste time.

Exercise: escaping from positions

Think about negotiating a career development step with your employer. Write down the things you think you would insist on as part of the deal. Then revisit the list, asking what basic position is really involved, and note some other ways in which your needs could be satisfied. This will demonstrate the way in which an apparently absolute condition can be changed – and might also reveal a few negotiating angles at the next pay round!

For example, you might originally specify a salary of at least £x. Other options might be:

- a package of equivalent value;
- training that will increase your future value;
- a long-term contract and enhanced pension;
- relocation to a lower-cost area;
- agreement that you can work from home;
- low interest loans;
- entry into share option plans.

Alternatively, you might originally require a position on the board, but decide on reflection you would settle for:

- direct accountability for a key business area;
- a high-status job title;
- board 'trimmings' – a larger office and so on;
- regular attendance at board meetings;
- agreement to formally review the situation after a fixed time;
- overseas experience;
- senior executive training.

Learn to reframe

The negotiations between Mark and his prospective client seem to have come to an end. Mark's product is fine, but they are stuck on price. The lowest Mark can go to is £100. The highest the buyer will settle for is £90. Will this impasse break the deal, or is there a way forward?

First Mark should invoke the 'don't get stuck' principle, and ensure that neither party is stuck over a declaration of position.

There has to be sufficient goodwill for a creative exploration of further options. Then there needs to be a 'reframing' of the issue to find what those options might be.

The classic tool for reframing is brainstorming, something most people will experience in their working lives, but not necessarily as a negotiating tool. The purpose is to produce as many ideas as possible. Brainstorming is a team exercise, usually with five or six people, and the key requirement is that it is non-judgemental. Off-the-wall ideas are encouraged as a way of giving a new perspective.

In general, you will undertake brainstorming in the negotiating context with a team from your own side, but there is no rule against brainstorming with the other side, provided the event is clearly distinguished from a negotiation session. The wild ideas that are thrown forward must be accepted by all participants as exploration of new avenues, not negotiating propositions.

The product of the brainstorming will be a list of ideas, usually starting life on a flip chart. Mark's job is now to refine the list and decide which to advance in his negotiation. To break the apparent deadlock over price, the session might for example have thrown up:

- 'bartering' in which payment is received in the form of the other party's products or services;
- changed payment arrangements;
- alternative packaging;
- different delivery dates;
- modified guarantees or service terms;
- longer term contract;
- purchase of higher volumes or other products in addition;
- part of the price linked to performance.

Advanced in the form of 'if' propositions, ideas like these can restart a process that seemed dead, and create opportunities for both parties to find a solution that satisfies everyone's needs.

Don't be dominated by price

A gift shop sold jewellery, ornaments and the like. A line of coral bracelets wasn't moving at all. Margaret, the owner, tried displaying them more prominently, producing interesting signs, cutting the price and so on, but to no avail. Finally, just before she went away on a week's holiday she instructed her staff to halve the price of the bracelets. When she returned the bracelets had indeed all been sold, apparently with ease. However it turned out Margaret's instructions had been misheard. The price of the bracelets had not been halved, but doubled!

Many studies show how a belief that the price of a product is too high is often in the mind of the seller, not the buyer. Cheap products can be associated with poor value, and can provoke the buyer to attempt to drive the price down even further. In launching a business area, we organized a series of free seminars to introduce our services. Then we discovered something surprising: when we charged for the seminars we had higher attendance than when they were free. Often a failure to charge appropriately high prices is a failure of confidence. We don't have the nerve to ask the price our products and services really warrant.

Gary Karrass tells of an experiment by Dr Chester Karrass in which 120 professional negotiators were paired off to negotiate a lawsuit. Some were told to aim for $700,000 or more, and some that they could settle for less than $700,000. Nothing else was different. The 'more than $700,000' group averaged settlements of $650,000. The 'less than $700,000' group averaged $425,000. The lesson is that price is a mind-set. Believing you will secure high prices is most of the battle.

The real question is not 'What is the price of your product?' but 'What is its value?' Does the customer really want it? Is it adequately differentiated from the competition? Too often negotiations become fixated by price, with the buyer relentlessly seeking reductions. The seller's job is to move to higher ground: to expect high prices, ask for them, and in return deliver what the buyer is really seeking.

Exercise: escaping the price trap

Imagine you have to sell your company's product at an exorbitantly high price. Develop some sales approaches that you can use when you are told it is 'too expensive'. This will encourage a value-based consideration of your products, and encourage a positive rather than defensive approach to developing sales strategy. For example, if the product is a set of encyclopaedias, the value propositions might be that they will:

- bring knowledge and wisdom;
- answer family arguments;
- enable you to enter prize-winning competitions;
- enable you to set up business as a quizmaster;
- look good in the bookcase, and impress friends;
- transform children's education.

Look for 'win-win'

The 'win-win' concept is widely known but little used. The idea is that a deal is reached in which both parties end up better off. It doesn't take much thought to realize that no other outcome makes sense, but we still often embark on negotiations with 'win-lose' as our goal. If that is the starting point of both parties, the negotiation will be tough, protracted, unimaginative and likely to fail.

'Win-win' involves more than finding a deal that delivers what both parties want. There is an important psychological element in helping the other side feel they have a good deal. Martin has just advertised to sell his caravan for £4,000 but would actually settle for £3,500. He has a phone call from someone who wants to view the caravan immediately. After a quick inspection, the buyer agrees to pay £4,000 and the deal is done, but Martin doesn't feel happy. He is worried that it was too easy and that he has probably sold cheap. Martin would actually have been happier if there had been some haggling and the buyer had slowly accepted £3,750. The real 'win-win' includes making the other party feel positive about the deal. Any good salesman knows that a buyer wants to be told they have a good deal. This psychological reassurance is probably much more important than the actual price. In a negotiation it works both ways, with the buyer and the seller both needing to feel good about the result.

One key to finding the 'win-win' position is to find elements of the deal that have a low cost but high value. In other words, find items that can be traded reasonably painlessly but that have real value to the other party. We had dinner with a colleague recently who was well versed in the art of negotiation. Unfortunately, his food arrived after a long delay, and David decided to negotiate a discount. The outcome was a free bottle of wine. This added real value to the meal (financial and psychological!) and did not cost the restaurant much. We ended up happy if slightly inebriated customers, and honour was done on all sides.

In a business negotiation, especially after a spell of brain-storming, many elements may have this low cost, high value property. Examples to consider might be:

■ improved delivery times;
■ 'branding' the product or service specifically for the customer;
■ volume discounts;
■ arranging joint PR or advertising.

In a real situation there are likely to be many more opportunities, provided you are not trapped by position or price, and the will to seek the 'win-win' deal has been established.

Don't be put off by tactics

These days we often find ourselves having to deal with a relatively recent business arrival, the professional buyer, whose job is to secure the best deal for their employer. There's nothing wrong with that, but be warned: they may well have 'win-lose' in mind (their win, your loss), and will know all the tricks of the negotiating trade. So what tactics are they likely to employ, and how can you deal with them? Let's consider a few approaches we might have to face:

■ *Bullying*. Intimidation can take many forms, from 'Can't you understand that?' through standing up and shouting to psychological warfare such as remaining silent for long periods or the unnerving avoidance of eye-contact. Don't be moved. All our interviewees displayed enough robustness and strength of character to see their way through an assault by bullies.
■ *Deception*. You may be deliberately misled into making false assumptions. The archetypal car salesman is notorious for claiming that a car has only been driven by one old lady on occasional Sundays, or failing to mention that it has been rebuilt after a major crash. Business-to-business negotiations may have more subtle deception but are unlikely to involve full disclosure about product weaknesses, impending take-overs, departure of vital people, legal actions and so on. In a significant exercise this is the role of the 'due diligence' process in which facts are checked, but many negotiations will not have that back-up safeguard, so an approach is needed that minimizes the likelihood

of deception. The technique is not to rely on trust, but to check key facts and not be deterred from this by bullying tactics. A questioning approach and a willingness to verify data will act as a deterrent to deception and limit the chance of being cheated.

■ *Consultation with others*. Andrew recently bought a new washing machine. He negotiated a good price, but resisted the purchase of a three-year extended warranty. The salesman took the line that, one, he had only dropped the price because he had assumed Andrew would buy a warranty, and two, he couldn't take moral responsibility for selling the goods without full insurance cover. Andrew was only fractionally moved by these arguments until the salesman declared that he would have to consult with his store manager. He disappeared for about 20 minutes and returned to announce that his manager too was anxious about the possible lack of cover.

Fortunately Andrew stood firm and is now the happy possessor of his new washing machine. It does not have an extended warranty, and it has not yet broken down. However, the 'consultation with others' tactic does have real power. It introduces delay when you think you are close to a deal, and can raise doubts because it puts the other party in a minority position.

Like Andrew you could stay resolute, but a better approach is often to bounce the tactic straight back. Andrew could have said, 'While you're consulting the manager, I'll go home and talk this over with my family.' The salesman would almost certainly have backed down rather than let a potential customer escape from the shop. In business, an attempt to delay by invoking others can be matched by, 'Okay, let's both think of this as an open situation and I too will let you know of any changes we feel we need.' This will either accelerate progress, or allow you to match the other side's changes with some of your own.

■ *Refusal to negotiate*. A common approach of professional buyers or sellers is to refuse to negotiate, but whatever they say, there is always some scope for negotiation. A good approach is to ignore the 'take it or leave it' statements and introduce a few 'if' propositions instead. 'If we stick with those prices, we could only include off-site service.' 'How would it be if we accept the prices, but settle for a three-year contract?' There is no reason to end the negotiation before it has started.

Take risks

There are always risks in negotiation, but willingness to confront the risks was rated by our interviewees as one of the key skills of success. Risk taking involves moving outside the safe box where things are done the way they have always been done, and finding some new approaches that give real differentiation from competition and take the business in exciting new directions.

Bridget was discussing some advertising proposals with a brand new agency. She realized that some of the ideas were genuinely radical and would give the business a positioning she had never thought of before. She was intrigued and excited and recognized that there was scope for the business to penetrate entirely new areas, but her potential deal was fraught with risk. The advertising company was new, with no track record. It might not survive. It might not deliver the quality it was promising. On the other hand, turning down the proposal would mean that the new ideas would be taken to a competitor. Should Bridget ditch the old, safe agency they had been with for years to pursue a high-risk strategy?

There is no sure answer, but somehow we know that the real business leaders would at least explore every angle of the new opportunity, would negotiate a deal with as much protection as possible, and would not be limited by lack of nerve or allegiance to the past.

Risk taking in negotiation adds authority. It encourages new thinking and results in deals based on true added value where both parties really move their business forward rather than closing just another conventional transaction.

TIPS FROM THE TOP

Sir Ian McAllister, Chairman and MD, Ford Motor Company

■ What were the principal things you had to learn to become successful?

Understanding finance was important to me when I started. But I really had to learn how to encourage risk taking and participation in the organization.

> - What challenges did you meet along the way?
>   *An accident returning from Glyndebourne meant being out of commission for two months. This experience has given me a perspective on life, a certain balance with less worry.*
> - What advice would you give to an aspiring manager?
>   *Breadth of experience in business and marketing, especially if that experience can be obtained overseas.*

Manage the relationship

A friend takes things she doesn't like back to the shop and always succeeds in getting her money back. Curious how she manages this, we studied her technique. The secret is that she is nice to people. People like dealing with nice people. Business relationships are perfectly real relationships and warrant proper respect and cultivation. It was interesting to see how 'nice' all of our successful interviewees were: charismatic, easy to relate to and, we presume, a pleasure to meet around the negotiating table.

Niceness is disarming. A business colleague has to deal with people who have complained about aspects of his employer's business. He has tried two approaches. The first is to be straightforward but tough. He puts the company's counter-position forward and argues over each point. The other is to put himself in the complainers' shoes and to sympathize with their concerns. Empathy wins every time. He has discovered something all good salespeople know, that the most satisfied customers of all are those who had a problem that was dealt with well.

There is a risk of being a soft touch. Indeed, Fisher and Ury have a section in *Getting to Yes*, 'Being nice is no answer'. They point out that being determinedly nice with someone determinedly nasty is destined to lead to failure. It will result in one-sided disclosure of information, yielding to pressure and accepting losses in the interests of agreement. If it is not possible to establish a relationship with the other side, it is important to settle for principled negotiation in which each step is carefully analysed and removed from any emotional inclination.

In general, though, managing the relationship is enormously helpful. Karrass describes this as 'the power of wooing'. He contrasts the success of the car salesperson who takes an interest in customers and goes out of the way to be helpful, with the relative failure of the salesperson who just gives the necessary facts and makes the customer feel they are a bit of a nuisance. It's the same product at the same price, but the customers who are wooed are much more likely to buy, likely to feel satisfied, and to come back again.

Another aspect of managing the relationship is making sure the other side thinks they have done well. As we noted in discussing 'win-win', we often need the reassurance that we are going for a good deal. Liz has just bought a television set and was very reassured that the salesman told her she had purchased a great set at a bargain price. What else was he going to say? But the fact was Liz had checked the reviews, found the cheapest supplier, and just needed the psychological push to complete the deal. If you have negotiated a good deal, which of course you will have done, don't gloat. Congratulate the other side on their professionalism and their hard-won bargain. You are in this for the long term, and a warm relationship should be part of your settlement.

Prepare for last-minute problems

Angela was as good as there. She had negotiated one of her company's biggest contracts, for the provision of design services to a high street retailer with outlets throughout the country. Every detail of the deal had been agreed. Angela had beaten off the competition. The buyer had faith in her company's design skills, and the negotiation had resulted in terms that suited both parties. They had shaken hands, and all that remained was the 'formality' of lawyers agreeing on the contract details.

A week or so later it was clear the deal was far from done. The telephone updates became more and more unsettling. The lawyers were not happy with the detail. It seemed to Angela they were querying points that had nothing to do with legal issues and had been fully covered during the negotiations, such as pricing detail. To make things worse, Angela's main contacts were becoming less positive. They didn't return her telephone calls and stopped radiating the enthusiasm they had shown a few days earlier.

This is a common problem. Last minute problems have a range of likely causes:

- The enthusiasm of the 'deal' might have given way to anti-climax, with no one managing to raise the energy to finalize the details.
- Interfering busybodies like company lawyers or professional buyers might be undermining the deal behind the scenes.
- Competitors, knowing the deal is almost done, might sneak in with a last-minute offer designed to undercut your proposal.
- Whoever has to actually sign off on the deal, the chief executive or the board of directors, might have challenged the whole concept.

Be prepared for the last-minute problems. Don't assume the deal is done on the handshake. To quote the baseball player Yogi Berra, 'It ain't over till it's over.' Angela needs to be psychologically ready for the telephone call that starts, 'Just a few little points.' She also needs to be ready for the whole thing to fall flat. The remedy here is to keep selling. Don't allow control to transfer to the other side. Keep up the initiative, set the timetable and arrange implementation meetings. Continue to stress the advantages of your deal and seek agreement to commence implementation. The post-deal coolness will pass and the problems will be resolved, but keep control.

Stay in control

The thirteenth and final principle is a re-emphasis of Angela's central challenge: stay in control. Control does not have to be bombastic or aggressive, but will ensure that the process moves at the pace and along the lines we need. Control should ideally be established early in the negotiating exercise. It involves more work and energy than allowing the other side to take charge, but pays real dividends. Here are some key stages where control can be introduced:

- Set the agenda. Issue written proposals for the next meeting's content and intended outcomes.
- Arrange the meeting. Suggest the venue and book the location.
- Chair the meeting. Take over quickly by seeking agreement to the agenda and reviewing the structure of the meeting.
- Issue minutes or details of the agreed action points.
- Summarize the agreement reached.

- Consult with individuals whose consent is needed to aspects of the deal.
- If at all possible, undertake the first drafting of the contract. This ensures inclusion of all the points you believe have been negotiated, and gives you the opportunity to follow the process through to final signature.

In most cases the others round the negotiating table will be only too thankful to allow you to take control. It is less effort for them, but for you it is the key to the whole process. It sets your agenda, and at the end of the day delivers your result. To borrow the title of Susan Jeffer's book on personal development 'feel the fear and do it anyway'.

Negotiating is not rocket science, but it demands effort, commitment and nerve. It is one of the key skills you will need on your path to the boardroom. Fortunately it can be learned, and your negotiating skills can be refined and polished. Good luck in negotiating your path to success.

Keys

- Be clear about your desired outcomes before starting to negotiate.
- Don't concede without getting something in return.
- Don't get stuck on unnecessarily inflexible positions.
- Take control of the negotiation.
- Keep the relationship – stay friends.

twelve

The tenth commandment: be confident

Some of the leaders in our sample seemed to be born confident whereas for others it came with the job. While few were completely nerveless, virtually all rated their confidence as high. This seems to be an essential requirement since they need to speak up for themselves, argue effectively with senior colleagues and be the focus of attention in a range of business situations. This final commandment will concentrate on how we think about ourselves, first impressions, body language and presentation skills.

Peter Jacobs, former CEO of BUPA Healthcare, has a theory that all chief executives are driven by a lack of self-confidence. We saw little sign of it in our sample. Asked if he had always been confident, Andrew Fraser of Invest UK said, 'Yes, appallingly so.' Chris Brown of Euromoney admitted that he was far too self-confident and Diana Parker, senior partner at Withers solicitors, replied, 'I am totally confident in myself'.

Others felt selectively confident. Lord Gordon of Strathclyde, CEO of Radio Clyde, explained, 'I am more self-confident than I should be in my ideas, less self-confident than I should be as a person.' Denise O'Donoghue of Hat Trick Productions is 'at work fearless but less so elsewhere'. Most certainly felt that even on bad days they had to look and act confidently.

Confidence is not arrogance. That strutting, boastful, bragging behaviour is often mistaken for confidence by those who are not, but it is actually based on profound insecurity. Confident people, comfortable in the knowledge of their talents, are relaxed and keen to listen and learn from others. The arrogant are self-oriented, keen to hear themselves talk, and so worried they are not good enough that they have to tell everyone how good they are. Never mistake this for confidence.

How confident are you? Answer 'yes' or 'no' to the statements in the confidence checklist (Table 12.1) and you will discover what areas you need to tackle. Note down the 'no's: they are your goals for change throughout this chapter.

Table 12.1   The confidence checklist

	Yes	No
1. Do you feel comfortable talking to strangers for the first time?	☐	☐
2. Do you make a good first impression?	☐	☐
3. Can you enter a roomful of strangers with aplomb?	☐	☐
4. Do you enjoy going to social events where you meet a range of new people?	☐	☐
5. Do you find it easy to make conversation with a wide variety of people?	☐	☐
6. Are you relaxed socially?	☐	☐
7. Are you an enthusiastic and motivated person at work and at home?	☐	☐
8. Is life fun for you?	☐	☐
9. Do you have high self-esteem?	☐	☐
10. Do you think positively about your attitudes as a person?	☐	☐
11. Do you tend to think positively about your future?	☐	☐
12. Do you focus on your successes rather than your failures?	☐	☐
13. When you encounter difficulties do you problem solve rather than become depressed?	☐	☐
14. Are you generally positive about other people?	☐	☐
15. Do you reward and compliment those around you?	☐	☐
16. Do you handle difficult people skilfully?	☐	☐
17. Do you handle your emotions well, directing them appropriately?	☐	☐
18. Do you cope with conflict and resolve it?	☐	☐
19. Can you speak in public with ease?	☐	☐
20. Are you successful at job interviews?	☐	☐
21. Do you put yourself forward for promotion?	☐	☐
22. Do you see yourself becoming a leader of a group, team or company?	☐	☐
23. In the past have you ever successfully changed any aspect of yourself – a bad habit for example?	☐	☐

Some of the questions on the confidence checklist have been covered in previous commandments: things like problem solving, meeting people, rewarding and complimenting. This chapter will tackle the bits missed out so far: thinking for confidence, your impact, confident body language and presentation skills. Business success is so intertwined with the skills for confidence that it is with some relief that the authors noted that it had been selected in our business leaders' top ten.

Thinking for confidence

Often we are so used to our thoughts that we believe they are fixed, but this is of course untrue: we are in charge of what goes on in our minds. To tap into your thinking style, complete the following exercise, being as honest as possible.

Exercise: labelling

Make a list of five words, phrases or traits that describe you best in each of these ways:

- as you see yourself;
- from the viewpoint of a superior at work;
- from the viewpoint of a relative or partner.

Give yourself about five minutes to complete this exercise. Do not deliberate too long, as first thoughts are best. When you have finished, judge whether your words, phrases or traits are positive or negative, and mark them with a plus or minus sign.

Did you have more positives than negatives overall?

Did more negatives cluster in one section more than the other two?

If you do have some negatives, why did you not consider a list of 15 positives? If you did consider it, what stopped you?

TIPS FROM THE TOP

Sir Christopher Harding, Chairman, United Utilities

- What was the principal thing you had to learn to become successful?

   To understand business – I wish I'd done a chartered accountancy course.

- What challenges did you have to meet along the way?

   Sorting out people issues – the wrong people in the wrong jobs. But I'm a people person and this is also the area of greatest satisfaction.

- What advice would you give to an aspiring manager?

   Do things well. Look confident. Develop a network of people you like, respect and trust.

This exercise is about self-esteem, which Chris Mruk describes in his book *Self Esteem* as a combination of worth and competence. If you selected 15 positive statements to describe yourself, congratulations. If you have a peppering of negatives, ask yourself whether these descriptions truly describe you now, or whether you have progressed in competence and worthiness beyond them. We may get so used to calling ourselves 'shy', for example, that it never occurs to us to challenge this even after we have given a speech to the board then gone on to a party to celebrate.

Take your labelling exercise list to a good friend and ask them to go through it with you. Ask them, 'Is the image I have of myself, the image that others have of me?' Be prepared to listen. Also note if you have negatives in the last two sections. Is this really how your superiors or family view you? Check this out. If you are wrong, change the way you think of yourself. If you are right, it's time for you to change your behaviour.

The labelling exercise shows that some of the labels you stick on yourself are outmoded, suitable only for a life you have developed beyond. Of course, some of the negatives might be true. If you believe they still describe you, either make this aspect of your personality a goal for change, or forget about it and concentrate on your strengths. Martin Seligman states in his book *Learned Optimism* that even the way we think about our problems will help us master them or lead us to feel helpless. Thoughts become habits. To make yours positive, write down as many personal strengths as you can bring to mind in two minutes. Remember you do not have to be the best in the world at these skills, just good. A list of 20 is good, but try for 100.

Your impact

The impact you make at work can have a profound effect, either drawing people to you or turning them off, putting you on the fast track to promotion or holding you back. Awareness of how you come across to others when you first meet or see them in the office every day is difficult to achieve, and people often live their lives without knowing how they impact on others.

Daniel Goleman, in *Emotional Intelligence*, places first impressions, gut reactions at the heart of interpersonal communication. This gut reaction can make us wary of dangerous or incompetent people, or drawn to those who are confident and with whom we feel comfortable. Discover the impact you make on your team by asking them to complete the 'feedback from your colleague' questionnaire. If you are feeling bold, ask your superior to complete 'feedback from your boss'.

Feedback from your colleague

Your colleague wishes to assess his/her working style and areas to work on. This questionnaire is to help improve his/her handling of you and the rest of the people in the business. Only through your total honesty can he/she begin to tackle his/her shortcomings.

Please answer all 18 questions. Consider the amount and the nature of the support your receive from your colleague. Rate this by circling the appropriate number on the scale 1 to 5, where 5 is high and 1 is low.

1. To what extent does your colleague appear to have confidence in you?
   Comments: 1 2 3 4 5
2. To what extent does your colleague try to help you to understand your work problems?
   Comments: 1 2 3 4 5
3. To what extent does your colleague try to help you to solve your problems?
   Comments: 1 2 3 4 5
4. To what extent is your colleague interested in your family and personal problems?
   Comments: 1 2 3 4 5

---

5. To what extent does your colleague try to help you with your family and personal problems?
   Comments: 1 2 3 4 5

6. To what extent do you feel your colleague is interested in you as a person?
   Comments: 1 2 3 4 5

7. To what extent does your colleague help you to improve your performance, eg by coaching, by discussing your work, by giving you constructive feedback?
   Comments: 1 2 3 4 5

8. How strong is the support from your colleague eg in defending you (and your work) against other people in the business?
   Comments: 1 2 3 4 5

9. To what extent does your colleague make time for discussions?
   Comments: 1 2 3 4 5

10. How often does your colleague ask for your comments or advice?
    Comments: 1 2 3 4 5

11. To what extent do you feel able to disagree with your colleague?
    Comments: 1 2 3 4 5

12. How open is your relationship with your colleague?
    Comments: 1 2 3 4 5

13. How confident are you that your colleague will not take offence at what you say?
    Comments: 1 2 3 4 5

14. How well does your colleague delegate to you?
    Comments: 1 2 3 4 5

15. How much do you think your colleague concentrates on the important issues as opposed to the trivial or irrelevant ones?
    Comments: 1 2 3 4 5

16. Please list three things you'd like your colleague to **stop** doing:

17. Please list three things you'd like your colleague to **continue** doing:

18. Please list three things you'd like your colleague to **start** doing:

Feedback from your boss

Your colleague wishes to assess his/her working style and areas to work on. This questionnaire is to help him/her improve his/her handling of you and the rest of the people in the business. Only through your total honesty can he/she begin to tackle his/her shortcomings.

Please answer all 25 questions. Consider the amount and the nature of the support your receive from your colleague. Rate this by circling the appropriate number on the scale 1 to 5, where 5 is high and 1 is low.

1. To what extent do you have confidence in your colleague?
   Comments: 1 2 3 4 5
2. To what extent does your colleague actively problem solve with you or his/her team?
   Comments: 1 2 3 4 5
3. To what extent is your colleague interested in your family and leisure pursuits?
   Comments: 1 2 3 4 5
4. To what extent is your colleague interested in you as a person?
   Comments: 1 2 3 4 5
5. To what extent does your colleague make time for discussions with you?
   Comments: 1 2 3 4 5
6. How good is your colleague at keeping you up to date with relevant information?
   Comments: 1 2 3 4 5
7. How often does your colleague ask for feedback and advice about his/her performance?
   Comments: 1 2 3 4 5
8. To what extent does your colleague feel able to disagree with you?
   Comments: 1 2 3 4 5
9. How open is your colleague's relationship with you?
   Comments: 1 2 3 4 5
10. How confident are you that your colleague will not take offence at what you say?
    Comments: 1 2 3 4 5

11. Can you delegate to your colleague with confidence?
    Comments: 1 2 3 4 5
12. How well does your colleague handle meetings in your organization?
    Comments: 1 2 3 4 5
13. How well does your colleague develop his/her staff?
    Comments: 1 2 3 4 5
14. How well does your colleague coach his/her staff?
    Comments: 1 2 3 4 5
15. How well does your colleague delegate to his/her staff?
    Comments: 1 2 3 4 5
16. How much does your colleague concentrate on important issues as opposed to trivial or irrelevant ones?
    Comments: 1 2 3 4 5
17. How elegantly does your colleague handle difficult work colleagues?
    Comments: 1 2 3 4 5
18. How positive is your colleague's thinking?
    Comments: 1 2 3 4 5
19. How good are your colleague's presentation skills?
    Comments: 1 2 3 4 5
20. How motivational is your colleague's leadership style?
    Comments: 1 2 3 4 5
21. How good is your colleague at handling stress?
    Comments: 1 2 3 4 5
22. How team orientated and participative is your colleague?
    Comments: 1 2 3 4 5
23. Please list three things you'd like your colleague to **stop** doing:
24. Please list three things you'd like your colleague to **continue** doing:
25. Please list three things you'd like your colleague to **start** doing:

Note the areas in which you received a score of 3 or less. These are the areas in which you will have to put most effort to change the impact you make on those around you. Pay particular attention to the last section of three things to stop, continue and start doing. That feedback is worth more than gold to you in your desire to progress.

TIPS FROM THE TOP

Andrew Fraser, former MD, Invest UK

- What were the principal things you had to learn to become successful?

  I have had to learn to be more patient when dealing with staff. However this needs to be countered by a very necessary impatience to get the job done.
- What challenges did you meet along the way?

  Not many. I have always been appallingly confident. Moving from the private sector, from Saatchi and Saatchi to that of the public investment arena has been interesting and different. But I just love the thrill of the chase.
- What advice would you give to an aspiring manager?

  You have to be confident and ambitious although I have to say my career has been more by instinct than planning. You must also know how to manage relationships.

Confident body language

How you look when you talk is of primary importance. Despite knowing how crucial body language is in terms of impact (see Mehrabian's estimate in Figure 12.1), we still focus too much of the time on what we say, not how we say it. Mehrabian's estimate might be deemed conservative, as other researchers suggest the impact of body language is nearer 80 per cent of communication.

Allan Pease, in *Body Language*, reminds us how profoundly visual we are. He cites Professor Birtwhistell's estimate of 10 to 11 minutes of conversation for the average person per day, with sentences lasting a mere average 2.5 seconds. The rest is non-verbal.

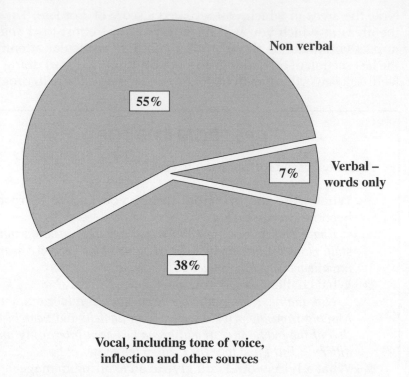

Figure 12.1 Human messages – the clues and signals we give

We often see people with strutting body language and mistake that arrogance for confidence. Of course the truly confident are very relaxed, comfortable with their view of themselves. The great and the good can be as insecure as any of us, but you know when you are in the presence of a master. When Placido Domingo was singing his hundredth Don José in an Edinburgh Festival production of *Carmen,* he did not boast of his musical prowess or complain about the size of his dressing room. The lesser-known tenors and sopranos strutted grandiosely, while Domingo celebrated his centenary with the chorus.

There is a view that body language reveals the hidden person, the unconscious impulse, mainly because we can 'choose our words carefully' but tend not to think of controlling our body language. This was revealed in a television series called *Confidence Lab* and the subsequent book *Confidence in Just Seven Days*. John, a participant from Glasgow, felt his lack of height contributed to his poor self-confidence. He had developed a very aggressive exterior to show people not to mess with him, and this tough carapace certainly worked: people did leave him alone, but then he felt isolated and unloved. His typical body language when entering a room or a bar was to scowl, look down towards the floor, avoid eye contact and move to a spot where no one was standing. He claimed that this was a Scottish macho thing that other cultures could not understand. This was challenged, since Scottish men and women are renowned for their friendliness and ability to talk to strangers. His belief system was personal and self-defeating.

When he practised entering a room in an open, friendly fashion the change was remarkable. He smiled, took time to look around the room, chose someone who appeared to be interesting, asked questions, listened and nodded approval. People were drawn to him and were less likely to create trouble than he feared, and much less likely to have the slightest concern about his height.

What stops us using such simple body language when we know it works so powerfully? Is it life, stress, absorption with our own agendas or just not caring? If you are to transform yourself into a confident communicator, you must care about the people around you: not just your intimate circle of friends and relations, but everyone – colleagues, acquaintances, people you have just met.

Confident people are 'inside out'. They focus on those around them, helping them to feel comfortable and being interested in what they have to say. The shy and insecure are so self-oriented, worrying about their sweaty palms and beating hearts, that there is no room for anyone else. One of the best ways to increase your confidence is to focus on others.

Many of us are brought up with the concept of being 'professional'. To many accountants, lawyers, engineers and doctors this seems to be an excuse not just to be serious but to be stiff and boring. It takes a lot of practice, and what a waste of time: hands behind the back, eyes to the ceiling, read from the text and your audience is either wondering what to have for lunch or is already dozing off. It is not just nerves. This formality has been elevated to a philosophy of professional behaviour which pervades entire organizations, so most meetings, presentations and conferences have to be endured rather than enjoyed.

There is a wonderfully simple rule about all of this. When you are 'yourself' your body language is congruent with your message, so what you say and how you look are fused into one powerful communication with no distractions. You also come across as genuine and honest, something we all wish to achieve.

Just as important as an awareness of our own body language is our ability to perceive and react to other people's. It is particularly useful to know if a client, customer, or boss is interested in what we are saying or if they have switched off.

TIPS FROM THE TOP

Denise O'Donoghue, MD of Hat Trick Productions

- What were the principal things you had to learn to become successful?

  I have had to become less knee-jerk in my reactions and really must become less amazed by my success. I normally don't admit to running the company.
- What challenges did you meet along the way?

  I'm a very shy, private person, but at work, I overcome that and become fearless.
- What advice would you give to an aspiring manager?

  Do a good job regardless of the task, present yourself well and get on with people.

In a business context it is important to understand what some particular nonverbal cues mean so that you can take appropriate action. A warning, though: look for body language clusters, not isolated bits of behaviour. Other information is important too. The list in Table 12.2 will help you not only achieve confident body language yourself, but notice positive or negative body language in others.

Presentation skills

In 1990 *The Times* carried out a survey of things the British most fear. Speaking in front of a group was top of the list, with death ranking only fifth! It doesn't have to be this way, especially since the ideas we are going to talk about can make presentations stress free, whether they are to a mother and toddler group or 2,000 business people.

Table 12.2 Body language and its meanings

Non-verbal cues	Possible processes
Negative body language:	
Furrowed forehead, knitted brows	Thinking, perhaps not positively
Tapping foot and/or drumming fingers	Impatience, irritation, anger, agitation
Avoiding eye contact	Anger, concern, sexual attraction
Rapid, light breathing	Anxiety, fear, distress
Irregular breathing	Approaching important issues, controlling feelings
Deep, slow breathing	Suppressing strong feelings
Physical stroking of face, arm and neck	Comforting self or holding back the need for comforting
Scratching, pinching, severe pressing	Punishing self, reflecting self-criticism or holding back from provoking or punishing someone else
Fast, high voice	Excitement, tension, fear
Tightness/rigidity in jaw, neck, shoulder	Holding back anger or upset
Clenching fists, tightness in arm	Holding back anger or upset
Body leaning forward, legs tightly crossed	Defending, uninvolved, unconcerned
Arms tightly folded, legs tightly crossed	Defending, putting up barriers, resistance
Lounging extravagantly in chair	Detachment, cynicism, discounting
Hand covering mouth	Hiding, playing games, uncertain
Finger jabbing	Critical, putting down, fencing
Confident body language:	
Smiling	Happy, at ease
Leaning forward	Interested in what the other person is saying
Direct gaze	Confidence in relationships
Head erect, good posture	High self-esteem
Open gestures	Open, honest person
Relaxed stance and gesture	Mental and physical ease
Head to one side	Listening positively
Nodding	Approval of another's point of view

The ability to present information to clients and at internal meetings is a skill essential to the upwardly mobile. Influencing people to tackle problems, produce results and change in the requisite direction makes the difference between success and failure. Let us start by working out what makes a good presenter. Complete the questionnaire in Table 12.3.

Table 12.3   What makes a good presenter?

	Positively agree	Agree	Disagree	Strongly disagree
1. What you say in a presentation is the most important element				
2. You always need to be anxious to keep on your toes and deliver an effective presentation				
3. How you look when presenting will be a major influencing factor for an audience				
4. Perfecting a good presentation means that you don't have to change it for each audience				
5. Humour and stories are out of place in a formal presentation				
6. Reading your notes is important as it means that you miss nothing out of your presentation				
7. Making mistakes will ruin a good presentation				
8. Enthusiasm for your subject will generally see you through				

Results

1. What you say is not as important as how you look: whether you are animated, smiling and generally engaging. This is reassuring, as we often get hung up about remembering every bit of our talk.
2. It is so much better if you are relaxed during your presentation. Then you attend to the audience, not your sweating palms.

3. We know from question 1 that how you look is very important.
4. Every presentation you give should be targeted at your audience and therefore different.
5. Humour and stories are fabulous in any presentation – surprisingly even at a funeral.
6. Never read notes. The spoken and the written word come from different planets and shouldn't be confused with each other and if you miss something out who knows except you?
7. Making mistakes is not important; recovery is. Everyone makes mistakes and it can be quite endearing not to be seen as perfect. The trick is not to be thrown.
8. Enthusiasm is essential. If you don't have it, get someone else to do the presentation who has.

The bottom line

- **People buy people**. It is a fact that if you are liked, your ideas will stand a better chance of success. Remember you have 30 seconds to make a good impression.
- **You are your best visual.** During a presentation your audience has plenty of time to assess you. Do you look the best you can, or have you been flung together? Be positive about your attributes. If you are not, who is going to be?
- **Enthusiasm conquers all** (well, almost all). Are you user-friendly as a presenter with an animated, friendly face and lively speech? If not, let us help you have fun.

First, let us show how you can put together a presentation in a couple of minutes on the back of an envelope, and look as if you had been working on it all week.

TIPS FROM THE TOP

Dame Stella Rimington, former Director General of MI5, now non-executive director of Marks and Spencer, BG and GKR among others

- What were the principal things you had to learn to become successful?

    I had to learn to be confident. I was a very anxious person when younger, being sick before exams and that kind of thing. I can trace that anxiety back to my experience of air raids as a child during the war.

    And I had to learn to be less self conscious and more orientated towards those I was leading. This was a gradual learning process as I achieved promotion through the ranks.

    I also had to manage risk, often on the basis of inadequate information.

    I had to learn to be even tempered as I was prone to be emotional when younger. I am therefore much better at handling difficult people now and will try not to have head on confrontations.

- What challenges did you meet along the way?

    The press were very intrusive in a quite inappropriate way when I first became Head of MI5. What I wore and where I bought it became the focus of many an article while I was trying to focus on national security. They found out where I lived and so forced me to move from a house in which I was very comfortable. I really resented that.

- What advice would you give to an aspiring manager?

    They need to become self-confident and learn to work with a wide variety of people. Developing the ability to work in and through teams is an essential skill today.

Good presenters are made, not born

This is the magic formula for putting together a presentation. Once you know how to follow it, presentations almost write themselves.

1. Researching.
2. Mind Mapping.

3.   Structuring.
4.   Topping and tailing.

Researching
You need to know who you are presenting to, so you can target your talk to suit. Phone up in advance and ask the following questions:

■   Who will be there? What are the backgrounds of those attending? Will they know anything of what you are talking about?
■   Numbers of people? Is it 5 or 50? You need to know in case any visual aids cannot be seen from the back of the room.
■   Where will it be held? Will your talk be at table or on a platform?
■   What equipment do you need and do they have it?

One consultant turned up at meeting which she thought five people were attending. Imagine her consternation when she opened the door to find 500 – and closed it again thinking she had gone to the wrong place. Not a good start or a confident entrance.

Mind Mapping
You were introduced to the concept of Mind Maps in Chapter 3, where it was seen to be useful for problem solving. Mind Mapping is also especially useful for presentations, either at the brainstorming information stage or during the presentation itself:

■   Mind Maps help us to memorize the key points in our presentation.
■   Mind Mapping is great for the preparation of information. Put anything that occurs to you onto paper in no set order, leaving your mind free to make connections and come up with ideas.
■   You can use this Mind Map, or a tidied-up version, during your presentations. It has the advantage of being on one piece of paper and the key concepts are all there in front of you as signposts.
■   A Mind Map allows you to target your presentation quickly and easily for each audience.

As an exercise, draw a Mind Map of a presentation you have to make.

Structuring
Once you have finished your mind map you must add some structure to your thinking. Here are some ideas for structuring your talk.

Be aware of the **WIFT** (what's in it for them) factor. Your mind map may have been a general look at yourself, a hobby or a product you want to sell. Now you must concentrate on the areas that will really interest your audience.

Mark McCormack, famous for his book *What They Don't Teach You at Harvard Business School*, was asked to speak at a conference in Northern Ireland. Throughout his talk he mentioned the way large multinational companies ran their businesses. This would have been fine had it not been a conference for small businesses. Part of his audience were bored, the other half angry. He failed to follow his own advice in Chapter 1 to 'read people'.

Look at primacy and recency. Select the two most important points from your talk and place them at the beginning and at the end. We remember probably only two things from presentations, and we tend to remember the first and the last things we hear.

Statistics and stories are very important. The left sides of our brains like facts and figures, the right stories and anecdotes. Since most of your audience will have two parts of their brain functioning, you need to include both. People enjoy hearing stories and anecdotes, especially believable personal ones, so tell your story as though you were there. Be very specific and give a few details. Do not be afraid to borrow stories and change the details. This can be seen as poetic licence.

If you make a joke but get no response, move on to your next sentence and pretend it was never intended as a joke. Your jokes are less likely to fall flat if you make sure the humour is relevant to your presentation. Never tell a tasteless joke: they are totally inappropriate in a speaking situation. At a Scottish Burns Night supper a speaker had not realized that it was not an all-male event and had included a lot of sexist jokes against women. The room got quieter and quieter with absolutely no one laughing. The speaker became more and more flustered. In the end he sat down, never to be invited back.

If the audience seem 'dead' as you begin, engage them in something active to get them going. Give them a question to discuss with you, a neighbour or in a small group: anything to shake off their passivity and get them involved.

Anecdotes engage your listeners. They can imagine the whole scene clearly and can enter into your story with you. It is best to tell a personal anecdote, since:

■ the audience won't have heard it before;
■ you won't forget it;

■ you'll be perceived as more sincere;
■ it will enliven both you and the presentation.

Topping and tailing
Your introduction must make people realize they are in for a treat. Follow the guidelines in Figure 12.2 and you will have them sitting on the edges of their seats.

You should have a zappy conclusion ready for the end, so if you're told you have run out of time, you can seamlessly go to it as if you meant to finish just at that moment. Figure 12.3 makes some suggestions.

Table 12.4 provides you with an overall structure. Just add your content and stir.

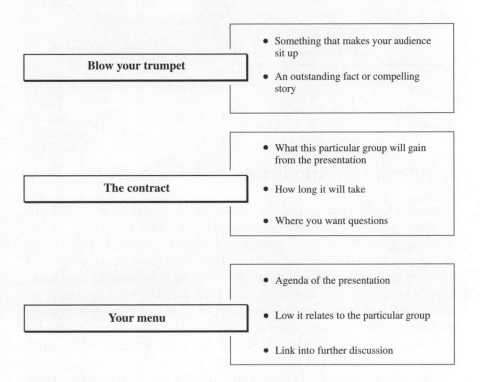

Figure 12.2 The introduction to your talk

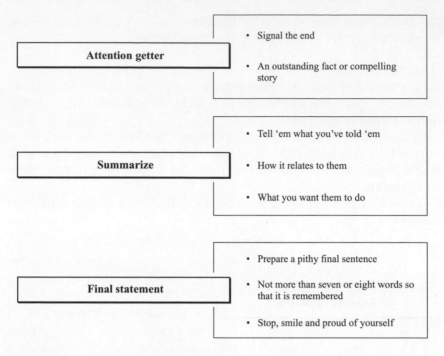

Attention getter
- Signal the end
- An outstanding fact or compelling story

Summarize
- Tell 'em what you've told 'em
- How it relates to them
- What you want them to do

Final statement
- Prepare a pithy final sentence
- Not more than seven or eight words so that it is remembered
- Stop, smile and proud of yourself

Figure 12.3   The conclusion to your talk

Nightmare questionnaire

Now you know how to put the presentation together, we can focus on you. Try the 'nightmare questionnaire in Table 12.5.

Most of the nightmares you might experience while presenting are owing to anxiety. Shuffling, fiddling and freezing are all part of being more tense than normal. Something happens to our body language when we are anxious. The words, which might be confident and credible, begin to be undermined by tense body language. The implication for our audience is that we look furtive at worst and ill at ease at best. These are not what we want to communicate if success is what we have in our sights.

The 'power minute' featured in Chapter 8 is a wonderful technique for relaxing before a speech or presentation. It also focuses the mind and helps you to concentrate on your audience, not your beating heart. In addition what really helps is to visualize success the week before that special presentation. You must practise this every day so that it becomes second nature, a part of you.

Table 12.4   Putting your talk together

Opening line:
The contract:

Relation to audience:
Agenda:

Discussion:
Main point 1:

Connection:
Main point 2:

Connection:
Main point 3:

Connection:
Main point 4:

Conclusion:
Summary:
Last sentence:

Table 12.5 Nightmare questionnaire

When giving your last presentation, did you experience any of the following?

	Yes	No
1. When asked to present did you just want to die?	☐	☐
2. When you started speaking did you feel and look awkward?	☐	☐
3. Did you gesture too much?	☐	☐
4. When tense, did you freeze like a statue?	☐	☐
5. Did you have the habit of looking at the ceiling, floor etc, anything except the audience?	☐	☐
6. Did you fiddle with keys or change in your pocket when speaking?	☐	☐
7. Did you tend to shuffle about as you spoke?	☐	☐
8. Did you look sombre and serious when you presented?	☐	☐
9. Did you have any of the following feelings:		
Breathlessness?	☐	☐
Rapid heartbeat?	☐	☐
Dry mouth?	☐	☐
Tense throat?	☐	☐
Blushing?	☐	☐
Tense face?	☐	☐
Sweating?	☐	☐
Butterflies in stomach?	☐	☐
Blotches?	☐	☐
Cold hands?	☐	☐
Nausea?	☐	☐
Feeling faint?	☐	☐
10. Would you be happy if you never had to give a presentation again?	☐	☐

Visualizing success

Visualization is using your imagination for positive outcomes. Follow these guidelines and you will float through your next presentation with ease. Using the power minute to relax, you can then imagine each phase of your talk very positively.

- Enjoy the preparation phase. Realize that you are communicating interesting and vital information which is distinctive for your audience.
- If any worries come into your mind, brush them aside and tell yourself you will worry about that later.

- Visualize arriving at the presentation venue very relaxed and in control.
- Imagine the introduction, with your audience gazing at you with rapt attention. They are captivated by your facts and stories.
- See yourself talking through your argument, the body of your talk. Heads are nodding as your points are being well received.
- You arrive at your conclusion with a flourish, leaving a pithy phrase in the minds of your audience that encapsulates your whole presentation.
- Visualize the clapping at the end, with people slapping you on the back saying it is the best they have ever heard you speak.

Visualizing success is what every famous athlete does to win a race. Entertaining failure increases the chance of it happening. Why take that chance?

Body language for presentations

You need a **bright, lively, interested expression** rather than a tense, serious face. Find something near the beginning of your talk to make you smile, either a story or a joke. Smiling is so captivating that it will get most audiences on your side instantly.

Your **eye contact** should be towards the audience, not your on notes or slides. Try to look at the audience as if you were talking to each individual. A Scottish chorus visiting the USA were conducted by Daniel Barenboim, who was exceedingly demanding. The chorus, though challenged, were determined to be the best they could be. After the concert was over, each member of the 200-strong group said, 'Did you see the conductor looking at me?' Daniel Barenboim had the wonderful knack of making eye contact with everyone on the stage, so they all gave the performance of a lifetime.

A **confident posture** with a straight, though not rigid, back is preferable to an apologetic one. Taking a deep breath and easing your shoulders back helps you to make an impact.

Gestures are good. They help to underline important points and add emphasis to your speech, so keep your hands out of your pockets and use open gestures.

At the end of a talk it is great to make **personal contact**. A hand-shake with the chair and members of the audience forges links for the future.

Make sure you are at a **useful distance** for easy scanning of your audience. Reorganize the room if you are uneasy about seeing every member of the group.

Confidence comprises an inner sense of high self-esteem, an ability to talk and think positively about our attributes, looking confident, and making presentations to any size of group anywhere with equanimity.

Keys

■ Make sure that the labels or names you call yourself are realistic and up to date. Play to your strengths.
■ Learn to sell yourself by being positive about your attributes.
■ Practise confident body language and become sensitive to other people's.
■ Follow the magic process for constructing successful presentations and remember that enthusiasm conquers all.

The **last chapter**

If you have reached this final chapter then you have read, or certainly glanced at, the 10 commandments for success. They may have surprised you in their orientation. Absent certainly were any traditional technical skills such as finance or IT. When asked about the paucity of these skills from their checklists, our successful people agreed that technical skills were undoubtedly important, but when you wished to rise to the elevated heights of running a business or heading up a government department, these 10 areas got their vote. They of course are oriented to problem solving, focusing on results and people skills.

Table 13.1 presents that list again. This time, rate yourself on these skill areas on a scale of 1 (poor) to 10 (proficiency). This will tell you which chapters you need to concentrate on. Of course you may not see yourself as others see you (who can?), so you may want to check your impressions with a colleague or manager. Ask them to complete the ratings for you, then discuss the discrepancies between their score and yours.

Mike was an engineer of long experience and distinction. He began to wonder why other younger engineers were promoted above him, especially when he deemed them less competent. He decided to ask his manager and the MD for feedback on his lack of progression. They both took the opportunity to tell him that he was inconsiderate of other staff, he failed to communicate what he was doing so his talent was never passed on, and he was very aggressive with the female supervisors. In fact one of the bosses described him as an 'animal'. You can imagine he was nonplussed: his view of himself was a rather cuddly technician and father of two. When he started to reflect on how he had become so lacking in people skills, he realized he was completely oriented towards machines. On the shop floor he would cast people aside in his bid to get to the machine. This feedback was the best thing that could have happened. He acquired the requisite training and is now known as the pussycat.

Table 13.1 The ten commandments rating scale

One: problem solve	1 2 3 4 5 6 7 8 9 10
Two: want to win	1 2 3 4 5 6 7 8 9 10
Three: deliver the goods	1 2 3 4 5 6 7 8 9 10
Four: relate	1 2 3 4 5 6 7 8 9 10
Five: trust the team	1 2 3 4 5 6 7 8 9 10
Six: de-stress	1 2 3 4 5 6 7 8 9 10
Seven: love change	1 2 3 4 5 6 7 8 9 10
Eight: know yourself	1 2 3 4 5 6 7 8 9 10
Nine: strike a deal	1 2 3 4 5 6 7 8 9 10
Ten: be confident	1 2 3 4 5 6 7 8 9 10

Changing is not that easy. On the other hand it is not impossible. You just have to follow some guidelines and the benefits will be yours.

First you must understand that there are different ways of learning to change. Some people will choose to learn online, some would want to read more about skills for success before committing themselves to a course of action, others still will want guidance from a specialist. Reflect how you have learned in the past and run with that method. You may even like a mixture: a bit of info online, a touch of reading and a lot of support from friends and trainers of all sorts. There is no use beating yourself up about not sticking to a plan of action if that plan is not to your liking from the start.

If there are a number of areas where you would like to be more skilled, you may wonder where to start. Here are a few rules of thumb.

- Start with something achievable. If you find it difficult to present at meetings, chose a small unimportant one to start with. You can work up to one the chief executive attends later on.
- Choose a skill that will make a real difference to your working life. Learning the techniques of problem solving with your team (rated as the first commandment of course) might be the most major skill to distinguish your team from the rest.
- Only select a couple of issues to work on at a time. It takes three weeks to change an old habit to a new behaviour, and another nine weeks to convert this behaviour into a new habit: not bad timing if you have had the habit for 10, 20, or even 30 years. Running with too many actions will confuse you and doom your plans to failure.

■ Persistence is important. Keep practising until the new skill happens like breathing. If you have learned to drive, think back to your first driving lesson. You had to think consciously to look in the mirror, take the handbrake off, put your foot on the clutch and the car into first gear. Now you doubtless jump into the car and scoot off without a conscious thought. So worry not that these new skills seem a little strange, uncomfortable or daring. With a bit of practice and slight tweakings to suit your lifestyle, you will become more skilled without even thinking about it.

Setbacks do of course occur. Analyse the situation with as much cool detachment as you can muster, or chat it over with a friend, then reset your plans. Perhaps you had to deal with a difficult colleague who seemed to be agreeable till the end of the meeting when he or she stormed out. Your debriefing of yourself should focus on whether you had said anything to upset this colleague, whether he or she had other stresses to deal with in his/her life, and how you can next ask him/her what happened. Do not always believe you are to blame. Ask why and take it from there.

The main thing to remember is that as soon as you start on the path to success it is great fun trying out your new-found skills in different contexts. The more often you counter setbacks, the stronger and more confident you will become. To help with these decisions, answer the following questions.

How to make a difference

1. What would make a difference right now to your success as a team member, team leader or manager?
2. Who might help you to acquire new skills?
3. Who will coach you when you are stuck with a problem?
4. Who, among those you know, inspires you to achieve?
5. What could you do to make life at work less frustrating?
6. What could you do to make work a more creative place?
7. What could you do to make life at work less routine?
8. What would motivate those around you?
9. What could you do to have more fun at work?
10. What could you do to develop personally?

If you want to be successful in any area of work you also need to have a distinctive vision, know what your values are, what you hold dear, and above all how you can make a difference. Then you need to talk about them to inspire others to follow your lead.

An acting head of a famous girls' school in Ireland was to be interviewed for the permanent post. She felt she lacked confidence, so we staged a panel of eminent educationalists to put her through her paces. When they asked about the Irish situation, its impact on young women's education and her vision for the future, she responded that politics was not an area she was comfortable with, and she had no view on such matters. At the debriefing she was told to have a view within five minutes about the political situation and how within this climate she was going to make a difference to modern education in Ireland. She got the message that when you are in a senior position you are part of a community larger than just your job or company. Politics, race, religion, ethics must become grist to your mill. You need to keep up to date with current affairs, the latest literature about organizational development and the impact on society. Top people in top companies have to deal with their country's leaders. As a recent advert challenged, if you sat next to Henry Kissinger on a transatlantic flight how long could you keep the conversation going?

The majority of our successful people had broad interests from football to the arts and could happily converse about both. They also had to learn about government agencies and be relaxed about the media.

A major finding from our interviews was that there was very little difference in results from the entrepreneurs and those who worked their way up through the ranks of corporations. All treated their companies as if they owned them. They identified with the output, and the company's success was their success.

The majority also did not set personal goals: aspirations to reach that rung of the corporate ladder by a particular time. This was viewed as unacceptable behaviour to be undermined and thwarted rightfully by colleagues. The naked self-interest so beloved by consultants and gurus the world over would have received minus marks on their top 10 list. However they did set goals for their teams, departments and companies. This approach led to their success.

Focus on your long-term work goals first – but probably no more than a year. Then think about how you are going to reach them using medium- and short-term ones. (See Table 13.2.)

Table 13.2 My work goals

My long-term goals (one year)	*When I want to achieve them*	*Examples*
		Motivated team Double-digit growth High profile New product or service Development of staff

My medium-term goals (three months)	*When I want to achieve them*	*Examples*
		Everyone completed IT training Ten new clients Four trade press articles Product development team formed Personal development programmes launched

My short-term goals (next month)	*When I want to achieve them*	*Examples*
		Meetings with each employee New literature Interviewed by *The Times* Appoint product development manager Agree staff development training programme

There is a lot to learn. However if you follow the ten commandments, working on the chapters that will make a difference to you, success will be yours.

references

Allen, R and Fulton, J (1999) *Mensa Know Yourself*, Carlton, London

Balke, E (1999) *Know Yourself*, Kogan Page, London

BBC (2001) *Quiet Britons Lose Out on Promotion*, Research for *Get Confident*

Belbin, M R (1996a) *Management Teams: Why They Succeed or Fail*, Butterworth-Heinemann, London

Belbin, M R (1996b) *Team Roles at Work*, Butterworth-Heinemann, London

Benton, D A (1999) *How to Think Like a CEO*, Warner Books, New York

Berne, E (1968) *Games People Play*, Penguin, London

Boucher Gilberd, P (1996) *The Eleven Commandments of Wildly Successful Women*, Macmillan Spectrum, New York

Boyett, Joseph and Boyett, Jimmie (1998) *The Guru Guide*, Wiley, Chichester

Brown, K (1999) article in *New Scientist*, 4 September, pp 36–39

Buzan, A (2000) *The Mindmap Book*, BBC Consumer Books, London

Clark, J (2000) *The Money or Your Life*, Century, London

Coleridge, N (1999) *Streetsmart*, Orion, London

Collins, J C and Porras, J I (1997) *Built to Last*, Random House, London

Cooper, C and Cartwright, S (1997) *Managing Workplace Stress*, Sage, London

Covey, S R (1999) *The Seven Habits of Highly Successful People*, Simon & Schuster, Hemel Hempstead

Crain's (1999) *New York Business Book of Lists*, Crain's, New York

Dellinger, S (1989) *Psycho-Geometrics*, Career Press, Franklin Lakes USA

Downie, R S and Telfer, E (1969) *Respect for Persons*, Allen & Unwin, Sydney

Eales-White, R (1996) *How to be a Better Teambuilder*, Kogan Page, London

Firestein, R (1996) *Leading on the Creative Edge*, Pinon Press, Colorado Springs

Fisher, R and Ury, W (1997) *Getting to Yes*, Random House, London

Francis, D (1994) *Managing Your Own Career*, HarperCollins, London

Garratt, R (1997) *The Fish Rots From The Head*, HarperCollins, London

Goleman, D (1996) *Emotional Intelligence*, Bloomsbury, London

Handy, C (1989) *The Age of Unreason*, Hutchinson, London

Hanson, P G (1988) *The Joy of Stress*, Pan Books, London

Harvard Business School (1998) *Harvard Business Review on Change*, Harvard Business School Press, Cambridge MA

Herzberg, F (1993) *The Motivation to Work*, John Wiley, New York

Holmes, T H and Rahe, R H (1967) The social readjustment rating scale, *Journal of Psychosomatic Research*, **11**, pp 213–18

Karrass, G (1987) *Negotiate to Close*, Simon & Schuster, New York

Kotter, J P (1996) *Leading Change*, Harvard Business School Press, Cambridge MA

McCormack, M II (1986) *What They Don't Teach You at Harvard Business School*, Fontana Paperback, London

Margerison, C J (1989) *How American Chief Executives Succeed: Implications for developing high potential employees*, University Press

Martin, P (1997) *The Sickening Mind*, HarperCollins, London

Maslow, A H (1987) *Motivation and Personality*, Harper & Row, New York

Mehrabian, A (1971) *Silent Messages*, Wadsworth Belmont CA

Mruk, C (1999) *Self Esteem, Research, Theory and Practice*, Free Association Books, London

Noller, R (1977) *Guide to Creative Action*, Scribner, New York

Office Angels (2000) Survey of Bosses (press release), Office Angels, London

Oliver, D (1996) *101 Ways to Negotiate More Effectively*, Kogan Page, London

Parnes, S J (1997) *Optimize the Magic of Your Mind*, Bearly, New York

Pease, A (1997) *Body Language*, Sheldon, London

Persaud, R (1998) *Staying Sane*, Metro, London

Peters, T (1989) *Thriving on Chaos*, Pan Books, London

Richer, J (1990) *The Richer Way*, Emap Business Communications, London

Selge, H (1946) The general adaptation syndrome and the diseases of adaptation, *Journal of Clinical Endorminology*, **6**, p 177

Seligman, M (1998) *Learned Optimism*, Pocket Books, London

Shapiro, M (1991) *Understanding Neuro-Linguistic Programming*, Hodder & Stoughton, London

Smith, D (1995) *Motivating People*, Barron, London

Taylor, R (2000a) *Transform Yourself*, Kogan Page, London

Taylor, R with Scott, S and Leighton, R (2000b) *Confidence in Just Seven Days*, Random House, London

Times (1996) *The Times 1 000*, Times Books, London

Wille, E and Hodgson, P (2000) *Making Change Work*, Mercury, Burien

Wilson, L and Wilson, H (1998) *Play to Win*, Bard Press TX

Personal Profile Analysis courtesy of Thomas International Ltd, Harris House, 17 West Street, Marlow, SL7 2LS

index